the
Dramatic Criticism of
Alexander Woollcott

MORRIS U. BURNS

The Scarecrow Press, Inc.
Metuchen, N.J., & London
1980

Library of Congress Cataloging in Publication Data

Burns, Morris U   1939-
  The dramatic criticism of Alexander Woollcott.

    Bibliography: p. 157
    Includes index.
    1.   Woollcott, Alexander, 1887-1943--Knowledge--Per-
forming arts. 2.   Dramatic criticism--United States.
3.   Theater--United States--History--20th century.   I.
Title.
PS3545.O77Z63   809.2   80-12935
ISBN 0-8108-1299-1

To Frances
for her love and support

Acknowledgments

My task of reading the entire body of Woollcott's writings was facilitated by the efforts of library staffs at the University of Kansas, Hamilton College, and Harvard University. They have my gratitude. A number of individuals aided me in quickly tracking down Woollcott material when they were closer to certain libraries than I was. Foremost among this group are Drs. Porter Woods, Paul Shepard, and Sally Morris. My thanks to them all. I am also grateful to Drs. William Kuhlke and Ronald Willis, both of the University of Kansas, for their reactions to this study, as well as their helpful suggestions.

For permission to quote from Woollcott's unpublished letter to Frank Sullivan, dated December 29, 1937, as well as from articles from Hamilton College's Alumni Review and Literary Magazine, I am indebted to Hamilton College. By permission of the Houghton Library at Harvard University, I have used a quotation from an unpublished letter of Woollcott to Leggett Brown, dated December 3, 1936. I acknowledge Viking Penguin Inc. for permission to quote a number of letters from The Letters of Alexander Woollcott, edited by Beatrice Kaufman and Joseph Hennessey. Copyright 1944 by The Viking Press, Inc., renewed 1972 by Joseph Hennessey. Reprinted by permission of Viking Penguin Inc.

My final acknowledgment goes to my wife, Frances, and our four sons, David, Aaron, Nathan, and Joel. Frances's constant encouragement enabled me to complete this study. Her editorial insights were also invaluable. My sons' willingness to share me with Woollcott was also appreciated.

iii

TABLE OF CONTENTS

Chapter 1

THE CAREER OF ALEXANDER WOOLLCOTT

Alexander Woollcott was born on January 19, 1887, in Phalanx, New Jersey, where almost forty-four years earlier his maternal grandfather, John Bucklin, had helped establish an agrarian, socialistic community. Although the community had ceased to exist as an economic and political entity thirty years before Woollcott's birth, fifty to sixty people did continue to live in the eighty-five-room common house that was Woollcott's birthplace. He was the fifth of five children born to Frances and Walter Woollcott, Walter being an English immigrant who worked in various positions, such as lawyer, accountant, government clerk, and stock exchange operator.

In 1889 the Woollcott family moved to Kansas City, Missouri. It was there that the young Woollcott made his theatrical debut at the age of four, playing the part of Puck in a scene from A Midsummer Night's Dream in a neighborhood tableau vivant. It was in Kansas City also that he attended his first play, a touring production of Sinbad the Sailor, starring Eddie Foy. Woollcott was not certain of the date of this historic event, saying in 1928 that it occurred when he was five,[1] and in 1939 that it was when he was six.[2] Regardless of Woollcott's exact age, that first trip to the theatre did convince him to be a newspaperman. His escort to see Sinbad was Roswell Martin Field, a neighbor who then wrote for the Kansas City Star. When Woollcott's family pointed out to him that Field's occupation enabled him to attend the theatre free, the youth decided on a newspaper career:

> Then and there I sensibly decided to be a newspaper man too, nor did I ever waver from that resolution, save for one brief period of apprehension during my last year at college when my defeatism expressed itself, as defeatism so often does, in a short-lived ambition to teach.[3]

1

Woollcott's formal education began in a Kansas City grade school, where his first teacher was Sophie Rosenberger, who guided him to reading Louisa M. Alcott. When the young scholar was eight she introduced him to "selected portions of Dickens."[4] Woollcott received additional encouragement in his literary interests from his home environment, his parents both being Dickens enthusiasts. In a letter to Laura E. Richards in 1932 Woollcott spoke of some of the books he read between the ages of nine and fourteen:

> I think I knew, when I first read them, that I
> would always like Huckleberry Finn and Little Wom-
> en, and Kenneth Grahame's The Golden Age, and
> Howard Pyle's Robin Hood, and Captain January.
> Mixed in with such treasures, and pretty much at
> the same time, was a good deal of addiction to
> Harrison Ainsworth [the English historical novelist]
> and to Charles Reade [the English novelist and play-
> wright]. But above all, and through all, and to
> this day, my dear Charles Dickens. My father
> started me when I was ten reading Great Expecta-
> tions to me. I still think it is the best of the lot.
> I had read all except Bleak House by the time I
> was twelve. Later I took on Jane Austen, and one
> of the reasons why I am not particularly well read
> today is because I have spent so large a part of
> the last twenty years rereading Dickens and Jane
> Austen.[5]

When Walter lost his Kansas City job with the Light and Coke Company in 1895, the Woollcott family returned to Phalanx, where Alexander continued his education. He finished grammar school in the Germantown section of Philadelphia, where Walter had taken a job with the gas company. In the fall of 1901 Alexander entered Central High School in Philadelphia. Woollcott spent most of the academic portions of his high school years as a boarder with various families. Summers were spent back at Phalanx, where Woollcott's mother resided after his father left the family.

Woollcott's interest in theatre and the newspaper world continued to grow during his high school years. He attended the theatre in Philadelphia and appeared there, at the age of sixteen, at the Chestnut Street Opera House in 1903, as a "super" in The Proud Prince, which was written for and starred E. H. Sothern. In his senior year he played Juliet in a parody of Romeo and Juliet that he had written. His

youthful desire for a newspaper career was encouraged when
he had book reviews published in the Philadelphia Evening
Telegraph and Record. In the spring of 1905, Woollcott's
senior year, his cousin Helen W. Sears, who was in charge
of the book review page for the Telegraph, turned the page
over to him for three weeks while she cared for her sick
father.

Three people were responsible for Woollcott attending
Hamilton College in Clinton, New York: Ivy Ashton, Edwin
B. Root, and Alexander Humphreys. Ivy Ashton, a playwright, had relatives living at the common house in Phalanx.
In the summer of 1905 she and her husband, Edwin B. Root,
visited those relatives. They took an interest in Woollcott,
who wanted to go to college but didn't have the necessary
funds. Root, whose family had been attending Hamilton for
years, was able to arrange for a scholarship to cover Woollcott's tuition. Alexander Humphreys, Woollcott's namesake
and President of Stevens Institute of Technology, loaned
Woollcott $3,000 to cover room and board and other expenses.

Woollcott's years at Hamilton, 1905 to 1909, did much
to further his literary and theatrical interests. As a freshman he contributed two book reviews, an article, and three
short stories to the Hamilton Literary Magazine, commonly
called The Lit. In his sophomore year he became one of the
editors and was editor-in-chief during his last two years.
During his freshman year he also won the Ninety One Manuscript Prize, which carried a $25 award. It had been es-
tablished that year by two Hamilton alumni, George M. Wean-
er, Jr., and Samuel Hopkins Adams, to recognize "the best
undergraduate writing in the extracurricular field."[6] He won
this award with a love story submitted to The Lit entitled
"The Precipice, A Story of Bohemia." He later submitted
the same story to The Bohemian, a pulp magazine, and received $12 for it. Woollcott also won the Ninety One Prize
in his senior year.

Woollcott's stage performances during his freshman
year were limited to monologues he delivered for the Glee
Club as "Mabel, the Beautiful Shopgirl," a Woollcott creation.
His theatrical activity picked up in his sophomore year, when
he revived the moribund drama club, which was thereafter
christened "The Charlatans." He devoted much of his attention to the club during the remainder of his college career.

In November of his junior year Woollcott wrote a

piece for The Lit entitled "Richard Mansfield. " The three-
page article was a prototype of other articles on theatrical
personalities that he was eventually to write for various magazines. Woollcott cited Mansfield's irascible personality as
one reason why the recently deceased actor had received so
little praise. He went on to laud the actor for continually
expanding his repertoire, foreshadowing the day when as a
critic he would write on the necessity of performers constantly challenging themselves. After pointing out Mansfield's
failures and successes, Woollcott questioned who would take
his place as "the great American actor. " Dismissing E. H.
Sothern and David Warfield as possibilities, he concluded:
"Mansfield's place seems destined to remain empty. "[7] It
wasn't until July 1920 that Woollcott found Mansfield's re-
placement. He was John Barrymore, whose performance
that season as Shakespeare's Richard III moved Woollcott to
write that he had "clearly become 'Mansfield's successor. '"[8]

Woollcott earned a Phi Beta Kappa key in his junior
year for his scholastic achievements. He also managed to
visit Utica to attend touring plays.

He left Hamilton with his Bachelor of Philosophy degree in 1909, but returned later as a lecturer, as a recipient of an L. H. D. degree in 1924, as a member of the College Board of Trustees, to which he was elected in 1936, and
as President of the College Alumni Society, a position he held
during the 1936-37 academic year. As these honors indicate,
he was a strong supporter of the college. He mentioned the
school many times in his articles and broadcasts. He was
particularly helpful to the Hamilton Chorus, giving it national
exposure on his Town Crier radio series, as well as paying
for its visits to New York. Nor did he forget the theatre at
Hamilton, making "The Charlatans" the overseers of an annual campus playwriting contest. Woollcott provided the $75
annual award to "the best play on a college theme written and
produced by Hamilton undergraduates. "[9] Along with Mrs. Edward Root he also sponsored an English composition prize.
Hamilton was grateful for Woollcott's patronage. In announc-
ing his election as a trustee, the Hamilton Alumni Review
stated:

> If Hamilton has had many friends as devoted as
> Alexander Woollcott, she has had few who have
> "done as much about it. " He is a man of special
> talents and gifts, who has used those talents and
> gifts generously for the benefit of his College. [10]

Woollcott had hoped to go to work immediately as a reporter for the <u>New York Times</u> upon graduating. He had persuaded Samuel Hopkins Adams to write a recommendation on his behalf to Carr Van Anda, managing editor of the <u>Times</u> and Adams's former boss. Years later Adams recalled that recommendation:

> So I wrote, on his behalf, to one of my old bosses of the <u>Sun</u>, Carr Van Anda, who, as managing editor was then raising the <u>Times</u> to the position of being the most important and influential newspaper in New York. To the best of my recollection and that of the recipient my support was on the cautious side. I guaranteed nothing, but gave my opinion, for what it was worth, that the young man had possibilities, and that it might be worth while to give him a trial. [11]

Unfortunately there were no openings at the <u>Times</u> when Woollcott graduated, and he had to settle for a job as a bank messenger at the Chemical Bank in New York, a job secured through the efforts of his old benefactor, Alexander Humphreys. With the exception of time off to recover from an attack of the mumps, Woollcott worked at the bank until September, when a reporter's job finally opened up at the <u>Times</u> for $15 per week. As a reporter, one of Woollcott's assignments was the criminal courts. It was his work here that probably led to his later interest in crime cases and murder mystery plays. His five-part series for <u>Look</u> magazine in 1940 on "Classic American Crimes" testified to this interest, as did the President's Crime Shelf of detective stories, which he drew up for Franklin Roosevelt in 1939. <u>The Dark Tower</u>, the murder mystery play he wrote in collaboration with George S. Kaufman in 1923, revealed again the influence of his criminal court reporting days, as did his propensity for explaining the plots of such plays in great detail in his reviews. In 1928 he humorously wrote of his interest in "murder dramas" in an article discussing the ones produced in New York that year.

> If the psychologists ever get around to studying my own addiction to such murder dramas, I suggest, as a clue for their researches, the possibility that I keep on going to them in the urchin hope that some day when the distracted heroine grasps the pearl-handled revolver, points it at the minor actor and fires, it won't go off. [12]

In addition to his criminal court reporting Woollcott covered a variety of other stories, such as the sinking of the Titanic; a World Series; and in 1909, his first play review, of The Bachelor's Baby, by Francis Wilson. Woollcott received this early experience as a Times reviewer when four plays opened simultaneously on Broadway the evening of Monday, December 27, 1909. Unsigned reviews of three of the plays appeared in the Tuesday, December 28 edition of the Times. Adolph Klauber, the Times's regular reviewer, undoubtedly wrote the review of the most important of the three productions, Know Thyself, by the French playwright Paul Hervie. The play derived its importance from the fact that it starred Arnold Daly. Klauber's review took up nearly three-quarters of the first column. In the third column of the page appeared a three-paragraph review entitled "Baby Makes a Hit in Wilson's New Play."[13] In his October 24, 1920, column for the Times Woollcott identified himself as the author, writing that it "was the first New York premier reported by your trusting correspondent, who wrote a gushing account under the impression that Baby Davis [a four-year-old performer in the play] was quite the most admirable little actress he had ever seen."[14] The review did little more than explain the play's plot and praise the child performer.

It was the strain of the reporter's beat, which culminated in the Rosenthal murder case in 1913, that moved Woollcott to give up his reporter's job and become a rewrite man for the Times. He remained in this position only until February 1914, when Klauber resigned his position to marry the actress Jane Cowl and become a theatrical producer. Woollcott did not apply for the vacated position but gladly accepted it when Carr Van Anda offered it to him. Van Anda recorded this reaction to Woollcott's acceptance of the $60-per-week job:

> I was agreeably surprised to learn that he was an ardent student of the drama for I was taking a chance without that knowledge, and equally surprised that, in spite of his bent, he had not applied for the place, which, it appeared, was due to youthful diffidence. He ultimately persuaded the world at large, I believe, that he was no longer so handicapped. [15]

At twenty-seven Woollcott was the youngest newspaper drama critic in New York. With the conclusion of the 1913-

14 Broadway season he departed for Europe, where he spent
eight weeks reviewing plays in London and Paris. Writing
from Paris in July, Woollcott told his Times readers of some
plays he had seen and some that were headed for New York.
This was the first of several trips that Woollcott would take
to see European theatre as well as Europe itself. Besides
keeping him up-to-date on the continental drama, it would
later in his career supply him with material for magazine
articles.

Woollcott was well settled in his new position on the
night of March 17, 1915, when he went to the 39th Street
Theatre to see a Shubert production of the farce Taking
Chances. His review in the Times the following morning
was to trigger a chain of events that would make him a center of controversy and at the same time bring him a great
deal of notoriety. Woollcott's objections to the production
were entirely with the script--and the monotone English of
the Frenchman Lou Tellegen, who played the male lead.
Woollcott did, however, have praise for Tellegen, saying,
"Much of his performance is deft and pleasing."[16] He also
praised the leading lady, the scenery, the direction, and the
company, which did not "feel called upon to roar or yell."[17]
In the review Woollcott immediately let his readers know his
opinion of the script: "it is not vastly amusing."[18] The play
told of a burglar who circumvented the law by seducing the
police chief's wife and using the seduction as blackmail to
ensure his escape. Woollcott faulted the play for being "quite
absurd" and "tedious, " and in his concluding paragraph referred to "moments when a puzzled audience wonders what it
is all about."[19]

The play didn't do much better with the other New
York critics, receiving only one good review (and that one
from the Shubert-owned New York Review). The play was
rejected by eight reviewers and received noncommittal notices
from six. The Shuberts proceeded to retaliate against Woollcott by barring him from their theatres. They accompanied
their complimentary tickets for their next production to the
Times with a note saying the tickets would not be honored if
proffered by Woollcott. The Times's managing editor returned the tickets and instructed Woollcott to buy his ticket
for the opening. Woollcott did so, but on the evening of
April 1, 1915, was turned away from the Maxine Elliott Theatre by Jack Shubert and his doorman. Backed by the Times,
Woollcott went to court and on April 3 received an injunction
against the Shuberts that restrained them from excluding him

from their theatres upon presentation of a paid ticket. The
Times also informed the Shuberts that it would no longer ac-
cept Shubert advertisements. That night, injunction in hand,
Woollcott attended the Shubert revival of Paul Trotter's Trilby.
Woollcott liked the production, saying, "Indeed, 'Trilby,' in
its present performances has much to please and is well
worth going to see...."20 The review was the first to carry
his byline.

In accordance with the injunction the Shuberts on April
7 presented reasons in court why the injunction should not be
continued. The court, however, ruled in favor of Woollcott
on May 18. The Shuberts did not give up. They brought the
case to the Court of Appeals, which on February 22, 1916,
ruled in their favor. The court, in a unanimous decision,
ruled that Woollcott's civil rights were not being violated.
He was not being barred because of his race, creed, or color.
As long as these rights were observed the Shuberts could seat
whom they wished. Although Woollcott lost the court battle,
he won favor both with the public and the Times. The latter
raised his weekly salary to $100, increased the space allot-
ment for his Sunday column, and gave him a Sunday byline.
In a year's time the Shuberts had felt the loss of their Times
advertisements, as well as reviews. After agreeing to admit
any reviewer the Times might send, the Shuberts again had
their productions reviewed in the Times and their advertising
accepted by the paper. In May 1929 Woollcott wrote of the
managers' attitude, which was the root of his problem with
the Shuberts. He noted that theatre managers were only interested in favorable reviews and had, through their advertising business, intimidated "the flabbier newspapers" into running only positive reviews. He further observed that audiences
for a play would not "be greatly increased by its hearty in-
dorsement in a journal which, for the sake of peace and a
little advertising, heartily indorses every play produced."21

In 1917 Woollcott expanded his professional activities.
He wrote a five-part series on Minnie Maddern Fiske for
Century magazine, which ran monthly from January through
May. The articles, with some additional commentary by
Woollcott, were then published in book form by the Century
Company in October as Mrs. Fiske--Her Views on Actors,
Acting, and the Problems of Production. In publishing the
articles in book form, Woollcott started a procedure he would
use frequently in his career.

In May 1917, anxious to serve his country in the war

effort, Woollcott enlisted as a private with the Medical Corps. In July he was shipped to Base Hospital No. 8 in Savenay, France. While there he wrote a one-act play, And Ye Took Me In, which told the story of a returning serviceman whose fiancée discovers his true character by disguising herself. The play was successfully presented at the base on Halloween.

In February 1918 Woollcott was transferred to Paris and the office of the Stars and Stripes, the Army's newly formed newspaper. He spent the remainder of his service career as a roving reporter, covering various battles and human interest stories. His discharge came on April 30, 1919, and the Times reported his arrival in New York aboard the Fabre liner Canada in its June 3 edition. [22] He resumed his reviewing duties in the August 6 issue of the paper with a review of Eugene Walter's The Challenge. He might have been speaking for himself when he wrote in the review:

> The ex-soldiers at "The Challenge" will be a little surprised to find themselves all suspectful of revo-lutionary infection, whereas most of them, of course, are so unaffectedly delighted to get back into civilian life that they cannot see anything the matter with it. [23]

Woollcott's return to the Times was marked by two changes: his reviews now regularly carried his byline, and George S. Kaufman was his assistant reviewer. During his first year back Woollcott's second book, The Command Is Forward, was published. Its subtitle aptly described its con-tents: "Tales of the A. E. F. battlefields as they appeared in The Stars and Stripes." The book contained thirty-five arti-cles Woollcott had written for the service newspaper.

In 1920 Woollcott was instrumental in the formation of the famous "Algonquin Round Table." The group got its start when Woollcott invited fellow newspapermen Franklin Pierce Adams and Heywood Broun to lunch with him at the Algonquin Hotel on New York's West Forty-fourth Street. The luncheon date turned into a weekly affair and eventually into a daily one. The original group of three expanded to include many fledgling authors, playwrights, columnists, editors, drama critics, pub-lishers, illustrators, cartoonists, artists, actors, and sculp-tors of the period. They were dubbed "The Algonquin Round Table" after the round table the hotel's manager Frank Case had installed for them in the hotel's Rose Room, their gather-ing place. In addition to the original three some of its mem-

bers were George S. Kaufman, Robert Sherwood, Ring Lard-
ner, Robert Benchley, Dorothy Parker, Marc Connelly, Edna
Ferber, Harold Ross, Art Samuels, Frank Crowninshield,
Herman Mankiewicz, John Peter Toohey, Harpo Marx, Paul
Robeson, Noel Coward, Alfred Lunt, Margalo Gillmore,
Peggy Wood, Tallulah Bankhead, Lynn Fontanne, Beatrice
Kaufman, and Charles MacArthur. In his book The Algon-
quin Wits Robert E. Drennan describes them:

> Generally speaking, all were young, fun-loving, and
> ambitious; all took a strong interest in theater,
> sports, politics, and social problems; and most
> noteworthy, all were gregarious, loquacious, ar-
> ticulate.
> Their common bond and peculiar genius was, of
> course, wit, although their excellence in conversa-
> tion, repartee, and bons mots may have caused
> them to undervalue their contributions to the com-
> munity of letters. [24]

The group gave Woollcott a natural outlet for his wit
and flamboyant nature. He also was a charter member of
another group that grew out of the Algonquin crowd in 1922,
the Thanatopsis Literary and Inside Straight Club. This was
a poker playing group that met at the Algonquin on Saturday
evenings and often would play well into Sunday. According
to Drennan, "Harpo Marx was popularly acknowledged as the
most proficient gamester; Woollcott was unanimously voted
the worst."[25] Among the other players, some of whom were
also members of the Round Table, were Franklin Pierce
Adams, Robert Benchley, Heywood Broun, Marc Connelly,
Harold Ross, Donald Ogden Stewart, and Herbert Bayard
Swope. It was probably at one of the group's sessions that
Charlie Chaplin made the following observation:

> I like to know the way writers work and how much
> they turn out a day.... The American critic Alex-
> ander Woollcott wrote a seven-hundred-word review
> in fifteen minutes, then joined a poker game--I was
> there when he did it. [26]

In addition to providing Woollcott with camaraderie the
Algonquin also provided him with material for the printed page.
In December 1923 he wrote a humorous article for Vanity
Fair, "The Passing of the Thanatopsis," in which he explained
why Heywood Broun, Marc Connelly, and he had resigned from
the poker playing club. Actually they hadn't, but Woollcott

was able to use "the white lie" to relate some comic incidents
that had happened at the club.   In January 1929 he wrote an
article for McCall's, "Wayfarer's Inn, " in which he told of
experiences some celebrities had at the hotel.   Besides these
two pieces Woollcott mentioned the Algonquin and the Round
Table in other articles.   One was a New Yorker "Shouts and
Murmurs" column containing mention of The Green Pastures,
by Round Tabler Marc Connelly.   He noted that the success
of the play must be annoying to those who think of the Algonquin Wits as a "huddle of sneering sophisticates":

> Yet from that Table, of all places, has issued a
> play, lofty, simple, and so strong in its loving
> kindness that it warms the heart.   "The Green
> Pastures" has all the sneering sophistication of the
> Twenty Third Psalm. [27]

By 1932 both the Round Table and the Thanatopsis had
ceased to exist.   The Depression has been cited as one of the
reasons for the latter's death, and a change of interests and
movement to other geographical areas by members have been
reasons given for the passing of the Round Table itself.

In 1921 Woollcott entered into a new phase of his professional career--book-reviewing.   That year he wrote two
reviews for Bookman.   The first, appearing in March, was
of The Gathering of the Forces, a two-volume collection of
newspaper articles written by Walt Whitman for the Brooklyn
Eagle.   The editors were Cleveland Rodgers and John Black.
Woollcott was quite critical of the book:

> The stuff was hardly worth the labor involved in its
> exhumation or, more positively, ... its republication
> would be a distinct disservice to the reputation of
> a great name. [28]

Despite this negative commentary Woollcott noted how some
of Whitman's evaluations of theatre reprinted in the book were
appropriate to Woollcott's own day.

Woollcott's second Bookman review appeared in June.
It gave his impression of The Invisible Censor, a collection
of articles by Francis Hackett written for the New Republic.
Woollcott complained of the articles' superficial quality.   However, he took part of the sting from his criticism by offering
the following reason for it: "Maybe, after all, this chafing
at Hackett comes from reading at one gulp a tight little pem-

mican style unsuited to anything but the brief excursions of
'The New Republic's' columns. "29

These represented Woollcott's first reviews outside
the Times.   In his "Second Thoughts, " of September 10, 1916,
he had reviewed an anonymously written book, The Truth
About the Theatre.   Woollcott rejected it:

> Of any real diagnosis of our theatre's ills, of any
> attempt to separate the transitory from the funda-
> mental weaknesses, of any suggestion of remedy or
> forecast, of any hint that the author knows the the-
> atre in time will punish its own offenders, the book
> is innocent.   Instead it is packed to the brim with
> what everybody knows, with what has been said
> again and again and again. 30

Woollcott continued to review books for various publi-
cations throughout his career.   His influence as a book reviewer was noted by Louis Kronenberger in 1935:

> Mr. Woollcott is not only a best-seller in his own
> right, but with a sentence or two he can make best-
> sellers of other men.   At present he is by far the
> most influential salesman of books in the United
> States. . . . 31

In October 1922 Woollcott left the Times to join Frank
Munsey's New York Herald, where he replaced Laurence Rea-
mer as the drama editor.   Money was the primary reason
for the move, an increase in salary from $100 per week to
$15, 000 per year.   Woollcott's final article for the Times
was on Sunday, October 8.   He made no mention of his departure until the last line: "Exit the First Grave-Digger.
Curtain. "32   "The First Grave-Digger" was a name given to
Woollcott at the Lambs Club in recognition of his critical
ability to bury performers.

At the Herald Woollcott introduced a new feature to
his writing schedule.   In those editions in which there was
no play review to be published he might write a column on
a theatrical or non-theatrical topic, anything from what to
give for Bon Voyage presents to the disappearance of theatrical boarding houses to reminiscences on the war.

Woollcott published two more books in 1922:   Mr.
Dickens Goes to the Play and Shouts and Murmurs.   The

first book was a natural project for Woollcott, who had always admired the author. As the title indicates, the book deals with Dickens's interest in the theatre. It contained three articles by Woollcott, letters by the novelist revealing his interest in theatre, excerpts from his work dealing with theatre, and a Dickens sketch, Sleight of Hand. With the exception of a six-page introduction, Shouts and Murmurs was a collection of previously published material on theatre that Woollcott had written for the Times and various magazines.

On April 30, 1922, Woollcott took to the boards of the 49th Street Theatre with some other members of the Algonquin Round Table for a one-night stand of a program entitled No Sirree! An Anonymous Entertainment by the Vicious Circle of the Hotel Algonquin. The program, a satire on the contemporary theatre, was made up of monologues, skits, short plays, and musical numbers totaling fifteen acts--all written by members of the company, although none claimed authorship on the program. Woollcott was quite active in the production, appearing in six of the acts. He appeared in the opening chorus, which included John Peter Toohey, Robert Benchley, George S. Kaufman, Marc Connelly, and Franklin P. Adams. He then played the part of the Second Agitated Seaman in "The Greasy Hog," a one-act satire of O'Neill's one-act sea plays. Next, he appeared as one of eleven first-nighters in a sketch called "Between the Acts." He then appeared as "Dreggs, a butler" in "Big Casino Is Little Casino." Subtitled "A Samuel Shipman Play," the piece satirized contemporary playwright Samuel Shipman's melodramas. Woollcott then enacted the role of Archibald Van Alstyne in his own sketch, "Zowie or the Curse of an Akins Heart." Parodying the romantic plays of Zöe Akins, the sketch dramatized the meeting between Zhoolie Venable and two of her former beaux, one of whom Woollcott played. Woollcott concluded his participation in the program by appearing with the rest of the company in the finale.

A morning-after account of the performance, by Laurette Taylor, appeared in the Times; "Actress Gets Back at the Critics." Taylor had some humorous words of advice:

> They [the members of the company] all gathered to
> show the actor how it should be done, and being a
> constructive critic I would advise a course of voice
> culture for Marc Connelly, a new vest and pants
> for Heywood Broun, a course with Yvette Guilbert
> [a French songstress] for Alexander Woollcott, and

> I would advise them all to leave the stage before
> they take it up. A pen in their hand is mightier
> than God's most majestic word in their mouths. [33]

Taylor's only comment on "Zowie" appeared in the July 1922 issue of Vanity Fair: "Ruth Gilmore in a splendid imitation of Ethel Barrymore made 'Zowie' something that was really satire at its best." [34]

In 1922 Woollcott also delivered a series of lectures at New York University on the subject of dramatic interpretation. Lecturing was to become one of his more frequent pursuits in ensuing years.

On March 20, 1924, Woollcott again changed newspapers. The New York Tribune purchased the New York Herald, and Woollcott was transferred to another Munsey paper, the Sun, where he replaced Gilbert Gabriel.

On May 19, 1924, Woollcott attended a musical comedy, I'll Say She Is, featuring the Marx Brothers. The headline over his review in the March 20 Sun read "Harpo Marx and Some Brothers." Woollcott liked the performance of the brothers, whom he referred to as "those talented cup-ups," but it was Harpo who captivated him:

> In particular it is a splendacious and reasonably
> tuneful excuse for going to see that silent brother,
> that shy, unexpected magnificent comic.... Surely
> there should be dancing in the streets when a great
> clown comes to town, and this man is a great
> clown. [35]

The show helped establish the Marx Brothers as legitimate theatre stars, with Woollcott's review undoubtedly helping. Harpo and Woollcott were to become close friends.

On September 6, 1924, Woollcott enthusiastically opened his review of What Price Glory? with this sentence:

> No war play written in the English language since
> the German guns boomed under the walls of Liege,
> ten years ago, has been so true, so alive, so salty
> and so richly satisfying as the piece called "What
> Price Glory" which was produced last evening by
> Arthur Hopkins. [36]

Audiences picked up Woollcott's enthusiasm and supported the play through 299 New York performances and a road tour that extended through 1927. In addition film versions of the play were made in 1926, 1936, and 1952. The success of the play must have been gratifying to Woollcott; it was he who had originally recommended it to Hopkins.

Woollcott's fourth book, Enchanted Aisles, was published in 1924. This too, was mostly a collection of previously published material on theatre.

When Woollcott's contract with the Sun expired in August 1925 he gladly accepted Herbert Bayard Swope's offer to join the World, where he replaced Heywood Broun for $15,000 per year, the same salary he was then receiving at the Sun. Woollcott's main dissatisfaction with the Sun was that it was an afternoon paper. As Edwin Hoyt explained in his book on Woollcott, the reviewer realized that the critics on the morning papers were the ones who decided the fate of shows. [37]

As for his working relationship with Frank Munsey, his mentor at the Herald and the Sun, who was noted for interfering with his former drama critic, Hamilton Owens, Woollcott offered these comments when Munsey died in December 1925:

> When one morning in the fall of 1922 this chronicler of the theatre sallied forth to report for duty for the first time at the office of the then unabsorbed "New York Herald," nearly every one he passed on the street stopped him long enough to tell him what trouble he was sure to have with Mr. Munsey, how constant the interference with his department would be, how disastrous would be the inroads on his independence as a critic. But during the three years which he then served under Mr. Munsey on the "Herald" (and, after that journal was shot from under him, on the "Sun"), he was quite unhindered by such interference--was indeed left as free as he could possibly have wished to say his say and do his work according to his own flickering lights. Today, therefore, he can do no less than say so. [38]

On January 25, 1925, the Saturday Evening Post published the first of five biographical articles by Woollcott, "The Story of Irving Berlin." G. P. Putnam's Sons then published

the articles in book form under the same title. As with his
Dickens volume, the Berlin book was a natural project for
Woollcott, since he admired the composer both professionally
and personally.

In the fall of 1925 Woollcott gave three talks under the
auspices of the Theatre Guild. The general topic was "current theatrical events. "[39]

Prior to the start of the 1927-28 Broadway season,
Woollcott's last as a newspaper reviewer, he was voted " 'the
most discriminating and stimulating critic' in New York"[40] by
a group of twenty-one actors representing Actors Equity. The
group included Ethel Barrymore, Jeanne Eagles, Ruth Gordon,
Leslie Howard, Walter Huston, Charles Ruggles, Lee Tracy,
and Blanche Yurka.

Woollcott's three-year contract with the World ended
in August 1928. Swope offered Woollcott a new two-year contract with a $1, 000 yearly raise. Woollcott declined the of-
fer. In a "Shouts and Murmurs" column for the New Yorker
in February 1929 Woollcott offered the congestion of Times
Square and the pressure of meeting deadlines as reasons for
his departure from the World and from newspaper criticism
generally. [41]

In the three-part New Yorker series that Wolcott Gibbs
did on Woollcott in 1939 he spoke of the time limitations put
on Woollcott at the World:

> The World, in a desperate effort to beat the other
> papers to the street, kept advancing his deadline
> until, unless Mr. Woollcott left before the curtain
> went down, he often had no more than twenty min-
> utes to turn out his copy. [42]

In a 1933 interview with Ward Morehouse Woollcott
gave another reason for his retirement:

> I reviewed plays for thirteen years and I quit be-
> cause I didn't want to spend the rest of my life in
> that company. Where can you find a gathering as
> dreary, as ruthless and as moronic as you do at
> a New York premiere? First nights have lost their
> charm and flavor. I never go any more. I won't
> sit in that company. The newspapers have helped
> to ruin premieres, and the theaters have let them

get away with it. Why for instance, should the
Times get six pair of first night seats? Absurd.
A premiere night should be a pleasant occasion but
it has become an unbearable one. You certainly
don't want your friends and relatives at a premiere. ... Yes, you can take this down: the premiere audience that you draw nowadays is composed
of nothing more than $$!!!!!!$$ (Ed. Note: Mr.
Woollcott's explosives will be translated upon request.)[43]

As late as 1942 Woollcott proffered another reason for
his retirement from journalistic criticism in a letter to an
English friend, Lady Sibyl Colefax: "I have managed to stay
out of it [New York], except for four or five weeks a year,
since 1928. Indeed, that was my chief reason for resigning
as a dramatic critic. "[44]

In his book on Woollcott Edwin Hoyt suggests that the
working relationship between editor Swope and critic Wo*oll-
cott was another factor in Woollcott's departure from the
World. Swope wanted Woollcott to spend all his working energies on the World and not spend time writing for the several magazines to which Woollcott contributed. This attitude
quite obviously was not pleasing to Woollcott, nor was Swope's
propensity for sending him memoranda regarding his reviews
and Sunday columns. [45] One incident that certainly didn't help
the relationship between the two men was the opening of
O'Neill's Strange Interlude. Scripts of the play were made
available to the critics prior to the play's opening on January
30, 1928. In the February edition of Vanity Fair, which went
on sale before the play's opening, Woollcott wrote a negative
review of the script, in which he faulted O'Neill's "clumsy
and paltry dramatic writing." He believed that O'Neill "had
attempted a task which called for more intuition and knowledge of the human animal than he possessed. "[46]

Believing it wasn't fair to send a critic to review a
play the script of which he had publicly criticized, Swope
sent Dudley Nichols to review Strange Interlude instead of
Woollcott. Woollcott, however, did get to have his say on
the production in his Sunday column following Strange Interlude's opening. The production did nothing to change his
view of the play:

Neither the really brilliant resourcefulness with
which the unhampered Guild brought the play to life,

nor the novelty of the archaic technique O'Neill had
resurrected for the writing of it, served to conceal,
even for the fleeting hours of the performance, what
often seemed to me the naive and tasteless pomposity of its speech and the fearful pretentiousness of
its heavily furrowed brow. Indeed, I thought that
the net result of all the patient and austere effort
that went into "Strange Interlude" as it was performed at the Golden Theatre on Monday last was
a resonant emptiness. [47]

Woollcott's final paragraph as a newspaper reviewer
was written with his typical sense of the dramatic and testi-
fied to his awareness that as a critic he was loved by some
and less than loved by others:

Now that some one has suggested that my new home
be called These Old Arms and now that the Shubert
house organ [the New York Review] has described
me as the Theatre Guild's "journalistic lackey"
(known to my intimates, I suppose, as Wilton), the
theatrical season of 1927-1928 may be said to be
on its last legs. The First Grave Digger looks up,
notes that date on the calendar and wipes the sweat
off his hands. With an uneasy glance over his
shoulder, he exits hurriedly, almost unnoticed, save
for a faint murmur in one corner of the scene where
Alfred Lunt, Harpo Marx, Mrs. Fiske and Ruth
Gordon sob quietly in chorus, as the curtain falls.
Then, to a great blare from the orchestra pit, it
rises again in a street scene. Enter Lee Shubert,
Walter Hampden, Ruth Chatterton, Lowell Sherman,
Billie Burke and a great happy throng tossing roses
into the air. They dance. Curtain. [48]

In 1928 Woollcott published two more books. The
first, Going to Pieces, was again mostly a collection of earlier published articles. The second, Two Gentlemen and a
Lady, was a collection of three stories about dogs.

No longer having the newspaper position, Woollcott
could devote his energies to new endeavors. In early 1929
he took on a weekly column for the New Yorker, which was
run by his friend and associate from Stars and Stripes days,
Harold Ross. Woollcott called his column "Shouts and Murmurs," the title used for his 1922 book and, for a time, his
play-reviewing column at the Herald. The column covered a

variety of subjects--the theatre, books, contemporary society, and personal reminiscences among them. He continued writing it with few interruptions through December 1934. In a 1932 letter to Laura Richards he wrote of the satisfaction the column gave him:

> After my flight from Times Square, I invented this page in The New Yorker where, as a kind of town crier, I can say anything that is on my mind. The trouble is that there isn't often much on it. But every once in a while I have the satisfaction, which is the breath of the journalist's nostril, of hearing bells ring all over the country. Then I know that I have had the good fortune to say something which a lot of people had wanted to have said. Said for them, that is. [49]

In addition to his "Shouts and Murmurs" column Woollcott also occasionally contributed a profile article on a celebrity for the New Yorker.

In September 1929 he made his debut in radio, the medium where he "found his largest and most obedient audience."[50] His first contract was for thirteen weeks with station WOR, an affiliate of the Mutual Broadcasting System. His guests on his first program were Clifton Webb, Fred Allen, and Libby Holman, who were appearing at the time in a musical called The Little Show. When the thirteen-week contract expired Woollcott's program was picked up for an additional thirteen weeks by the Gruen Watch Company. It was the beginning of a career that would extend throughout most of the rest of his life. As radio's "Town Crier" he would eventually earn up to $3,500 per broadcast. Like his New Yorker column, his fifteen-minute Town Crier program might cover a variety of subjects. For a time he also had a book-review program, The Early Bookworm. The reason for his success as a radio personality was suggested in a 1943 eulogy:

> But perhaps Mr. Woollcott's greatest gift to radio over a period of years, was style.... In the slightest of the Woollcott programs there was style, a conscientious writer's care for the exact word, for balance and mood and structure. "This is Woollcott speaking***" his program began, and you knew that he was not going to talk down to you. And unless one is very much mistaken, this explained in

no small degree his enormous popularity on the air.
He honored his listeners by assuming that they too
were literate, and they need not be addressed in
words of one syllable merely because radio is a
mass medium. The listeners were obviously grateful; and the moguls of Radio Row, though they are
apt to think of the radio public in terms of the low-
est common denominator, ought to be impressed,
if only because his recommendation of a book or
a play virtually assured its success. [51]

In addition to his radio debut Woollcott also made his
debut as a Broadway playwright in 1929. With his former
assistant at the Times, George S. Kaufman, he wrote The
Channel Road, a comedy based on "Boule de Suif," a short
story by Guy de Maupassant. Arthur Hopkins produced the
play, thus verifying a statement Woollcott had made in
1917:

Certainly one who has never written a play... and
who gives his word of honor that he never will
write one, may be permitted to say that if he
should, he would a little rather have it fall into
the hands of Arthur Hopkins, than into those of
any other producer in America. [52]

The play, set in the time of the Franco-Prussian War,
told of a French prostitute who gave herself to a Prussian
lieutenant in the hope that he would let her fellow travelers
continue their journey. Opening on October 17, the play received mixed reviews and ran for only fifty performances.
The reaction of Brooks Atkinson in the Times was typical:

It is in many respects a library drama with a weakness toward fine writing and sentimental phrase-
making; and it is not helped by a performance which,
with the exception of two splendid actors, leaves the
comedy reclining languidly on the stage. But it has
moments of strength and beauty--a gallant climax
to the second act when everything that has been
brewing suddenly makes for magnificence, and a
modestly majestic final curtain. [53]

Some critics were quick to point out the negative contribution made to the play by Woollcott. Francis Bellamy,
the Outlook and Independent:

For years Alexander Woollcott, erstwhile Broadway dramatic critic, has been defending the omniscience of the critic against the assault of the outraged playwright by the simple statement that a man can tell a good egg from a bad one without being able to lay one. Last week he presented a play, written in collaboration with George Kaufman, and entitled The Channel Road. And proved at least part of his contention. He cannot lay the egg.

Indeed, to judge from what his play reveals, Mr. Woollcott is infinitely more a humorist than a critic. Else we doubt he could have perpetrated in the name of wit the crimes against human character which now stain the stage at the Arthur Hopkins Theatre.

The demon of the wise crack has been loosed by Mr. Woollcott on de Maupassant's simple tale of the German occupation of France in 1870. And he appears without warning in the guise of nearly every person in the play. Their faces as they converse may be the faces of de Maupassant's people; but the voice is the voice of Mr. Woollcott talking brightly to himself. [54]

John Hutchens, Theatre Arts Monthly:

It may be assumed that the play... belongs largely to Mr. Woollcott, for long a dramatic critic presiding over his own gracefully romantic school. But Mr. Woollcott's style, utterly gay as it may be elsewhere, has come down heavily on this story, blotting out much of its sting under the sort of fine writing that turns to lead in the theatre. [55]

Joseph Wood Krutch, who liked the play, commented: "the nostalgic sentimentality of The Channel Road (1929) is such pure Alexander Woollcott that Mr. Kaufman can have contributed nothing except his technical skill. "[56]

Besides being notable for his debut as a radio personality and Broadway playwright, the year 1929 was also important in Woollcott's life for his financial losses in the stock market crash. Wolcott Gibbs wrote in his articles on Woollcott that he lost more than $200,000. He also noted that in the next ten years after the crash Woollcott recovered financially, earning over $700,000 through his work as a writer, playwright, actor, radio personality, and endorser of various commercial products. 57

On November 9, 1931, at New York's Belasco Theatre, Woollcott opened another facet of his career by appearing in the role of Harold Sigrist in Brief Moment, a comedy by S. N. Behrman. The play told the story of the romance and marriage of a socially prominent young man and a cabaret singer. Behrman had described Woollcott's role as follows: "Sigrist is very fat; about thirty years old, and lies down whenever possible. He somewhat resembles Alexander Woollcott, who conceivably might play him. "58 Woollcott simply played himself, and most critics thought he did a good job of it. John Mason Brown of the New York Evening Post thought Woollcott was better than the play:

> Though he is neither a second Duse, nor another
> Minnie Maddern Fiske, Mr. Woollcott is a shrewd
> and accomplished comedian; as amusing on the stage
> as he is in print....
>   He is immensely funny. But even he, uproarious
> and delicious as he is and truculent as are his lines,
> cannot hide the sorry fact that he is walking away
> with a play that Mr. Behrman forgot to write. 59

Stark Young, reviewing for the New Republic, saw the possibility of a good acting career for Woollcott:

> Mr. Woollcott's performance errs on the side of
> isolation, a slant somewhat allowed by the role of
> modern oracle, but likely to dislocate the senses.
> He has, nevertheless, genuine comic gifts and he
> brought something invaluable to the play. His sense
> of the audience clicked with every moment he had to
> manage. It is more than obvious that he may turn
> out to be in his time one of our best character ac-
> tors. 60

Joseph Wood Krutch was quite critical: "Though Mr. Woollcott is amusing and doubtless better than any other dramatic critic would be, he is nevertheless an amateur who keeps one constantly reminded of the fact that he is. "61 Brooks Atkinson's appraisals pose somewhat of a contradiction. In his review of the play for the Times he was rather complimentary:

> For Mr. Woollcott professional acting consists in

speaking rather more deliberately than he does in the
aisles and lobbies, for the stage is invariably a
trifle more sluggish than life. Otherwise, Mr.
Woollcott is himself again. Cast in the play as an
obese sybarite, with a passion for reclining on
couches and the gift of a flowering literary style,
he makes amusing observations on the contemporary
scene with a kind of resigned cynicism. It is good
talk both merry and malicious, which is a strange
combination; and Mr. Woollcott tosses it across the
footlights with a relish that the audience shares. If
he enjoyed himself as much as the audience last
night enjoyed him, he must have been having a
good time. 62

In his 1970 book Broadway Atkinson gave a somewhat
different impression of Woollcott's performance: "Having
been a frustrated actor for years, he became a sort of virt-
uoso fat man. He gave colorless amateur performances as
a fat man in two of S. N. Behrman's plays--Brief Moment
and Wine of Choice. "63

In a newspaper interview during the week of the play's
New York opening Woollcott himself offered observations on
his acting and his role:

I'm not an actor. God no!...I'd have been a
pretty bum dramatic critic for some ten years if
I didn't know that much. I may protray an "obese
sybarite" on the stage. I may be "pontifical" or
even a "Cheshire Woollcott, " as some of the critics
termed me. Those are matters which can stand
debate.... But I'm not an actor....
The part I play doesn't need acting. The character has absolutely no emotions. Any one with a
good speaking voice could walk through it. In fact,
I'll venture to state that any actor living, with the
possible exception of Walter Hampden, could play
the role as well as I do....
That doesn't mean to say I haven't a good time
in the part. I've had a lovely time and enjoyed it
thoroughly. 64

In another interview the next day Woollcott gave his
interpretation of the desires of the opening night audience:

Here... is a play which is a delicate piece of

writing--acted by two superb young artists [Robert
Douglas and Francine Larrimore] and directed by
one of our first stage directors [Guthrie McClintic].
But an entire first-night audience comes to the theater only to see me. They are hoping against hope
that I will make an ass of myself. They have no
interest in anything until I appear. Then they sit
up and pay the keenest attention not to the character I am playing but to Alexander Woollcott acting
out. I make an exit--the play goes on--the thread
of plot spins along, but the audience sits back.
They came to see Alexander Woollcott--to the devil
with them.

Now mind you ... this will not occur again. A
decent, normal, play-loving audience such as one
gets in New York after that dreadful first-night
gathering of repressed exhibitionists will put me
in my proper place and I shall become simply a
modest part of the production and the play will become the thing, as it should be. [65]

The play itself received mixed reviews, but did have
a New York run of 129 performances and a national tour.
Woollcott's presence in the cast was undoubtedly the main
drawing card.

In 1933 Woollcott again collaborated on a play with
George S. Kaufman, whom Woollcott described as "the most
patient, the most considerate and the most courteous worker
I have ever known. He emanates a benign radiance. He
treats all the players after his own honor and dignity."[66]
A comic murder mystery, The Dark Tower dramatized the
murder of the villainous husband of a promising young actress and the ensuing search for the culprit. The play received a mixed critical reaction. Foremost among the complaints were its length and implausability. Brooks Atkinson
made one of the most poignant criticisms:

Before the authors have gotten around to unmasking
their murderer you begin to suspect that Mr. Woollcott could have related the story more pungently in
his bouncing, Dickensian prose without having to
shake his fist at the theatre....

"The Dark Tower" had, accordingly, a pleasant
appearance and a jovial manner. But it has more
time at its disposal than most theatregoers have.
Mr. Woollcott could tell the gist of it more vigor-

ously in his New Yorker series without having to
stir away from his desk. Dark doings in gloomy
towers can lie down more comfortably in those columns than in the three capacious acts of a loosely
woven drama. [67]

The most frequently mentioned attributes of the play
were its wit and polished writing--qualities one might expect
from its authors. The play wasn't much more successful at
the box office than The Channel Road. It opened on November 26 and had a run of fifty-nine performances. In a letter
to Burns Mantle Woollcott discussed his work as a playwright:

What's all this nonsense of classifying as a playwright one who (on the most liberal of interpreta-
tions) is no more than five-sixths of a playwright?
I did write half of one play (with G. S. K.) and (with
G. S. K. and G. deM.) a third of another. When I
recall their fate it irks me to be called upon for
enough clairvoyance to tell what I think about my
first success. [68]

In a newspaper interview shortly after The Dark Tower's opening Woollcott spoke rather humorously about the
writing of the play: "The best writing in 'The Dark Tower'
is that detective scene in the last act. The fact that George
Kaufman wrote every line of that scene throws me into a
state of mild confusion. "[69]

In 1934 Woollcott entered yet another field of endeavor,
motion pictures. He was featured in a short for R. K. O. Pictures, Mr. Woollcott's Little Game. The film depicted Woollcott playing a word game that had as its object the writing of
the most words beginning with a given letter in a minute's
time. Woollcott's opponents in the game were a dumb blonde
and a headwaiter. Reviewing the film for the New York
Times, Mordaunt Hall wrote: "Mr. Woollcott is quite at
his ease before the camera and the microphone. One might
hazard that he seems to be enjoying the letter and word game.
It is a frail piece of work which seems ended all too soon. "[70]

Another collection of Woollcott articles, While Rome
Burns, appeared in book form in 1934. His radio work con-
tinued to occupy his time, as a letter he wrote to Alfred
Lunt and Lynn Fontanne in February humorously revealed:
"My life as a broadcaster, which completely enthralls me,
also leaves me so little time that, except for an occasional

trip to the water-closet, I do nothing else. "[71] Woollcott's
time-consuming radio schedule came to an abrupt halt in late
1935, when he became involved in a dispute with his sponsor,
Cream of Wheat. He had made comments on the air about
Hitler and Mussolini that the company thought might antagonize
"large racial groups. " Woollcott's letter to Paul Harper,
whose agency handled the Cream of Wheat account, presented
his stand:

> Now, in these broadcasts the Town Crier has for
> several years been freely reporting his likes and
> dislikes on the books, plays, pictures, prejudices,
> manners and customs of the day. In undertaking
> such an oral column, he could not with self-respect
> agree in advance never to take pot shots at such
> targets as Hitler or Mussolini. Or, for that mat-
> ter, at any other bully, lyncher or jingo whose head
> happened to come within shooting distance. If he
> did embark upon a series thus hamstrung in advance,
> his own interest in the broadcasts would so dwindle
> that they would deteriorate in short order. [72]

Woollcott and Cream of Wheat were unable to resolve
their differences. Rather than submit to political censorship
he gave up the lucrative radio contract. The interest in political and social affairs that this incident reveals exhibited
itself other times during Woollcott's public life. For example,
he campaigned for Franklin Roosevelt in the 1936 and 1940
elections and spoke out in a May 25, 1941, broadcast against
Charles Lindbergh and other members of the America First
Committee, who wanted the United States to stay out of the
European war. Woollcott argued: "In this world today there
is no such thing as neutrality. You are either for or against
him [Hitler]. You either fight him or you help him. "[73]

Woollcott appeared in another film in 1935. The
Scoundrel starred Noel Coward; Woollcott played a very minor
role, which like his stage appearances called for him to be
himself. William Troy, reviewing for the Nation, was one
of the few critics to evaluate his performance: "It's rather
strange that the best scenes are those in which Alexander
Woollcott, conspicuously in the flesh, presides over sessions
of one of the more elegant cenacles of Park Avenue Bohemia. "[74] Andre Sennwald advised his New York Times readers: "You will find Alexander Woollcott perishing languidly
in a sea of tired epigrams. "[75] In a letter to Dorothy Parker,
Woollcott gave this reaction to film work:

> It did seem likely that, with Charlie [MacArthur]
> and Ben [Hecht] directing in their cockeyed fashion
> and Noel [Coward] fluttering about the studio..., it
> might be fun. It seems I was wrong about this,
> but, as they won't need me more than four days
> all told, the damage is inconsiderable. [76]

The 1935 trial of Bruno Hauptmann for the kidnapping
and slaying of Charles Lindbergh's son brought Woollcott
briefly back to journalistic reporting for the New York Times.
From the trial site in Flemington, New Jersey, he wrote two
articles on the proceedings.

Woollcott entered a new area in 1935, when he became
an anthologist of works other than his own. The Woollcott
Reader consisted of sixteen pieces, among them a biography,
a play, some essays, long stories, and a short story. The
represented authors included J. M. Barrie ("Margaret Og-
ilvy"), Thornton Wilder (The Happy Journey to Trenton and
Camden), William Allen White ("Mary White"), Clarence Day
("In the Green Mountain"), and Evelyn Waugh ("A Handful of
Dust"). In the foreword to the collection Woollcott explained
his choices:

> Assembled in this volume for you to have and to
> hold--not I hope too costly to have nor too unwieldly
> to hold--are certain of the minor masterpieces from
> the literature of my own day which have given me
> the deepest and most abiding satisfaction. [77]

The success of the volume led in 1937 to the publication of Woollcott's Second Reader. In January of that year
he returned to the air for a season as the "Town Crier," with
two weekly fifteen-minute broadcasts. A month before the
series began he expressed his elation in a letter to Leggett
Brown, his secretary at the time: "I am to have music if
and when I feel like it. The sponsors are the Chesterfield
people and the product is the Granger pipe tobacco. All the
conditions seem to me so auspicious that I am crossing my
fingers in sheer apprehension."[78] In another letter of March
of that year Woollcott revealed to Harpo Marx that along with
Beatrice Kaufman, George S.'s wife, he had bought the production rights to Steinbeck's Of Mice and Men,[79] thus adding
another dimension to his career. The play had been published in February of that year and reached the stage on November 23, 1937. It enjoyed a run of 209 performances,
while winning the Drama Critics Award.

In the summer of 1932 Woollcott had reminisced in a magazine article about his performance earlier that year in Brief Moment. He related that his mind had wandered during a performance and a fellow actor had fed him a line to get him back in place. Contemplating his future as an actor he concluded:

> So if I never return to the stage it will be because I feel myself unequal, after years of self-indulgence, to the strain of complete attention. Of course, I may never have another role offered to me. It is conceivable that the question will never come up. [80]

The question did come up in 1937, when another Behrman play, Wine of Choice, was being cast. The part of Binky, described by one writer as "the cosmopolite Pygmalion who nurses the artistic careers of young women and acts as sort of male Elsa Maxwell to Long Island society, "[81] was offered to Woollcott. Woollcott's lecture schedule prevented him from accepting the role, but he attended the play's premiere in Chicago because he was there on business. The play wasn't received well by the Chicago critics, and the Theatre Guild, which was producing it, got Woollcott to take over the part of Binky in hopes of bolstering the play. Behrman was also rewriting. In a letter to an old newspaper friend, Frank Sullivan, two days after he opened in the play in Philadelphia, Woollcott explained why he accepted the role: "It may not have escaped your attention that I am acting again. My own official version is that I did it to help Behrman, but I guess it was just exhibitionism. "[82] Just prior to the New York opening in a letter to Rebecca West he wrote again of his joining the production:

> It is difficult for me now to recall just why I went into it, but I did so lightheartedly in the not unreasonable conviction that the whole thing would blow up in two or three weeks. Instead, it has gone on and on, gathering strength as it went. [83]

Whatever momentum the production had gathered quickly dissipated with the New York opening, for the play ran a total of forty-three performances. As with Brief Moment Woollcott fared better with most of the critics than did the play. Brooks Atkinson saw some improvement in Woollcott's acting since his appearance in Brief Moment:

> If there is little to blame at this stage in his [Behr-

man's] comedy's fortunes, there is little to praise
beyond a taut and sparkling performance by a band
of first-rate professional actors with the portly
Alexander Woollcott tossed in for groaningly full
measure. The Town Crier is steadily improving
his feet and his mettle most of the evening now....
     Although his [Woollcott's] rhythms in acting have
none of the liquefaction of his Town-Crying out loud,
he comes closer to being an actor than he did in
"Brief Moment." At least he is noticeable, which
is more than you can say for long stretches of
"Wine of Choice. "84

Joseph Wood Krutch, who had referred to Woollcott as
an "amateur" in his review of Brief Moment, also noted improvement: "And if Mr. Woollcott, who shares with Leslie
Banks and Claudia Morgan the chief roles, still 'behaves'
somewhat more than he acts, his behavior is very appropriate
and he has increased considerably in skill since his last appearance on the stage. "85 Stark Young, who had been favor-
ably impressed by Woollcott in Brief Moment, said of his
Wine of Choice performance: "Through personal magnetism,
a flair for the stage, and a growing technique of acting, he
gives a very entertaining performance. "86 Woollcott did not
completely captivate the critics, as Edith Isaacs's comments
for Theatre Arts Monthly illustrate:

> Mr. Woollcott never was an actor, but the exhibition
> he gives in Wine of Choice is surely the theatre's
> revenge for his years of exhibitionist dramatic crit-
> icism. It is so amateurish a performance as to put
> the rest of the acting completely out of focus. 87

In a 1942 letter to Lady Sibyl Colefax, Woollcott was
critical both of Behrman and himself:

> I played in two plays, both by S. N. Behrman, re-
> writing my parts in each from beginning to end be-
> cause his dialogue simply cannot be spoken. In
> each case I succeeded only in throwing the play out
> of shape and the star into hysterics.... 88

Lawrence Langner, founder of the Guild, wrote of
Woollcott's rewriting of Wine of Choice prior to his debut
in Philadelphia:

> Alec Woollcott... scorned to criticize where he

thought he could create. His method of showing
his dissatisfaction [with the play] was to take his
typewriter and rewrite all his scenes using his own
dialogue--which, considering how light and limber
was his usual conversation, was singularly heavy
and repulsive. 89

On October 16, 1939, Kaufman and Hart's The Man
Who Came to Dinner opened at the Music Box Theater in New
York City. It told the story of Sheridan Whiteside, a famous
radio personality and lecturer who takes over the Stanley
household when he is forced to stay with that family after in-
juring himself on their icy doorstep. Obviously Woollcott was
the model for Whiteside. The play was a critical and box office success, running 739 performances in New York. Atkinson opened his Times review by writing:

> Whether or not it is the funniest comedy Moss
> Hart and George S. Kaufman have written is prob-
> ably a matter of opinion. But it is a fact that "The
> Man Who Came to Dinner, " which opened at the
> Music Box last evening, is the funniest comedy of
> this season, and is likely to remain so long after
> the competition has grown stiffer. 90

Joseph Wood Krutch wrote for the Nation:

> There is no doubt about the fact that "The Man
> Who Came to Dinner" (Music Box Theater) is one
> of the best and funniest of the farces which Mr.
> Kaufman has written with either Mr. Hart or any
> of the other numerous collaborators with whom he
> has worked. 91

Questioned by Time magazine on his reaction to the
character of Whiteside, Woollcott replied: "I only review
plays for money. "92 He wrote of the play in private, however, in a letter to Lady Sibyl Colefax, explaining to her that
he had remarked to Moss Hart after one of his Behrman performances that he "yearned some time to tour the country in
the central part of a play, so that if I could succeed in being
funny it wouldn't disturb the other actors. "93 He went on to
say:

> After one of my absences [from New York]... I
> came back to find the boys [George S. Kaufman and
> Moss Hart] with an act and a half written and puz-

zlingly guilty-looking as they arranged to read it to
me.   It had been my parting instruction that my
role should be as different from me as possible.
I was considerably taken aback to find they had
done a cartoon of me.   They had found it so easy
and entertaining that they could not resist.   They
did not wish even to go ahead with it without my
consent.   I said I would take a week to think it
over, my hesitation being based solely on the effect
my playing would have on the play.   It struck me
that it would be alienating and even offensive for
me to come forward and say in effect, "See how
rude and eccentric I can afford to be.   Dear, dear,
how amusing I am, to be sure."   Besides, I had a
sneaking notion that the play would be a success, in
which case I might have to stay in New York for two
years.   I have managed to stay out of it, except for
four or five weeks a year, since 1928....   However, I thought the play very funny and told George
Kaufman that once the joke had been sprung I would
not at all mind heading a second company. [94]

   Woollcott did head a second company in the spring of
1940.   Clifton Webb took one to Chicago, and Woollcott opened
with another on the sixth of March in Santa Barbara, Cali-
fornia.   On April 23 the company was appearing in San Fran-
cisco when Woollcott suffered a heart attack.   The tour, which
was booked through the first of June, was canceled.   A recovered
Woollcott reopened the tour again in Philadelphia in January
1941 and played into May.   Reviewing his performance in
March, Brooks Atkinson wrote:

      Mr. Woollcott takes disarming pleasure in acting
      it.   The same expansive style that attends his myr-
      iad activities as writer, speaker and friend gives a
      kind of merriment to his performance.   He is Fa-
      ther Christmas and Foxy Grandpa rolled in one.
      As an actor he is no virtuoso.   There is none of
      this nonsense about holding the mirror up to life in
      his performance.   He never once stops staring at
      the audience, and his eyes rove the galleries as
      though he were hunting deer.   His gestures are as
      deliberate as a first lesson in dancing; you can al-
      most hear teacher counting "one, two, three."   But
      Mr. Woollcott reads his lines very well indeed,
      speaking the words distinctly, throwing the emphasis
      where it will do the most good and timing the re-

> torts sagaciously. Since he has no secrets from
> the audience every one knows at once what he has
> in mind when he speaks a line or whirls his chair
> around. The audience dotes on him and understands
> him. [95]

Woollcott continued his acting career in August 1941,
appearing in The Yellow Jacket with Harpo Marx in a summer production at Marblehead, Massachusetts. First produced in 1912, the play tells how a Chinese mother and son
escape the evil intentions of the father and ultimately emerge
triumphant. Although written by Americans J. Harry Benrimo and George C. Hazleton, the play incorporated oriental
features, such as property man and chorus. Woollcott had
admired the play since he had first seen it on Broadway in
1912. In this production he played the rather small role of
the chorus, who commented on the action of the play. Marx
played the property man, who moved about the stage supply-
ing properties to the characters. Reviewing the 1941 summer
theatre season, Life called the production the "most interesting of the 150 shows produced so far this summer...."[96]
The article did not evaluate Woollcott's performance.

In the fall of 1941 Woollcott went to England for a
series of six broadcasts. His topics covered such personalities as Julia Ward Howe, Oliver Wendell Holmes, Jr.,
Benedict Arnold, and Stephen Foster. [97]

The year 1942 saw the appearance of the film version
of The Man Who Came to Dinner, starring Monty Woolley.
It also saw Woollcott hospitalized by another heart attack, in
March. In June he was in the hospital again for a gall blad-
der operation. When his illnesses permitted, Woollcott wrote
articles for such magazines as Good Housekeeping, the Atlantic Monthly, and the Reader's Digest. He also served the
Reader's Digest as "roving editor." He worked on two books,
as well. As You Were was an anthology of prose and poetry
gathered by Woollcott especially for servicemen. Long, Long
Ago was a collection of four of his broadcast scripts and a
number of previously published articles. Both books were
posthumously published in 1943.

On January 23 of that year he was invited to partici-
pate in a radio program in New York called "People's Plat-
form." The round table discussion topic that evening was the
tenth year of Hitlerism in Germany. He became ill during
the program and was unable to finish the broadcast. He was

taken to Roosevelt Hospital, where he died shortly before midnight.

As might be expected, there was a flood of obituaries. Probably no line from those obituaries would have pleased Woollcott more than one written by Edmund Wilson: "The idea that 'social betterment' and the 'elevating' effects of the arts were the most important things in the world and causes to be served gratuitously was always alive in his mind...."[98]

Notes

[1]"How a Critic Gets That Way," Collier's, February 25, 1928, p. 12.

[2]"In Memoriam: Rose Field," Atlantic Monthly, May 1939, p. 643.

[3]Ibid.

[4]Samuel Hopkins Adams, A. Woollcott, His Life and His World (New York: Reynal and Hitchcock, 1945), p. 30.

[5]The Letters of Alexander Woollcott, eds. Beatrice Kaufman and Joseph Hennessey (New York: Viking, 1944), pp. 108-9.

[6]Adams, p. 49.

[7]"Richard Mansfield," Hamilton Literary Magazine 42 (November 1907):103.

[8]"The Success of the Season," Century, July 1920, p. 418.

[9]"New Trustees," Hamilton Alumni Review 1 (January 1936):38.

[10]Ibid.

[11]Adams, p. 53.

[12]"Murder at 8:30 Sharp," Collier's, March 17, 1928, p. 49.

[13]"Baby Makes a Hit in Wilson's New Play," New

York Times, December 28, 1909, p. 6.

[14]"Second Thoughts on First Nights," New York Times, October 24, 1920, Sec. 6, p. 1.

[15]Adams, p. 65.

[16]"Lou-Tellegen in a German Farce," New York Times, March 8, 1915, p. 11.

[17]Ibid.

[18]Ibid.

[19]Ibid.

[20]"An All-Star 'Trilby,'" New York Times, April 4, 1915, Sec. 2, p. 5.

[21]"The Exclusive Managers," Vanity Fair, May 1929, p. 130.

[22]"Alex Woollcott Home," New York Times, June 3, 1919, p. 12.

[23]"The Play," New York Times, p. 7.

[24]The Algonquin Wits (New York: Citadel, 1968), p. 15.

[25]Ibid., p. 17

[26]My Autobiography (New York: Simon and Schuster, 1964), p. 389.

[27]"Shouts and Murmurs," New Yorker, March 22, 1930, p. 34.

[28]"Walt Whitman--Dramatic Critic," Bookman 53 (March 1921):75.

[29]"Excursions with Mr. Hackett," Bookman 53 (June 1921):362.

[30]"Second Thoughts on First Nights," New York Times, Sec. 2, p. 5.

[31]"Down with Woollcott," Nation, December 18, 1935, p. 720.

[32]"Second Thoughts on First Nights," Sec. 6, p. 1.

[33]New York Times, May 1, 1922, p. 20.

[34]Ibid.

[35]New York Sun, p. 18.

[36]"'What Price Glory' Magnificent," New York Sun, p. 3.

[37]Edwin P. Hoyt, Alexander Woollcott: The Man Who Came to Dinner (New York: Abelard-Schuman, 1968), p. 165.

[38]"Second Thoughts on First Nights," New York World, December 27, 1925, p. 2M.

[39]"Alexander Woollcott to Lecture," New York Times, October 29, 1925, p. 28.

[40]"Actors Vote on Critics," New York Times, August 3, 1927, p. 29.

[41]New Yorker, February 16, 1929, p. 40.

[42]"Big Nemo-II," New Yorker, March 25, 1939, p. 27.

[43]"Broadway After Dark," New York Sun, December 9, 1933, p. 10.

[44]Woollcott, Letters, p. 322.

[45]Hoyt, pp. 174-88.

[46]"Giving O'Neill Till It Hurts," Vanity Fair, February 1928, p. 48.

[47]"Second Thoughts on First Nights," New York World, February 5, 1928, p. 3M.

[48]"Second Thoughts on First Nights," New York World, May 20, 1928, p. 3M.

[49]Woollcott, Letters, pp. 107-8.

[50]"Town Crier," New Sweek, February 1, 1943, p. 63.

[51]John K. Hutchens, "The Late Town Crier," New York Times, January 31, 1943, Sec. 2, p. 9.

[52]"Second Thoughts on First Nights," New York Times, May 13, 1917, Sec. 8, p. 7.

[53]"The Play," New York Times, October 18, 1929, p. 24.

[54]"The Theatre," Outlook and Independent, November 6, 1929, p. 389.

[55]"In Many Moods," Theatre Arts Monthly 13 (December 1929):881.

[56]American Drama Since 1918 (New York: Braziller, Inc., 1957), p. 140.

[57]"Big Nemo-III," New Yorker, April 1, 1939, pp. 22-6.

[58]Brief Moment (New York: Farrar & Rinehart, 1931), p. 3.

[59]"The Play," New York Evening Post, November 10, 1931, p. 14.

[60]"Three More Plays," New Republic, December 2, 1931, p. 70.

[61]"Drama, the Kinds of Comedy," Nation, December 2, 1931, p. 622.

[62]"The Play," New York Times, November 10, 1931, p. 28.

[63]Broadway (New York: Macmillan, 1970), p. 253.

[64]Morton Eustis, "'I'm Not an Actor,' Says Mr. Woollcott," New York Post, November 14, 1931, Sec. D, p. 4.

[65]Anita Loos, "Miss Loos Pays a Call on a Rising Young Actor," New York Times, November 15, 1931, Sec. 8, p. 1.

66"That Benign Demon, George S. Kaufman, " New York Times, December 3, 1933, Sec. 9, p. 5.

67"The Play, " New York Times, November 27, 1933, p. 20.

68Hoyt, p. 155.

69Morehouse, "Broadway After Dark, " New York Sun, December 9, 1933, p. 10.

70"Two Merry Pictorial Musical Comedies, " New York Times, May 6, 1934, Sec. 9, p. 3.

71Woollcott, Letters, p. 128.

72Ibid. , p. 153.

73"Woollcott Takes Lindbergh to Task, " New York Times, May 26, 1941, p. 12.

74"Films, " Nation, May 22, 1935, p. 612.

75"The Screen, " New York Times, May 8, 1935, p. 23.

76Woollcott, Letters, pp. 142-43.

77The Woollcott Reader (New York: Viking, 1935), p. vii.

78Alexander Woollcott to Leggett Brown, December 3, 1936, Alexander Woollcott Collection, Harvard University, Cambridge, Massachusetts.

79Woollcott, Letters, p. 182.

80"I'm Glad I'm Absent-Minded, " American Magazine, July 1932, p. 74.

81Lloyd Lewis, "Woollcott Speaking, " Chicago Daily News, December 29, 1937, p. 17.

82Alexander Woollcott to Frank Sullivan, December 31, 1937, Alexander Woollcott Collection, Hamilton College, Clinton, New York.

[83]Woollcott, Letters, p. 203.

[84]"The Play," New York Times, February 22, 1938, p. 18.

[85]"Drama," Nation, March 5, 1938, p. 281.

[86]"Theatre Guild Fore and Aft," New Republic, March 9, 1938, p. 132.

[87]"Fresh Fields, Broadway in Review," Theatre Arts Monthly, 22 (April 1938):253.

[88]Woollcott, Letters, p. 231.

[89]The Magic Curtain (New York: Dutton, 1951), p. 267.

[90]"The Play," New York Times, October 17, 1939, p. 31.

[91]"Drama," Nation, October 28, 1939, p. 474.

[92]"The Theatre," Time, October 30, 1939, p. 42.

[93]Woollcott, Letters, pp. 321-2.

[94]Ibid.

[95]"Town Crier on Stage," New York Times, March 23, 1941, Sec. 9, p. 1.

[96]"Summer Theatre," Life, September 1, 1941, p. 53.

[97]Hoyt, p. 320.

[98]"Woollcott and Fourier," Nation, February 6, 1943, p. 196.

Chapter 2

WOOLLCOTT ON ACTORS AND ACTING

Woollcott followed the careers of many performers during his tenure as a reviewer. By examining his comments on those who elicited the greatest amount of his commentary, this chapter will help define Woollcott as a reviewer and provide a profile of his view of the theatre and acting.

Minnie Maddern Fiske

Woollcott first reviewed Fiske in 1916 in her role as Juliet Miller in Marian de Forest's comedy, Erstwhile Susan. In his initial review and subsequent commentary he made three observations that he would repeat in later evaluations of her work: (1) she was the first artist of the American stage;[1] (2) she was "the most brilliant comedienne of the American stage";[2] and (3) she was appearing in poor material. [3] Woollcott's main weakness as a reviewer was a failure at times to provide specific reasons for his evaluations. Such was the case with his first two observations on Fiske. He did, however, elaborate on the third point:

> In all this there is no room, of course, for the genuine emotional power that is hers in abundance, no room for the mute tragedy that made memorable her great first act in Sheldon's drama of the slums [Salvation Nell], nor for such spiritual radiance as glorified her great last act in "The Pillars of Society," a great moment in her performance as Lona that made it one of the finest achievements in sheer acting that the modern stage has known. [4]

In that characteristically lengthy statement Woollcott attributes to Fiske three abilities that he deemed important to the actor's art: the ability to convey emotion; the ability to express oneself without the aid of language; and the ability

39

to impart a spiritual radiance. In criticizing Erstwhile Susan for not allowing Fiske to display "spiritual radiance," Woollcott was referring to a quality he highly regarded. He wrote of it in his book on Fiske in 1917 while describing her performance in Salvation Nell, which he saw prior to his career as a reviewer: "It was the outgiving of a dynamic being, an inspirational, communicable emanation, a transcendant expression of the spirit. This, it seems to me, is acting in its highest estate, and this, I think, is the genius of Mrs. Fiske."5

Having pointed out her role's deficiencies in Erstwhile Susan, Woollcott praised Fiske for her "potency of gesture" and the "vocal variety" that she demonstrated in the production. 6 He considered her voice to be one of her most valuable tools, describing it as "heart stirring in trajedy and indescribably infectious when it ripples with unheard laughter, ...the most thrilling voice in America."7

Woollcott's review of Fiske's next Broadway appearance, in Hatcher Hughes and Elmer Rice's 1921 comedy Wake Up, Jonathan!, is noteworthy for his praise of her ability to listen on stage. He believed that listening was half the secret of good acting and thought that Fiske could "listen as none of our players can."8 When she opened in Lillian Barrett's The Dice of the Gods in April 1923 he chided her for appearing in a "third rate company."9 Along with her propensity for appearing in poor plays, this was his most frequent criticism of her. 10

Woollcott also criticized Fiske's performance in Barrett's play for her nervousness and inaudibility. 11 Altogether these criticisms demonstrate that Woollcott was a more critical observer of Fiske's work than he admitted to being. Referring to himself in the third person, he wrote in 1923:

It might be admitted...that he is a poor judge to send to any theatre where Mrs. Fiske is playing. If her play is a poor thing or the role beneath her, he comes away raging as if some singularly atrocious felony had been committed and for days afterward he can be head [sic] muttering something about boiling oil. But if, on the contrary, she has a role which gives rein to the mad comedy which is in her, then he rushes jubilant into the night and there is dancing in the streets that night if he has to do it all alone. 12

Woollcott reviewed Fiske for the final time as a journalistic writer in 1928, when she appeared as Mistress Page in Shakespeare's The Merry Wives of Windsor. Again he labeled her as "the foremost artist of our stage" and praised her comedic ability: "I know no actress in the English-speaking world who is half so good a comedienne."[13] This evaluation echoed his initial one of her in Erstwhile Susan in 1916. In neither case did he provide specific reasons for his pronouncements.

The high esteem in which Woollcott held Fiske was tempered by his regret over her choice of plays and companies. He also registered his regrets over the choice of plays of other performers. Foremost among these were the Barrymores.

The Barrymores

Ethel, John, and Lionel Barrymore were all part of the Broadway scene during Woollcott's tenure as a daily reviewer. He first reviewed Ethel in 1914, when she appeared in a revival of Sardou's A Scrap of Paper. Woollcott believed that the play didn't demand the most of her and found her as a result to be "at her charming second best."[14] As with Fiske, the failure to appear in challenging roles was Woollcott's most frequent criticism of Barrymore.[15] He found her voice to be the most praiseworthy dimension of her acting, citing its beauty, enchantment, and ability to capture emotion.[16] After her voice, her beauty was praised most frequently.[17]

Believability was the foremost criterion by which Woollcott judged acting. Once he listed what he believed were the "real questions" to be asked in evaluating a performance:

> The need or lack of need of such disguises [those achieved through make-up], the use or failure to use outward aids--these are really immaterial points. Does he stir you? Does he convince you? What of the illusion? These are the real questions.[18]

Barrymore's performance in the 1915 production of The Shadow, by David Niccodemi and Michael Morton, answered Woollcott's questions in a positive manner: "This long and difficult role [Berthe Tregnier] Miss Barrymore

plays without a note that is not sure and true."[19]   When she
next appeared on Broadway, in Our Mrs. McChesney, Woollcott praised another quality of her acting that he esteemed,
her ability to present emotion:

> But to the one or two moments in the play that in-
> vite it she brings that genuine emotion which is act-
> ing in its best estate.... If ever in an idle mo-
> ment you have foolishly said that Miss Barrymore
> brings only a pleasing personality to a part, go to
> the Lyceum and watch her work in the scene where
> she hears her boy is suspected of thieving, where
> she rallies her faith to his aid and is able to meet
> him soon with the charge disproved. Watch this,
> wipe your eyes, and then write your letter of abject
> apology.[20]

In addition to revealing his praise for Barrymore's
emotion Woollcott's comments also reveal his sentimental
nature. He once described himself as possessing a "foolish
and romantic heart,"[21] and thus his favoring of sentimental
plays is not surprising.[22]

Barrymore's only Broadway appearance in the 1916-17
season was in James M. Barrie's The Twelve Pound Look,
a play she appeared in periodically throughout her career,
often in vaudeville houses. Her performances permitted
Woollcott to address her comedic ability. He described her
as "that expert and fascinating comedienne," and after noting
that she had appeared in the same role six years earlier, he
wrote: "Her impersonation... was then a delightful bit of comedy acting, but last night it seemed even more free and more
deft. Every look, motion and intonation counted."[23]   This
was the extent of Woollcott's delineation of Barrymore's comedic acting ability. As with Fiske, he was content to label
without elaborating.

After returning from the service, Woollcott first reviewed Barrymore in her performance as Lady Helen Haden
in Zöe Akins's Déclassée. For a change, Woollcott could not
only rave about her performance but about the play as well.
"At the zenith of her powers and in the fullness of her queenly
beauty, Ethel Barrymore came back to town last night in the
richest and most interesting play that has fallen to her in all
her years upon the stage."[24]

After a successful season on Broadway Barrymore

toured in Déclassée, opening in Buffalo, New York, in September 1920. Woollcott was against Barrymore tying herself up in the play "at the zenith of her career." Furthermore he mused that she could be creating new roles from new or old plays instead of touring. Woollcott blamed both the theatre system and Barrymore herself for her decision to continue in Déclassée, but did not provide a rationale for his opinion. 25 As Woollcott's reaction to the Déclassée tour implies, he saw the long run as a detriment to the actor. In 1921 he gave his reasons:

> Obviously it is a curse to the hopeful young actor who plans to grow in ability and reputation by being seen in many roles, and who finds himself booked for endless months in one unchanging part. Then it is none too welcome to a player of established reputation who, nevertheless, is ambitious to experiment in various characters and who, also, may be too restless a spirit to play the one role night after night without suffering a boredom inexpressible. 26

Barrymore's next Broadway appearance was in 1923 in another Akins play, A Royal Fandango. He praised her performance but noted that there was a nervousness that marked her acting in the first scene. 27 Two years later, when she portrayed Portia in The Merchant of Venice, he would again note a nervousness in her performance, although again he praised her acting. 28

In summarizing Woollcott's attitude toward Ethel Barrymore, one is struck by the same complaint he had of Minnie Maddern Fiske, that she appeared in plays that did not offer enough challenge. He did, however, believe Barrymore to be a great actress who displayed emotion well and possessed a voice he described at various times as "beautiful," "lovely," and "of enchanting melody." In the spring of 1923 he showed the high esteem in which he held her by including her in a group of performers he believed would still be stars in twenty years. 29 Time obviously proved his confidence to be well placed.

Woollcott first reviewed John Barrymore when he opened in Kick In, by Willard Mack, on October 19, 1914. Barrymore played the role of Chick Hewes, an ex-convict trying to reform. Woollcott's comments on his performance were limited to the review's last paragraph: "The demands

of the role of Chick Hewes are met to the full by Mr. Barrymore, who plays with intelligence and vigor and imparts to
it a deal of charm. "[30] These comments have an air of po-
liteness that does not mark Woollcott's enthusiastic responses
to performances that truly enthralled him. This was not the
case when he reviewed Barrymore's next performance in John
Galsworthy's Justice in April 1916. He correctly saw his
portrayal of William Falder as a milestone in Barrymore's
career: "They [the audience] saw John Barrymore play as
he never played before, and so by his work as the wretched
prisoner in 'Justice' step forward into a new position on the
American stage."[31] In the review's last paragraph he praised
the manner in which Barrymore was transformed from "his
debonair self" to the "undernourished underclerk of Mr. Galsworthy's story."[32] He was particularly impressed by the
"extraordinary power" Barrymore displayed, a dimension of
his acting that he would praise in the future.[33]

When Woollcott was particularly impressed by a play,
production, or performance he might discuss it further in a
Sunday column following his initial review. Such was the
case with Barrymore's performance in Justice. He wrote of
it again in two Sunday columns. Rejoicing over Barrymore's
use of his ability, Woollcott wrote on Sunday, April 23, 1916:

> Barrymore is enjoying now the reward which only
> doing well a thing worth doing at all can give. It
> is what the theatre can bestow on those who serve
> it loyally. This comes now to a player who has
> long been a favorite but many of whose years in
> the theatre have been lackadaisical.[34]

In the same column Woollcott praised the "development in his voice of a strain of pure cockney" for the performance.[35] As with Ethel, Woollcott found John's voice to
be the most praiseworthy dimension of his acting.[36]

Woollcott's only negative commentary on Barrymore's
performance in Justice came in this column. He believed
Barrymore projected too much fear in the first act and subsequently was limited in the depth of fear he could reveal
through the rest of the play.[37] His criticism notwithstanding,
Woollcott described Barrymore's Falder at the end of the
1915-16 season as "probably the performance of the year."[38]

Before entering the service Woollcott reviewed Barrymore's performance in the title role of the dramatization of

Du Maurier's novel Peter Ibbetson, which also featured Lionel Barrymore. Woollcott referred to John as leading "the
company with his resourceful, finely imaginative playing...."[39]
Although he believed Barrymore did not physically fit the
"gigantic stature" the role demanded, he was impressed by
the combination of "tenderness, romantic charm and wistful-
ness" together with the "fine black rage" that he brought to
the role.[40] The performance was also marked by a spiritual
quality, which Woollcott, as his comments on Fiske revealed,
esteemed highly: "Particularly in the first act last night,
... there was a notable spirituality in his sensitive performance that gave the play its tone."[41]

Woollcott was still in military service when John and
Lionel Barrymore opened in The Jest in 1919. The production took a two-month summer break, and Woollcott was back
at his reviewing post when it reopened in September 1919.
His comments reveal, however, that he had seen the production in June, prior to resuming his position at the Times:
"Indeed, in the two all-engrossing roles the performance
seems to have gained, if anything, in richness--gained certainly over the work that was being done [in June]." Woollcott proceeded to note the progress he saw John making: He
"seems with each passing month to gain little by little in his
mastery of the instrument he is still visibly and wonderfully
perfecting."[42]

Before reviewing John's next performance, Woollcott
cited him, Lionel, and Laurette Taylor as the "only three
stars of the first magnitude which have risen in the American
firmament in the last ten years."[43] When John Barrymore
opened in his first Shakespearean play, Richard III, in March
1920 Woollcott continued to note the advancement he saw the
actor making: The performance, he wrote,

> marked a measurable advance in the gradual process
> of bringing his technical fluency abreast with his
> winged imagination and his real genius for the the-
> atre. Surely it was the highest point yet reached
> in that rapid unexpected ascent which began four
> years ago with the production of Galsworthy's "Jus-
> tice" and which has been unparalleled in the theatre
> of our time.[44]

Woollcott believed that the character of Richard was
more than inhuman. He believed there must be a touch of the
superhuman in him: "It is a Richard of such stature that

Barrymore in his new-found and still developing power creates for us. "[45] Using one of his favorite reviewing techniques, comparative criticism, Woollcott ranked Barrymore's performance with Ada Rehan's Katherine and Forbes Robertson's Hamlet. Ever conscious of the vocal dimension of a performance, Woollcott noted a marked improvement in Barrymore's voice:

> Now he has acquired, out of space, a voice. His voice three years ago was dry and monotonous, his speech slovenly and sometimes common. All that is largely changed. He entered upon the Shakespearean task with a patiently acquired voice, one rich, full and flexible. This is really the advance of which he may be proudest.[46]

For Woollcott Barrymore's portrayal of Richard III was the first time the actor achieved a high level of performance throughout a play. He proceeded to raise the question of Barrymore's replacing the vacancy created by Richard Mansfield's death, a vacancy he had earlier indicated was being filled by Fiske. Woollcott maintained that Barrymore could not fill the vacancy until he had "carried the best he has to offer outside the pleasant and preposterous city of ours. "[47]

Referring to Barrymore as "the foremost actor ... of our day," Woollcott uttered his hopes of seeing him play Iago, Malvolio, and then a role that Barrymore was eventually to play: "And we hope some day to see his Hamlet. If he be minded to take the last step of his ascent, he could be the finest Hamlet of our time. "[48]

Woollcott believed that after Barrymore's success in Richard III he would only do roles suited to his talents. His next portrayal, however, of Gwymplaine in Clair de Lune in April 1921, was disappointing:

> John Barrymore was interesting to watch and hear-- or at least he was intermittently so. But these two [Ethel Barrymore also was in the show] are possessors and guardians of a little genius. Not in recent seasons has it been so squanderously wasted as it was last evening.[49]

In his Sunday column of October 10, 1920, Woollcott had written of his dream theatre, in which John Barrymore would play Hamlet.[50]   On November 16, 1922, the dream became a reality.   Woollcott thought that Barrymore's Hamlet fulfilled his earlier prediction of being the best of the time: "One who has seen all the Hamlets that have been given in this country in the last twenty-five years must give over the very front of his report to the conviction that this new one is the finest of them all."[51]

In the first paragraph of his initial review of the production Woollcott demonstrated three abilities that help to characterize his style: his ability to capture the feeling of a moment on stage, his ability as a raconteur, and his facility with language.   The paragraph speaks for itself:

> It lacked but twenty minutes of midnight last evening when the four tawny clad captains of Fortinbras lifted the slim, young body of the dead Prince of Denmark to their mailed shoulders, bore it slowly up the great stone steps of Elsinore and out of the brilliant, gory, earthy castle into the cool of the moonlight.   They stood there for an instant, they had their burden silhouetted for us as a final memory.   There was a wail of trumpets in the distance, the lights faded out and the curtain fell.   Thus ended an evening that will be memorable in the history of the American theatre.[52]

Addressing Barrymore's performance specifically, Woollcott praised the understanding he brought to the role, the absence of stage tricks, and the originality of his conception.   The soliloquies for Woollcott "seemed for once just a lonely, unhappy man's thoughts walking in the silent darkness."   Barrymore's Hamlet was the "realest" one Woollcott had seen.[53]   Writing of the performance again in his Sunday column, Woollcott added the adjectives "masculine," "princely," and "whimsical" to his description of the portrayal.   He thought Barrymore's conception was "a little nearer the sweet prince" Shakespeare had envisioned than the one theatregoers were accustomed to--namely, "a withered fellow though surprisingly supple and well preserved and one given to recitations when alone."[54]

A second viewing of the production brought additional accolades from Woollcott.   Barrymore's performance brought the play's "humanity and its beauty ... to life as never before."[55]   Woollcott also praised the casting of Barrymore in the title role:

> Here for once in these recent years, is the role
> appropriately cast according to the standards which
> the living playwrights exact of the producers when
> their own pieces are taking form in the theater.
> Call it the quest of types, if you will, but remem-
> ber that here it is a case of an affinity between
> part and player that reaches far beneath the sur-
> face. From a performance of such rare understand-
> ing you do come away with the notion that had Barry-
> more been a loitering student at Wittenberg to whom
> Horatio, drawing his breath in pain to tell the story,
> would have brought back the outline of the tragedy,
> he, far more clearly than Horatio himself, far more
> clearly than all the rest, would have divined what
> of inner torment and sensitive, bruised distaste had
> bred the woe at Elsinore. 56

Before viewing Hamlet a third time Woollcott wrote of
the rise of Barrymore and referred to him as "the heir-ap-
parent of the American theatre."57 In his third viewing of
the production Woollcott sensed a freer performance, a product, he believed, of the actor's loss of self-consciousness in
portraying a role made famous by other performers. 58

A fourth viewing of the performance in November 1923
found Woollcott again praising its improvement: "It is a better performance, richer, more fused, more mellow." Trying to account for the change, Woollcott wrote:

> Perhaps it is merely because "Hamlet" has become
> easy second nature to one who knows it better and
> is freed by the mere familiarity. Perhaps it is be-
> cause Barrymore is in better form. Certainly he
> looks more fit and more serene than he has seemed
> in fifteen years. 59

By January 1925 Woollcott's enchantment with Barrymore had diminished considerably--not because he believed
Barrymore's ability had decreased, but rather because of
Barrymore's failure to perform. Woollcott offered this ex-
planation:

> Usually the playgoers can rely on the good old
> law of supply and demand to keep their players work-
> ing for them. Hunger and the inner urge of exhi-
> bitionism will attend to the matter. But since a
> mere casual eight weeks in "Hamlet" nets Mr. Bar-

rymore something like $59,000, he presents a more
difficult problem, complicated by the fact that he
really doesn't like to act at all. Indeed the careers
of both the Barrymores [John and Lionel] have been
distorted by their unusual reluctance in the theatre
--a deep aversion made up of such odd ingredients
as sheepishness, schoolyard taboos, an aspiration
for some higher form of expression, etc., etc.
This fundamental reluctance helps to keep John
Barrymore off the stage for long stretches of
time.... 60

The memory of Barrymore's Hamlet remained with
Woollcott, however, and in writing of the Hamlet of Horace
Liveright in January of 1926, he referred again to Barrymore's Hamlet as "the best Hamlet of them all."[61] Woollcott
seemed to take real delight in following the career of John
Barrymore. He repeatedly noted the transformation his career had taken beginning with his appearance in Justice and
culminating in Hamlet. Along the way Woollcott praised Barrymore's intelligence, vigor, charm, imagination, voice, believability, and understanding, among other qualities. He
held Barrymore in such high esteem after the Hamlet production that it was natural for him to be disappointed by Barrymore's absence from the stage with the close of the production.

As previously noted, the production of Peter Ibbetson
in April 1917 included both John and Lionel Barrymore in its
cast. It was the first production in which Woollcott reviewed
Lionel, and although he said little about his performance, it
was all positive. He thought his playing of Colonel Ibbetson
was "an admirable thing" and used such adjectives as "graph-
ic," "telling," "arresting," and "ingenious" to describe it.[62]

The next month Woollcott included Lionel Barrymore
in a group of theatre personalities he thought had grown in
stature during the 1916-17 season. He applauded Barrymore's
return to the stage "after an absence of virtually fifteen years"
and saw him building a new reputation with a new generation
of playgoers by his performance in Peter Ibbetson.[63]

While Woollcott was still in military service Lionel
portrayed Milt Shanks in Augustus Thomas's The Copperhead,
a performance that brought him stardom. In September 1919
he performed the last act from the play for an Actors Equity
Association program. In his praise of Barrymore's perform-

ance Woollcott revealed his belief that the actor was the primary theatre artist:

> Surely this is the essential thing. If all the managers of our time were to retire tomorrow, the theatre would go on. If all the playwrights of our time were to throw away their pens to write no more, the theatre would go on. If the scenery were to be forgotten, the music to be stilled, the lights to be turned out, the theatre would go on. If every playhouse in America were to burn to the ground this night, the theatre would still go on, so long as each generation sees reborn the essential thing--the art of such an actor as Lionel Barrymore. [64]

As previously noted, the Barrymore brothers appeared in The Jest in 1919. Woollcott thought Lionel's voice and emotion in a September performance were superior to a June performance he viewed as a mere spectator. [65] Barrymore opened in The Letter of the Law, by Eugene Brieux, on February 23, 1920. Woollcott liked him but not the part: "It is a performance of consummate skill which he gives in an undistinguished part...."[66] As with Minnie Maddern Fiske and Ethel Barrymore, Woollcott most frequently criticized Lionel Barrymore for appearing in poor material. [67]

On February 17, 1921, Barrymore opened in Shakespeare's Macbeth. Woollcott was "shocked that Lionel Barrymore, while often good and occasionally very good ... never once ... brushed greatness in all the length and breadth of the play."[68] He described Barrymore in Macbeth as "curiously and perhaps deliberately suggestive of yokelry, a genial-looking fellow of somewhat monotonous speech, but fine and barbaric in build and so intelligent an actor even at his second or third best as to command respect."[69] The "respect" diminished considerably by February 27, when Woollcott's comments on Barrymore's performance were limited to the following words: "For Mr. Barrymore's monotonous and unimaginative Macbeth--precious little can be said."[70] Woollcott thought Barrymore did considerably better in the role of Achille Cortolon in a revival of Henri Bernstein's The Claw, which opened on October 17, 1921. Barrymore played a man who declines from "the vigor of his middle years to the decay and whimpering senility of old age and death."[71] Woollcott thought Barrymore's performance was the only worthwhile reason for the production: "Mr. Barrymore's virtuosity in such a tour de force is extraordinary and lends to 'The Claw' its only interest. "[72] Describing Barrymore's performance, Woollcott wrote: "He seemed last night to be playing with uncommon skill, marking the several stages of Cortolon's degeneration with an expertness few of our actors can command, varying and coloring the portrait with an ease fascinating to watch. "[73]

Barrymore's appearance in November 1923 in Laugh, Clown, Laugh moved Woollcott to write: "His ... appearance ... deepens an old conviction that they do not make many actors like him in any one generation. "[74] Woollcott's only other comment was that his role was "skillfully played. "[75]

Woollcott was not pleased with Barrymore's next appearance. It was as Bernie Kaplan in The Piker, by Leon Gordon, which opened on January 15, 1925. Woollcott labeled the piece "a generally second rate crook play. "[76] He charged Barrymore with being "slovenly and negligent in his choice of plays" and continued sarcastically: "Vide 'The Piker.' Or rather, don't. "[77]

Barrymore's last Broadway appearance was in Man or Devil?, by Jerome K. Jerome, which opened on May 21, 1925. In his opening sentence Woollcott referred to Barrymore's "tireless and groping search for a play of his own caliber. "[78] Woollcott didn't think that the search was successful, as his last paragraph revealed:

> But the play is three full-length acts floridly crowded with nothing at all, and such stature as he has enjoyed in the American theater cannot long stand the whittling process of such a season as he has just passed through. [79]

The "whittling process" stopped, for with the close of Man or Devil? after twenty performances Barrymore abandoned the theatre for films. As with Fiske and Barrymore's sister Ethel, Woollcott thought Lionel was a great performer who was not often challenged enough by the roles he played. This frequent lament would also be made about the career of Helen Hayes.

Helen Hayes

In 1914, at the age of thirteen, Helen Hayes appeared in The Prodigal Husband. She played the part of Simone, a

little girl who has been left alone in the world by the death
of her mother. It was her first role to be reviewed by Woollcott. His comments were short but positive: "The younger
Simone, she of the tears and the first act, is played to per-
fection by Helen Hayes Brown [Hayes had not yet adopted her
stage name]--but her presence on the stage is of the brief-
est."[80] When Woollcott returned from military service he
first reviewed Hayes again in the role of Cora Wheeler in
Booth Tarkington's Clarence. He foresaw a future for her:

> Probably Glen Hunter [who played Hayes's brother]
> and the beguiling Helen Hayes as the youngsters
> would be the most difficult to replace. They could
> scarcely be improved upon. Little Miss Hayes, who
> won all hearts in the neighborhood last Spring as
> the gentle, wide-eyed might-have-been daughter in
> "Dear Brutus," reveals her versatility by her shin-
> ing success in this totally different role. She is a
> seventeen-year-old Marie Tempest, with the world
> at her feet. [81]

Besides containing Woollcott's first forecast of stardom
for Hayes his review of Clarence also demonstrates his ability
to project enthusiasm:

> Write it on the walls of the city, let the town crier
> proclaim it in the commons, shout it from the house-
> tops that "Clarence," the new and capitally acted
> play which so vastly amused its first New York
> audience at the Hudson Theatre Saturday night, is
> a thoroughly delightful, American comedy, which
> the world and his wife and children will enjoy.
>   It is as American as Huckleberry Finn or pump-
> kin pie. It is as delightful as any native comedy
> which has tried to lure the laughter of this com-
> munity in the last ten seasons. And yet it is by
> Booth Tarkington. [82]

Woollcott praised Hayes again two months later in
writing of the successful players of that season. He described her as "the little sister in 'Clarence,' the most interesting and most promising new star that can be descried
now in the theatrical firmament. The world seems to lie at
this girl's feet."[83] Two months later Woollcott wrote of the
problems child actors face securing roles when they grow up.
Once again he found an opportunity to laud Hayes and also
wonder about her future:

But the wonder of the season is none of these
[other young performers he mentioned]. It is Helen
Hayes, an extraordinarily gifted and skillful actress
who is just eighteen. Her "technique" is so re-
markable that older and more famous actresses sit
open-mouthed and wondered where and how she
learned to do it.... At eighteen she is a marvel--
no less. What will she be at twenty-five? The
Maude Adams of her day or an obscure and happily
married woman, unknown to fame? In 1926, shall
we all be besieging the box-office of some Central
Park West Theatre buying seats far ahead for Miss
Hayes in "The Rescue of Violet" or will one of us
be saying: "That little Hayes girl who used to play
in those Tarkington comedies--she was a wonder,
wasn't she? I wonder whatever became of her?[84]

While describing Hayes as "an extraordinarily gifted
and skillful actress," Woollcott did not specify what aspects
of her acting warranted his evaluation other than the passing
reference to her technique.

Hayes next appeared in the title role of Edward Carpenter's Bab, which opened on October 18, 1920. Woollcott
praised her performance as being "enchanting and uncannily
expert. "[85] After noting that she was a natural choice for
the role after her performance in Clarence, Woollcott again
marveled at the talent she had for one so young:

Her equipment as a commedienne is extraordinary
and the sight of her easily and instinctively doing
the things it takes most players years and years
to learn must give the older folk of the theatre a
little pang of envy and wonderment. At nineteen
she has the kind of flawless precision of playing
which usually makes amends for crow's feet around
the eyes and a persistent matronly aspect. [86]

Her performance also drew some negative commentary:

It would be easy to find fault with some of the
things she does in "Bab." Indeed, it would be impossible to see it without wondering if she were not
working too hard without feeling the slight fatigue
that is begotten in spectators when any player strives
too ardently to please them. The tendency to over-
stress was reported in her work as the long run of

"Clarence" settled into its stride at the Hudson last winter. It is marked in "Bab." Perhaps the sight of her name in giant lights outside the theatre bore in upon her the notion that she ought to do a little bit more. Some day it will dawn on her that she ought to do a little bit less. Then she may be starred. [87]

Woollcott then proceeded to take some of the sting from the criticism by proposing that the play, being the type that rested heavily on one character, may have "goaded" her to act too ardently. [88] Woollcott noted that Hayes dropped her "ardent" approach in her next appearance, as Scoby in Booth Tarkington's The Wren: "What there is of it [the play] is charmingly played ... by the winsome Miss Hayes, who has foregone her naughty trick of insisting on herself too ardently...." [89] In November 1921 Hayes appeared as the female lead in the comedy Golden Days, by Sidney Toler and Marion Short. Woollcott thought she enhanced the play:

And those comments [the good ones] would be a good deal less than they are--as you may imagine-- without the winning personality and easy acting of Helen Hayes. It will not be surprising to those who know her to report that she gives the country girl a charm of manner and definiteness of characterization that make her consistently convincing. [90]

Hayes next appeared that season in George S. Kaufman and Marc Connelly's comedy To the Ladies. His initial comment on her indicates that he believed she had returned to her former fault: "All through the first two scenes the adroit and winning Helen Hayes to some extent ... took sledgehammers to the little playfulnesses of the Messrs. Kaufman and Connelly.... But thereafter the performance abated considerably...." [91] Speaking of her performance a few weeks later, however, Woollcott found no fault with it: "Helen Hayes continues to be uncannily good at every task assigned her and will, we suspect, be a great personage one of these days." [92] In 1923 he included her in a list of performers he thought would still be stars in twenty years. [93]

On March 11, 1924, Hayes opened in Israel Zangwill's We Moderns. Woollcott's comments on the careers of Minnie Maddern Fiske and the Barrymores revealed his firm belief that in order to develop the actor needed to be continually challenged. Hayes's appearance in We Moderns provided

Woollcott with an opportunity to note her lack of progress in this regard. On March 12 he described We Moderns as "a shallow and sententious play without the accent of life in it."94 After noting that her only good roles had been in Clarence and Dear Brutus he wrote: "One cannot help wondering how long her rare and exquisite talent will survive such misfortune."95 Later in the month he commented further on We Moderns and Miss Hayes's career:

> The chiefly regrettable thing about the "We Moderns" episode was its further waste of the precious talent of Helen Hayes. Here is one of the three most promising talents among the younger people in the American theater; yet since the production of "Clarence" nearly five years ago that talent has been frittered away on the most paltry of plays. Helen Hayes seems to us a second Mrs. Fiske, which coming from this quarter, is almost hysterical praise. No one could make her a bad actress, but some one has succeeded in making her a tremendously unimportant one. Her days in the theater have been fearfully mismanaged.96

In December Woollcott was not overly impressed with Hayes's next vehicle, Quarantine, an English play he described as "an inconsequential comedy cut from an old pattern."97 Hayes's performance, however, did impress him:

> But never did she seem to play with a greater felicity of tone and gesture, never did her every inflection, her every flick of the finger and toss of the head seem to say so much and say it with such sparkle and such unquenchable gayety. A fine actress is Miss Hayes and no mistake. There are some of us who mean to live thirty years longer if for no other reason than to totter over to Newark some day and attend her performance of Mrs. Malaprop in "The Rivals."98

On April 13, 1925, Hayes opened in the Theatre Guild's new theatre as Cleopatra in Shaw's Caesar and Cleopatra. Woollcott limited his comments on her to saying she "was so inevitable a choice for the sixteen-year-old mixture of child and queen whom Shaw had in mind when he wrote the play that no one else was thinkable."99 A year later she opened in the role of Maggie Wylle in a revival of James M. Barrie's What Every Woman Knows. Hilda Trevelyan was the

original Maggie in the September 1908 London opening, and
Maude Adams portrayed the role of the engaging wife in the
American premiere in December of the same year. Woollcott
believed that Hayes's performance bettered theirs: "Never
before was the role of Maggie Wylle played with the glow and
the grace and the unfailing art which Helen Hayes brought to
it last night. "[100] The performance confirmed Woollcott's belief in Hayes's ability:

> There was a great hubbub in the house when the
> curtain fell after the third act. It was for her.
> Often and beautifully has this commedienne played
> in our town. ... In her honor your correspondent's
> hat has more than once left its occasional post on
> your correspondent's head. But never was I half
> so sure as I was last night that Helen Hayes is a
> fine actress. [101]

After pointing out the "immense mediocrity" of the
supporting cast Woollcott proceeded with his praise: "Helen
Hayes by some magic has found just the right tide of loving
kindness, just the right wind of wintry charm, just the lacy
quality of a prim old valentine. "[102]

In November 1926, after the play completed its 252nd
performance and was about to close in New York prior to its
road tour, Woollcott recalled his 1920 article for Everybody's
Magazine in which he wondered where Hayes would be in 1926:
"Well the seven years have come and gone. ... But, anyway,
here it is 1926 and here, if you please, is Helen Hayes entering unchallenged into the heritage of the Maude Adams
repertory. "[103]

A year later Hayes was starring as Norma Besant in
Coquette, by George Abbott and Ann Bridgers. In his review
Woollcott noted the reputation that Hayes used to have:

> There was an era when the managers seemed to
> think of her as a cunning little kitten of an actress
> who would perch rather than merely sit on the grat-
> ified furniture. If a script revolved around an in-
> genue who always addressed her mother as "Mumsie"
> and even "Mumsie-wumsie," the manager could be
> counted on to pause at this point in his tearful read-
> ing of it and direct his secretary to put in a call
> for Helen Hayes. [104]

Woollcott then proceeded to note the change in her career:

This era seems to be passing, thanks be. Her performance in "What Every Woman Knows," exquisitely competent and wise with an uncanny, gnome-like wisdom put an end, I hope, to all that nonsense. And now in "Coquette," which Jed Harris presented to New York for the first time last night at Maxine Elliott's Theatre, she is summoned to scenes of tumult and heartache for which the average impresario would engage only some pulsating creature officially catalogued as "an emotional actress." Miss Hayes is superb in them.105

Coquette was the last play in which Woollcott was to review Hayes before his retirement as a newspaper reviewer. The memory of her performance in it stayed with him through the years. In a 1931 article for Pictorial Review he noted that the play "established her as an actress of true trajic force."106 In the same article he named her and Lynn Fontanne as the best young American actresses, not being able to choose between the two. In receiving this "title" from Woollcott, Hayes seemed to have fulfilled the potential the critic had seen in her back in 1919, when he wrote that she was "the most interesting and most promising new star that can be descried now in the theatrical firmament. The world seems to lie at this girl's feet."107 Two other performers who were to fulfill the potential that Woollcott foresaw for them were Alfred Lunt and Lynn Fontanne.

The Lunts

The most famous acting team in the American theatre during Woollcott's tenure as a daily reviewer was Alfred Lunt and Lynn Fontanne. Woollcott had reviewed individual performances of both of them before their New York debut opposite each other in the Theatre Guild's 1924 production of The Guardsman. He first reviewed Fontanne in her American debut in a play titled The Harp of Life, which starred Laurette Taylor. It opened on November 27, 1916, with Fontanne playing the role of Olive Hood, an ingenue of eighteen who suffers an affair of the heart. It was a minor role, but Woollcott was greatly impressed by the performance: "But next to Miss Taylor's performance the outstanding performance of the evening is given by Lynn Fontanne...."108

Lynn Fontanne's next Broadway appearance was in another Laurette Taylor vehicle, Out There. Opening on March 27, 1917, it was a war play by Hartley Manners, which

Woollcott described as "an unbeflogged study in patriotism."[109]
Fontanne played the role of "Princess" Lizzie, who thought
less of the war than did her patriotic sister, Annie, played
by Taylor. Woollcott's reference to Fontanne in his review
was brief but positive: "Again Lynn Fontanne strikes 13--
this time as Annie's exceedingly maternalistic little sister."[110]
Writing of her performance in a Sunday column after the
play's opening Woollcott said she played with "brilliant skill
and finesse."[111]

At the end of the 1916-17 season Woollcott devoted a
Sunday column to theatre people who showed great promise
during the season. One such person was Fontanne:

> Lynn Fontanne plays with telling precision and
> great nervous force. Her touching work as Olive
> in "The Harp of Life" and her truly glittering per-
> formance in "Out There," have been received with
> an acclaim that would have agitated a less serene
> and disinterested star than Laurette Taylor.[112]

Woollcott didn't review Fontanne again until well after
his return from the army. The occasion was her 1921 opening in the role of Dulcinea in Marc Connelly and George S.
Kaufman's comedy Dulcy. Describing her performance as
"brilliant," Woollcott was moved to speak of her future: "It
was apparent from the first that she was an actress of uncommon quality, and not even the rich role of Dulcy, which
offers her first full-size opportunity, measures up to her
suspected stature. She can do great things--and perhaps she
will.[113] A week later he described her as "an actress of
extraordinary gifts"[114] but did not elaborate on what these
gifts were. Woollcott did not find Fontanne faultless prior
to her joining Lunt. For one thing, he found her English
accent to be a limitation:

> One of the most conspicuous and important of these
> [limitations] is a permanent incapacity to fool you
> for one moment into thinking of her as an American.
> Her English accent in "Dulcy" which disturbs no one
> but which you can cut with a knife is presumably
> ineradicable.[115]

As his remarks on Fontanne imply, Woollcott had a
sensitive ear, and his reviews are sprinkled with notes ad-
vising actors to correct faulty pronunciation and poorly ex-
ecuted or inappropriate accents.[116]

The main fault Woollcott found with Fontanne was her failure to appear in the proper roles, a complaint he had registered about Fiske, the Barrymores, and Hayes. After her 1921 appearance in Sweet Nell of Old Drury, which he described as "a gaudy piece of rubbish,"[117] and her 1923 appearance in In Love with Love, he wrote:

> What does matter ... is that circumstance in the American theatre seems to have seized upon a singularly intense, vital, brilliant and slightly sinister actress and hurled her into comedies as heroines who are not any too bright.... She is playing a girl who is an empty babbling bit of gush who hasn't had an important thought since the spring of 1907. This, mind you, with an actress who could play Hedda Gabler and Rebecca West.[118]

Just as Woollcott had reviewed Fontanne before she starred with Lunt in The Guardsman, so did he review Lunt before that production. In each of these reviews Woollcott praised Lunt, using such words as "exceedingly good" and "magnificent."[119] There was no elaboration as to what specifically informed Woollcott's evaluations. Likewise there was no description of what manners Woollcott found annoying in Lunt's performance in Clarence (1919) and in Intimate Strangers (1921), although he did find them absent when Lunt appeared in Banco in 1922.[120]

Having each established something of a reputation on Broadway, the Lunts (Alfred and Lynn married in 1922) willingly sacrificed their usual fees for the opportunity of appearing in the Theatre Guild's production of Ferenc Molnar's The Guardsman. The production opened on October 13, 1924. In praising their performance Woollcott wrote of a possibility that became an eventuality:

> Wreaths rakishly askew on their damp brows are the portion to-day of Alfred Lunt and Lynn Fontanne, appearing together now for the first time, unless you choose (as we do not) to count the brief entanglement they shared in the revival of "Sweet Nell of Old Drury." They have youth and great gifts and the unmistakable attitude of ascent and those who saw them last night bowing hand in hand for the first time may well have been witnessing a moment in theatrical history. It is among the possibilities that we were seeing the first chapter in a partner-

ship destined to be as distinguished as that of Henry Irving and Ellen Terry. Our respective grandchildren will be able to tell. [121]

Continuing his evaluation of their performance, Woollcott wrote that Lunt "was admirable, playing with infinite zest, and all his new freedom." He had additional praise for Fontanne, but also a word of criticism:

Miss Fontanne played last evening with deep humor, now and again achieving a fleeting instant of such delicacy and shining rightness that the lover of good acting glowed to the point of incandescence. There were one or two moments, it is true, when she nervously mislaid her speeches and some such mishap seemed last night to derange the beat of the second act so that, after a long scene of comedy kept high and true, it fumbled and ended in blur and flurry. [122]

In December Woollcott wrote again of the promise of the Lunts:

In The Guardsman Alfred Lunt and Lynn Fontanne are equal to all the demands of this high comedy and by their performances suggest afresh how sagely and how inevitably the American Theatre will rely on them during the ten years that lie just ahead. [123]

In the ensuing years Woollcott's esteem for the Lunts' acting abilities grew. He followed their joint ventures in productions of Arms and the Man, The Goat Song, The Brothers Karamazov, The Second Man, and The Doctor's Dilemma. When they appeared separately--as Lunt did in such productions as Juarez and Maximilian, Marco Millions, and Volpone, and as Fontanne did in Pygmalion and Strange Interlude--he was equally attentive. Woollcott's most perceptive analysis of their acting together did not come until after he relinquished his daily reviewing post. In a 1933 article he wrote: "Their scenes together have that perfect dovetailing which directors dream of. The word is inadequate. A scene they play is a fabric in which you cannot see where the one begins and the other leaves off."[124] This description of their ensemble work was one of the few times he took the trouble to be specific in his evaluation of their performances. In Goat Song he saw Fontanne reaching new heights but did not detail what they were. [125] He described Lunt's performance in

Juarez and Maximilian as "a notable achievement" but did not
elaborate on what made it notable.[126] He praised them both
in The Brothers Karamazov without informing his readers as
to what informed his opinion.[127] When he was more specific
Woollcott praised Lunt's "handling of light comedy" and believable portrayal of exhaustion in Arms and the Man.[128] In the
same production he lauded Fontanne's "vitality" and "richly
comic" performance.[129]

Woollcott's enthusiasm for the Lunts did not prevent
him from criticizing them just as he had done prior to their
joining forces. He thought Fontanne's nervousness in the
first act of Arms and the Man "made her inarticulate and a
little laborious."[130] He faulted Lunt for being initially "overstrained"[131] by his role in Goat Song and was critical of the
"almost hypnotic weariness"[132] that he brought to his role in
Marco Millions.

In his biography of the Lunts Maurice Zolotow wrote
of Woollcott's propensity for socializing with performers and
the threat this practice might bring to a reviewer's objectiv-
ity:

> Before Woollcott, it was considered bad form for a
> drama reviewer to mingle socially with actors. Was
> one not in danger of losing one's critical detach-
> ment? Aleck, however, was enraptured by actors.
> He would rather be in the company of actors than
> any other sort of people. Besides the Lunts, he
> was enamored of Minnie Maddern Fiske, Maude
> Adams, Laurette Taylor, John, Ethel and Lionel
> Barrymore, Harpo Marx, Helen Hayes, Katherine
> Cornell and Ina Claire.[133]

As this examination of Woollcott's reviews indicates,
he was capable of criticizing as well as praising performers
he held in high esteem. Woollcott's constant campaigning for
performers to appear in challenging pieces was evidenced in
his comments on Fontanne prior to her joining Lunt. It was
also manifested after their union, when he complimented them
on their appearance in Goat Song after their frequent appearances in lighter plays. He thought the acting "in this extraordinary trajedy 'Goat Song' must come as a memorable experience, meat to men who have been on a long diet of mac-
aroons."[134] Woollcott's disenchantment with the idea of the
Lunts touring in Reunion in Vienna in 1934 was reminiscent
of his comments on Ethel Barrymore's 1920 tour in Déclassée.

It also expressed once again his conviction that the actor
should constantly be challenged:

> But it would mean another year's confinement to
> roles of which the Lunts have already exhausted
> the most important satisfactions. Their own pleas-
> ure in their profession and their growth in their art
> alike demand that they turn to the refreshment of
> new tasks. [135]

As his comments on Reunion in Vienna indicate, Woollcott continued writing about the Lunts after he retired as a
daily reviewer. In March 1929 he had written an article on
Lunt in which he observed:

> A trace of awkwardness impairs all his perform-
> ances in a comedy, and keeps him from being quite
> so good an actor in such pieces as this season's
> Caprice, or The Second Man, or even Arms and
> the Man, as he is in plays of pity and terror like
> The Brothers Karamazov, or Goat Song, or Juarez
> and Maximilian, or Outward Bound, or Robert E.
> Lee. [136]

In this same article Woollcott addressed himself to
the playing of comedy and tragedy:

> The man in the street thinks that comedians and
> tragedians are of different species, in which notion
> the man in the street is, oddly enough, in error.
> Indeed, as a rule, Macbeth can only be played by
> someone who would also be, or have been, a good
> Charles Surface, and only because he was also a
> delightful comedian was John Barrymore able to be-
> come the best Hamlet of his day. [137]

In this article Woollcott never elaborated on the shared
acting qualities required for the enactment of tragic or comic
roles. Nor did he in 1920, which was the first time that he
stated a good actor could play both tragedy and comedy. [138]

Despite Woollcott's belief that Lunt performed better
in serious roles, he still found him to be the leading actor
of the day in the English-speaking world, as his left-handed
compliment of 1929 indicated:

> Indeed, such is our poverty in the art of acting,

that this Wisconsin product who, with Lynn Fontanne, now heads the Acting Company of the Theatre Guild, is I suppose, the leading actor in the English speaking theatre. Certainly I know that if I were sentenced to spend the next five years in a town with only one theatre in it, but would be allowed to name the personnel of that theatre's stock company, the first player I would choose for its roster would be Alfred Lunt. And furthermore I think that if you were to take a poll of all the producers, critics and playwrights now in New York, a vast majority of them would, perhaps to their own surprise, make the same first choice. [139]

Four years later Woollcott again hailed Lunt as "the foremost actor in the English-speaking theatre."[140] In 1931 he honored Fontanne in superlative terms by offering her name along with Helen Hayes's as the best young American actress. In presenting Fontanne's name he wrote:

Miss Fontanne came to us in 1916, when Laurette Taylor brought her from London. She was emaciated, gawky, and astringent, but an infallible artist even then. Ellen Terry had been her teacher. After the odd jobs in Miss Taylor's company, she made rapid, fortunate, and enlarging progress, and since it seemed an important thing in the theater, she decided to be beautiful, too, achieving a transformation by sheer act of will, I think.

As first lady of the Theatre Guild, she has had a variety of opportunity such as has fallen in our time to no other actress in the English-speaking theater. Thus she has grown in grace and stature. Thus she has acquired merit in the long ascending pathway of her art. [141]

These evaluations and his praise of their ensemble acting demonstrated that the Lunts had fulfilled the promise he had seen in them in The Guardsmen in 1924.

In writing of Lionel Barrymore, Woollcott had first revealed his attitude that the actor was the primary theatre artist. An examination of his commentary on Minnie Maddern Fiske, the Barrymores, Helen Hayes, and the Lunts provides a composite of qualities he valued in a performer, none of which is surprising. Believability heads the list. The ability to project emotion was highly regarded, as was

proficiency in non-verbal skills, such as listening on stage
and the ability to express oneself through the use of the body.
He believed that the good actor could do both comedy and
tragedy. Speaking more amorphously, he maintained that acting at its best was characterized by a "spiritual radiance"
emanating from the actor.

In addition to providing insights into his tastes in acting Woollcott's remarks on performers help provide an image
of him as a reviewer and commentator on theatre. The foremost characteristic of Woollcott's work was his concern for
the welfare of the theatre. This concern is vividly illustrated
in his advice to performers. In telling people like Fiske, the
Barrymores, and Hayes to appear in challenging roles, he not
only demonstrated a concern for their individual development
but also for the theatre's enrichment. His disdain for the
actor's appearance in a long run also reflects this attitude.

Viewed from our perspective, Woollcott's responses to
the performers he covered reveal him to be quite perceptive.
In one of his Sunday columns for the Times he wrote:

> So entirely is a young actor's advance left to the
> hazards of each season that none of us can say of
> any of them whether he is a rising star or just a
> meteor streaking across the theatrical firmament.[142]

Nevertheless, in viewing early performances in the
careers of Helen Hayes and the team of Alfred Lunt and Lynn
Fontanne, he predicted stardom, and time proved him to be
correct.

In addition to seeing Woollcott's perceptiveness in his
ability to foresee stardom one can also see it in his evaluation
of performances. His opinion of John Barrymore's portrayal
of William Falder in John Galsworthy's Justice best exempli-
fies this. In his review on April 4, 1916, Woollcott told his
readers: "They [the audience] saw John Barrymore play as
he never played before, and so by his work as the wretched
prisoner in 'Justice' steps forward into a new position on the
American stage."[143] Contemporary theatre historians in reviewing Barrymore's career have made similar assessments
of the importance of his performance in Justice. Barnard
Hewitt in Theatre U.S.A. wrote: "John Barrymore demonstrated for the first time that he was an actor to be reckoned
with in serious drama."[144] Brooks Atkinson in Broadway
wrote: "In Justice a clever actor began to look like an important one."[145]

In addition to revealing his concern for theatre and his critical and prophetic abilities Woollcott's comments on performers also show him to be demanding of theatre artists. A pattern presents itself when one looks at his comments on Minnie Maddern Fiske, the Barrymores, and Helen Hayes. In each case there is initial praise followed by criticism. The criticism usually was that the performer was not appearing in challenging enough roles. No one represents this pattern better than Fiske. He showered her with praise in the first two productions he reviewed, Erstwhile Susan in 1916 and Wake Up, Jonathan! in 1921. In November 1921, however, he faulted her for spending her time acting in such poor material as these two plays represented in his eyes:

> When such players as these [Julia Marlowe and David Warfield] jog along in the same old roles year after year, as when Mrs. Fiske spends four seasons trying to give such cheap tinsel as her last two plays Erstwhile Susan and Wake Up, Jonathan! the look and lustre of gold, they are yielding the leadership of the stage to others. 146

Woollcott's comments on Fiske's choice of roles demonstrates his belief that what truly mattered for a performer as well as the theatre was the quality of the material with which one succeeded.

Accenting Woollcott's critical characteristics was his love of theatre. The enthusiasm marking his reactions to performances he truly admired reveals a commentator who never considered himself a mere functionary performing a task. There was a joy that projected through his work and immediately communicated to the reader his commitment to the subject matter about which he wrote.

Notes

1"Second Thoughts on First Nights," New York Times, January 23, 1916, Sec. 6, p. 6.

2"Mrs. Fiske Returns in Delightful Role," New York Times, January 19, 1916, p. 12.

3Ibid. For additional references to these points see "The Play," New York Times, January 18, 1921, p. 14; "Second Thoughts on First Nights," New York Times, November 6, 1921, Sec. 6, p. 1; "Shouts and Murmurs," New York

Herald, April 6, 1923, p. 12; "Mrs. Fiske in Helena's Boys," New York Sun, April 8, 1924, p. 24; "Plays and Players in These Parts," New York Sun, March 14, 1925, p. 5; "The Story of Mrs. Fiske," Collier's, November 21, 1925, p. 20; and "The Stage," New York World, March 20, 1928, p. 13.

4"Second Thoughts on First Nights," New York Times, February 27, 1916, Sec. 2, p. 7.

5Mrs. Fiske--Her Views on Actors, Acting, and the Problems of Production (New York: Century, 1917), p. 228.

6"Second Thoughts on First Nights," New York Times, February 27, 1916, Sec. 2, p. 7.

7"Shouts and Murmurs," New York Herald, October 7, 1923, Sec. 7, p. 1. At times Woollcott spelled tragedy with a j--"trajedy."

8"The Play," New York Times, January 18, 1921, p. 14.

9"Shouts and Murmurs," New York Herald, April 6, 1923, p. 12.

10See "Plays and Players in These Parts," New York Sun, March 14, 1925, p. 5; "The Story of Mrs. Fiske," Collier's, November 21, 1925, p. 20; and "The Play," New York World, January 11, 1927, p. 17.

11"Shouts and Murmurs," New York Herald, April 6, 1923, p. 12.

12"Shouts and Murmurs," New York Herald, September 12, 1923, p. 8.

13"The Stage," New York World, March 20, 1928, p. 13.

14"A Scrap of Paper Yellow with Age," New York Times, May 12, 1914, p. 11.

15See "Emma McChesney Goes on the Stage," New York Times, October 20, 1915, p. 11; "Second Thoughts on First Nights," New York Times, October 24, 1915, Sec. 6, p. 6; and "Shouts and Murmurs," New York Herald, February 13, 1923, p. 10.

[16]See "Ethel Barrymore in a Fine Play," New York Times, January 26, 1915, p. 11; "Emma McChesney on the Stage," New York Times, October 20, 1915, p. 11; "Second Thoughts on First Nights," New York Times, September 26, 1920, Sec. 6, p. 1; "The Play," New York Times, April 19, 1921, p. 15; "The Reviewing Stand," New York Herald, December 28, 1922, p. 6; "The Stage," New York Herald, October 12, 1925, p. 13; and "The Stage," New York World, November 30, 1926, p. 13.

[17]See "The Play," New York Times, October 17, 1919, p. 22; "The Play," New York Times, April 19, 1921, p. 15; "Second Thoughts on First Nights," New York Times, April 24, 1921, Sec. 6, p. 1; "The Reviewing Stand," New York Herald, December 28, 1922, p. 6; "Shouts and Murmurs," New York Herald, November 13, 1923, p. 9; and "The Stage," New York World, October 12, 1925, p. 13.

[18]"Second Thoughts on First Nights," New York Times, December 5, 1915, Sec. 6, p. 6.

[19]"Ethel Barrymore in a Fine Play," New York Times, January 26, 1915, p. 11.

[20]"Second Thoughts on First Nights," New York Times, October 24, 1915, Sec. 6, p. 6.

[21]Woollcott, Letters, p. 77.

[22]See Woollcott's reviews of Young America ("Young America Has Wide Appeal," New York Times, August 30, 1915, p. 7); Evidence ("Joy of New Play an Aged Actress," New York Times, October 8, 1914, p. 11); and The Fool ("The Reviewing Stand," New York Herald, October 25, 1922, p. 8) for examples of his praise of sentimental plays. While demonstrating a liking for plays that appealed to the emotions, Woollcott was aware of the misuse of their appeal and spoke out against it. See "The Play," New York Times, December 11, 1919, p. 11.

[23]"Ethel Barrymore Returns," New York Times, May 26, 1917, p. 11.

[24]"The Play," New York Times, October 7, 1919, p. 22.

[25]"Second Thoughts on First Nights," New York Times, September 26, 1920, Sec. 6, p. 1.

26"The Long Run as a Curse," Everybody's Magazine, May 1921, pp. 26-7.

27"Shouts and Murmurs," New York Herald, November 13, 1923, p. 9.

28"The Stage," New York World, December 28, 1925, p. 11.

29"Shouts and Murmurs," New York Herald, April 22, 1923, Sec. 7, p. 1.

30"Good Melodrama at the Longacre," New York Times, October 20, 1914, p. 13.

31"'Justice' Done Here with Superb Cast," New York Times, April 4, 1916, p. 11.

32Ibid.

33See "Second Thoughts on First Nights," New York Times, April 9, 1916, Sec. 2, p. 8, and "The Play," New York Times, March 8, 1920, p. 7.

34"Second Thoughts on First Nights," New York Times, Sec. 2, p. 8.

35Ibid.

36See "The Play," New York Times, September 20, 1919, p. 14; "Second Thoughts on First Nights," New York Times, March 21, 1920, Sec. 6, p. 6; "The Play," New York Times, April 19, 1921, p. 15; and "The Reviewing Stand," New York Herald, November 17, 1922, p. 8.

37"Second Thoughts on First Nights," New York Times, April 23, 1916, Sec. 2, p. 8.

38"Second Thoughts on First Nights," New York Times, May 21, 1916, Sec. 2, p. 6.

39"An Acting Edition of 'Peter Ibbetson,'" New York Times, April 19, 1917, p. 13. Woollcott proceeded to praise Barrymore's use of imagination in this portrayal in later commentary on this performance (See "Second Thoughts on First Nights," New York Times, April 22, 1917, Sec. 9, p. 3). He also praised this dimension of his acting in writing of his portrayal of Richard III (see "The Play," New York Times, March 8, 1920, p. 7).

40Ibid.

41Ibid.

42"The Play," New York Times, September 20, 1919, p. 14.

43"Second Thoughts on First Nights," New York Times, October 5, 1919, Sec. 4, p. 2.

44"The Play," New York Times, March 8, 1920, p. 7.

45Ibid.

46"Second Thoughts on First Nights," New York Times, March 21, 1920, Sec. 6, p. 6.

47Ibid.

48Ibid.

49"The Play," New York Times, April 19, 1921, p. 15.

50"Second Thoughts on First Nights," New York Times, October 10, 1920, Sec. 6, p. 1.

51"The Reviewing Stand," New York Herald, November 17, 1922, p. 8.

52Ibid.

53Ibid.

54"The Reviewing Stand," New York Herald, November 19, 1922, Sec. 7, p. 1.

55"The Reviewing Stand," New York Herald, December 3, 1922, Sec. 7, p. 1.

56Ibid. In regard to typecasting, Woollcott believed that actors often were best served by being cast in parts in which they closely approximated the "age and general appear-

ance" of the characters to be portrayed. See "Second
Thoughts on First Nights," New York Times, December 6,
1914, Sec. 9, p. 2. He drew the line at such casting pro-
cedures, however, when the quality of performance was sacrificed. See "Three Negro Plays Played by Negroes," New
York Times, April 6, 1917, p. 11.

57"Are We Out of the Woods?" Vanity Fair, January
1923, p. 35.

58"Shouts and Murmurs," New York Herald, February
2, 1923, p. 12.

59"Shouts and Murmurs," New York Herald, December 1, 1923, p. 9.

60"Plays and Players in These Parts," New York Sun,
January 21, 1925, p. 14.

61"Hamlet In Mufto," Vanity Fair, January 1926, p.
70.

62"An Acting Edition of 'Peter Ibbetson,'" New York
Times, April 19, 1917, p. 13.

63"Second Thoughts on First Nights," New York Times,
May 13, 1917, Sec. 8, p. 7.

64"Second Thoughts on First Nights," New York Times,
September 7, 1919, Sec. 4, p. 2. This was the first occa-
sion on which Woollcott expressed his view on the supremacy
of the actor's art, a view he reiterated on other occasions.
See "Second Thoughts on First Nights," New York Times,
April 18, 1920, Sec. 6, p. 2; "Shouts and Murmurs," New
York Herald, January 28, 1923, Sec. 7, p. 1; and "The
Story of Irving Berlin," Saturday Evening Post, February 21,
1925, p. 36.

65"The Play," New York Times, September 20, 1919,
p. 14.

66"The Play," New York Times, February 24, 1920,
p. 11.

67See "Plays and Players in These Parts," New York
Sun, January 21, 1925, p. 14, and "Lionel Barrymore Once
More," New York Sun, May 22, 1925, p. 4.

[68]"The Play," New York Times, February 18, 1921, p. 16.

[69]Ibid.

[70]"Second Thoughts on First Nights," New York Times, February 27, 1921, Sec. 6, p. 1.

[71]"The Play," New York Times, October 18, 1921, p. 20.

[72]Ibid.

[73]Ibid.

[74]"The Stage," New York Herald, November 29, 1923, p. 15.

[75]Ibid.

[76]"Lionel Barrymore Returns," New York Sun, January 16, 1925, p. 20.

[77]Ibid.

[78]"Lionel Barrymore Once More," New York Sun, May 22, 1925, p. 24.

[79]Ibid.

[80]"Mrs. Drew Appears in a Patchy Play," New York Times, September 8, 1914, p. 11.

[81]"The Play," New York Times, September 22, 1919, p. 8.

[82]Ibid.

[83]"Second Thoughts on First Nights," New York Times, November 23, 1919, Sec. 9, p. 2.

[84]"The Child-Actor Grows Up," Everybody's Magazine, February 1920, p. 57.

[85]"The Play," New York Times, October 19, 1920, p. 12.

86Ibid.

87Ibid.

88Ibid.

89"The Play," New York Times, October 11, 1921, p. 22.

90"The Play," New York Times, November 2, 1921, p. 20.

91"The Play," New York Times, February 21, 1922, p. 20.

92"Second Thoughts on First Nights," New York Times, March 12, 1922, Sec. 6, p. 1.

93"Shouts and Murmurs," New York Herald, April 22, 1923, Sec. 7, p. 1.

94"Shouts and Murmurs," New York Herald, March 12, 1924, p. 9.

95Ibid.

96"Shouts and Murmurs," New York Sun, March 29, 1924, p. 4.

97"Helen Hayes in 'Quarantine,'" New York Sun, December 17, 1924, p. 30.

98Ibid.

99"Shaw's 'Caesar and Cleopatra,'" New York Sun, April 14, 1925, p. 22.

100"The Stage," New York World, April 14, 1926, p. 17.

101Ibid.

102Ibid.

103"Second Thoughts on First Nights," New York Herald, November 14, 1926, p. 3M.

[104]"The Stage," New York World, November 9, 1927, p. 13.

[105]Ibid.

[106]"Who Is the Best Young American Actress?" Pictorial Review, April 1931, p. 92.

[107]"Second Thoughts on First Nights," New York Times, November 23, 1919, Sec. 9, p. 2.

[108]"Beauty and Truth in 'The Harp of Life,'" New York Times, November 28, 1916, p. 11.

[109]"'Out There' Power Most Appealing," New York Times, March 28, 1917, p. 11.

[110]Ibid.

[111]"Second Thoughts on First Nights," New York Times, April 8, 1917, Sec. 8, p. 5.

[112]"Second Thoughts on First Nights," New York Times, May 13, 1917, Sec. 8, p. 7.

[113]"The Play," New York Times, August 15, 1921, p. 14.

[114]"Second Thoughts on First Nights," New York Times, August 21, 1921, Sec. 6, p. 1.

[115]Ibid.

[116]See "Leah Kleschna After Twenty Years," New York Sun, April 22, 1924, p. 18, and "Reicher Presents Hauptmann Play," New York Times, December 15, 1915, p. 15.

[117]"Shouts and Murmurs," New York Herald, May 19, 1923, p. 7.

[118]"Shouts and Murmurs," New York Herald, August 7, 1923, p. 8.

[119]See "The Play," New York Times, September 22, 1919, p. 8; "The Play," New York Times, September 21,

1922, p. 18; and "The Stage," New York Herald, January 8, 1924, p. 9.

120See "The Play," New York Times, September 22, 1919, p. 8; "The Play," New York Times, November 8, 1921, p. 8; and "The Play," New York Times, September 21, 1922, p. 18.

121"Gayety in Thirty-fifth Street," New York Sun, October 14, 1924, p. 28.

122Ibid.

123"The House of the Second Chance," Vanity Fair, December 1924, p. 116.

124"Luck and Mr. Lunt," Cosmopolitan, April 1933, p. 56.

125"The Stage," New York World, August 26, 1926, p. 13.

126"The Stage," New York World, October 12, 1926, p. 15.

127"The Stage," New York World, January 4, 1927, p. 4.

128"The Stage," New York World, September 15, 1925, p. 18.

129Ibid.

130Ibid.

131"The Stage," New York World, August 26, 1926, p. 13.

132"The Stage," New York World, January 10, 1928, p. 15.

133Stagestruck: The Romance of Alfred Lunt and Lynn Fontanne (New York: Harcourt, Brace and World, 1965), p. 142.

134"The Stage," New York World, February 1, 1926, p. 11.

[135]"Miss Kitty Takes to the Road," Saturday Evening Post, August 18, 1934, p. 15.

[136]"The Haunted House of Lunt," Vanity Fair, March 1929, p. 60.

[137]Ibid.

[138]See "Second Thoughts on First Nights," New York Times, August 22, 1920, Sec. 6, p. 1.

[139]Woollcott, "The Haunted House of Lunt," p. 60.

[140]"Luck and Mr. Lunt," Cosmopolitan, April 1933, p. 56.

[141]"Who Is the Best Young American Actress?" Pictorial Review, April 1931, p. 90.

[142]"Second Thoughts on First Nights," New York Times, March 12, 1922, Sec. 6, p. 1.

[143]"'Justice' Done Here with Superb Cast," New York Times, p. 11.

[144](New York: McGraw-Hill, 1959), p. 320.

[145](New York: Macmillan, 1970), p. 146.

[146]"Second Thoughts on First Nights," New York Times, November 6, 1921, Sec. 6, p. 1.

Chapter 3

WOOLLCOTT ON PLAYWRIGHTS AND PLAYWRITING

Shakespeare

In the course of his career Woollcott reviewed twenty-one of Shakespeare's plays. As with his commentary on performers, Woollcott was not always explicit in presenting the reasons for his opinion of playwrights. An examination of Woollcott's reviews of Shakespearean productions and his articles dealing with Shakespeare reveals very little in the way of his evaluation of the Bard's strengths or weaknesses. However, individual positive and negative qualities of the plays can be noted in his reviews, and taken as a whole they do provide some notion of Woollcott's attitude toward Shakespeare.

Spirit is one quality of the comedies that Woollcott noted more than once. Reviewing As You Like It for the first time in 1914, he called it "the happiest of Shakespeare's comedies" and wrote of the play's spirit in commenting on the character of Rosalind: "'As You Like It' is mostly Rosalind. Its spirit is her spirit and its charm her charm."[1] Describing Margaret Anglin's performance as Rosalind, he said, "she is a Rosalind who is all joyousness."[2] Furthermore, he found that the actors let "the rolicking, romping spirit of the pastoral comedy come through."[3]

Spirit is also referred to in Woollcott's review of The Merry Wives of Windsor. Having found the character of Falstaff "bemused and duped and depreciated ... beyond all true semblance of Prince Hal's companions," Woollcott still described him as "the most durable spirit" in the play.[4]

Another quality of the comedies that Woollcott commended was their magic. He described A Midsummer Night's Dream as possessing the "magic of a fantastic play."[5] He described The Tempest as the "airiest flight of Shakespeare's fancy."[6]

He praised As You Like It for its beauty: "There is beauty here [in the setting] which is part and parcel with the youth in Summer time that is Rosalind and 'As You Like It' ";[7] Twelfth Night for its songs: "some of the loveliest songs Shakespeare ever wrote ... ";[8] and The Taming of the Shrew for being "a gay, rapid, rattling farce, richly Elizabethan in its flavor and full of fun for an audience of this day and city...."[9] He found the poetry of The Tempest to be "lovely," including "here and there" some of the "matchless things in the English language."[10]

Woollcott identified The Merchant of Venice as the most successful Shakespearean comedy in the theatre, but in typical fashion did not elaborate as to the reasons.[11] Perhaps he was thinking in terms of number of productions, as it was the Shakespearean play he reviewed the most, a total of eight times.

The most frequent negative quality Woollcott found in the comedies was a dullness which he described by using such words as "dreary," "tedious," "trying," and "dull." Plays so categorized were The Merry Wives of Windsor, The Comedy of Errors, As You Like It, and The Taming of the Shrew.[12] In regard to the last two plays Woollcott's initial positive reactions to them in 1914 had changed to negative ones in 1923 for As You Like It and in 1927 for The Taming of the Shrew. In neither case did Woollcott provide reasons for his change of opinion.

The two most frequently cited qualities of the tragedies were their difficulty of production and the inexhaustible depth of their material. He described Macbeth as the "most difficult and exacting of the Shakespearean tragedies."[13] Julius Caesar struck him as being "an exhausting and inexhaustible play."[14] Woollcott also used the word "inexhaustible" to describe Hamlet.[15] King Lear was described as "a play so ungainly and so difficult that it has not been attempted more than once or twice in our time and has not been attempted successfully at all."[16]

Hamlet was the tragedy Woollcott commented upon the most. He believed the play contained a humanity and beauty that John Barrymore's portrayal enabled him to feel "as never before."[17] He believed that "there never was a play which one could see so often. The sap of eternal life is in its lines as it is in the lines of the twenty-third Psalm."[18]

With respect to Hamlet himself, he believed that the character possessed a sense of humor and charm that heightened the pathos and poignancy of his tragic situation.[19] Hamlets who lacked this quality were duly chided.[20] He also called for "a fine brawling, besotted court, with a lascivious King and Queen forming a gaudy, bawdy background to the black, fastidious figure of a Prince suffering chiefly from distaste."[21] He made the request in 1925 and never noted that it was fulfilled.

The extent of Woollcott's examination of Hamlet was the exception rather than the rule in his reviews and commentary on Shakespeare's plays. His usual course was to be very brief in his analysis of the play. What occupied more of his time was relating the plot, providing background information on the play and actors, and commenting on the acting and production problems in general.

Admonishing those who employed a declamatory style of acting, Woollcott advocated a more believable "spirited" portrayal. His comments on Margaret Anglin's 1914 production of As You Like It make this clear: "Much of the artificiality that has grown up around the acting of Shakespeare through the centuries is here stripped away and the rollicking romping spirit of the pastoral comedy is left to work its will with the audience."[22] Woollcott wanted the actor to perceive the spirit of the play and perform in light of it:

> It is important, of course, that any modern performance of a Shakespearean play should be academically correct in its detail or, at least that it should not be academically incorrect. Devotion to the footnotes shall have its reward. But it is a hundred times more important that the spirit of a performance should be right, and it is in creating the spirit of the comedies that these [Anglin's] players have been so conspicuously successful....[23]

In 1916, the year of the Shakespearean Tercentenary celebration, Woollcott bemoaned the state of Shakespearean acting in our country, quoting William Winter:

> "It is deplorably true that, although fine individual impersonations become occasionally visible, no complete all-round performance of a Shakespearean play can anywhere be seen in America. The custom of acting Shakespeare has been permitted to dwindle.

The necessary and valuable traditions have been,
in a great measure, allowed to die. There should
be a revival before it's too late."
Thus Mr. Winter himself writing some five years
ago a paragraph which he might repeat with heavier
emphasis today....24

Woollcott did not end his discourse on a negative note,
however:

But one may be permitted to wonder whether
there might not be grounds for consolation in the
death of sacrosanct traditions, some value in a
fresh start and some hope that for such a start,
it can never be "too late."25

In regard to the producing of Shakespeare, Woollcott
demonstrated a primary concern with the pacing of the plays
in his comments on a 1916 production of The Tempest:

The production is notable first for the swift succes-
sion of the scenes, so that the play moves on its
way at a lively and enlivening pace.... For most
of us there is only one factor in the theatre of this
actor-dramatist that need be preserved, and that is
a stage so fashioned that the fine, full text of his
plays may unfold rapidly without long, tedious, in-
terrupting, disillusioning waits between the scenes. 26

As his remarks indicate, the tempo of a production
was a matter of concern for Woollcott. His reviews faulted
both actors and directors for the absence of the proper tempo
in productions. Woollcott never revealed what enabled him
to decide who deserved the blame. The blame was laid nevertheless. 27

Woollcott was not a "purist" in regard to the staging
of Shakespeare, as his comments on a 1927 modern-dress
production of The Taming of the Shrew indicated:

For more and more am I convinced that it is the
release of the actors from the swagger of doublet
and hose which makes these modern-dress revivals
move with such spirit and vitality. Just let a
troupe wear their own clothes when they are turned
loose in an Elizabethan play and, in this unaccus-
tomed comfort, they seem suddenly to discover that

after all their own Will did write about human be-
ings. [28]

On another occasion Woollcott had ventured to say that
Shakespeare "would have enjoyed" changes in his script: "He
was so good a showman that probably he has resented only
those solemn mountebanks who, from time to time, have in-
sisted on making his plays seem dull. "[29]

Woollcott believed that in Hamlet, Shakespeare wrote
"the masterpiece of the dramatic literature of our tongue. "[30]
He thought that at his worst, as in The Comedy of Errors,
Shakespeare was "witless and unspeakably dreary. "[31] His
reviews of Shakespeare's work reveal Woollcott himself working at his best and his worst. In the series of reviews of
Barrymore's Hamlet Woollcott details his view of the play in
a precise and enthusiastic manner. In reviewing a play like
The Winter's Tale, he ambles on without addressing the script
specifically at all. [32] Such fluctuation of attention and uneven
quality are not apparent in Woollcott's treatment of other
great playwrights who came under his scrutiny.

George Bernard Shaw

In his review of the first two parts of Back to Methuselah, produced by the Theatre Guild in 1922, Woollcott wrote
that a group such as the Guild "owes it to such a dramatist
as Shaw to give voice to any play that he may choose to
write. "[33] Woollcott's directive to America's most respected
producing organization of that time revealed the esteem in
which he held Shaw. At the end of the 1922-23 season Woollcott again expressed his admiration for Shaw by citing him as
one of the three best contemporary playwrights. (James M.
Barrie and Eugene O'Neill were the other two. [34]) When
praising Shaw, Woollcott most frequently cited the entertainment value of his work. [35] Descriptions of Pygmalion "as
simply entertaining a piece as the author has ever deigned
to write"[36] or Caesar and Cleopatra as Shaw's "endlessly
delightful comedy, "[37] demonstrate Woollcott's recognition
of Shaw's ability to regale his audiences.

The Shavian wit was praised for being "fresh and abundant, " as well as "matchless. "[38] Woollcott seemed particularly impressed by the apparent fact that time did not dimin-
ish the effectiveness of Shaw's wit. He voiced his opinion
in an April 1915 review of a revival of the 1896 comedy You

Never Can Tell and in a May 1915 review of the 1894 comedy Arms and the Man. [39]

Woollcott also lauded Shaw's ability to invigorate his audiences intellectually. He applauded Major Barbara for being "genuinely stimulating,"[40] Getting Married for its "intellectual vigor,"[41] and Back to Methuselah for "some searching ... things."[42] The beauty of Shaw's work was also extolled in Back to Methuselah[43] as well as Saint Joan.[44]

If Woollcott found much to praise in Shaw's work, he also found much to criticize. He most frequently faulted Shaw's prolixity, a problem he noted in nine of the nineteen Shavian plays he reviewed.[45] A much more substantive complaint was of Shaw's play-constructing abilities. He found The Doctor's Dilemma to have "a loose and straggling dramatic method."[46] He described Major Barbara as "a little ungainly and discursive,"[47] and while praising it for being "genuinely stimulating," he wished that Shaw had made it "dramatically forceful."[48] Woollcott's disenchantment with Shaw led him to address the dramatist's inability to use the theatre effectively as a medium. In his 1916 review of Getting Married he described it as "one of the most talkative and forgettable plays Shaw ever wrote" and noted that nothing about it made amends "for Mr. Shaw's deliberate perversion of the theatre, his bland refusal to make use of the theatre's incomparable means for driving home an idea by use of a dramatic story unfolded in a dramatic way."[49] Four years later Woollcott did not see any change:

> What has decidedly gained ground is the feeling
> that a mighty satirist and a great provocative teacher
> has strayed into the theatre, where the exhausting
> and seemingly futile effort to point out to him that
> he might say his say a hundred times more effec-
> tively, if only he would consider the limitations and
> potentialities of his medium, has come to be re-
> garded as wasting breath that might more handsomely
> and more intelligently be spent in acclaiming his con-
> sent to use any medium at all.[50]

Woollcott also was critical of Shaw's mixing moods in his plays, believing this to demonstrate a lack of taste and insensitivity to his audience's needs. He made this observation in his review of Getting Married:

> But best of all is Henrietta Crossman, who brings

riches of vitality to the role of Mrs. George, and
reads with fine skill and understanding the poetic
trance-utterance wherein the clairvoyante gives
voice to woman's age-old protest against her ignoble
treatment in a selfish, unapproachable world of men.
This is one of the most exalted and poignantly beautiful passages in contemporary English dramatic literature and it is characteristic of Shaw that he
should have dumped it into this sprightly and face-
tious comedy. It is part of his chronic indifference
to the dissonance of incongruity; part, in short, of
his basic lack of taste.

Shaw has no patience with the sensitive playgoer
who needs to have his mood prepared for such a
scene. For his own part, he lives to mix things
promiscuously, and he has always been contemptuous
of those who like their dramatic fare done up in
neat little separate packages. [51]

In 1920 Woollcott voiced his reservation about the universality of much of Shaw's work. He wrote:

Reviewing most of Shaw's old plays is a little like
fighting in last year's trenches; ... the journalistic
element in Shaw's work, while endowing it with
much of its present force and value and significance,
at the same time dooms it to grow stale like the
headlines of yesteryear. [52]

Woollcott's treatment of Shaw is much more substantive
than his treatment of Shakespeare. Perhaps the process of
covering a living playwright provided more of a stimulus to
register detailed analyses. Woollcott's propensity for not being specific at times still can be observed in his coverage of
Shaw, however. His original enthusiastic evaluation of Pygmalion in 1914, "as simply entertaining a piece as the author
has ever deigned to write," [53] changed to "a characteristic
example of Shaw at his second best" [54] in 1926 without explan-
ation. Of all Shaw's plays Woollcott was most enamored of
Candida. In a 1925 review he described it as "the best comedy ... which has been written for the modern English
stage." [55] In three other reviews of the play he was just as
laudatory, [56] but in none of his reviews did he elaborate on
the reasons for such high esteem. Nor did he explain what
led him to describe the role of Candida as "the role of roles
--surely the loveliest feminine role in the modern theatre." [57]

Perhaps Woollcott's review of the 1923 opening performance of St. Joan best encompasses his general attitude toward Shaw. He found it to be "beautiful, engrossing and at times exalting,"[58] although he found fault with both the length and direction of the play. In typically Woollcottian fashion he would not let reservations prevent his outpouring of praise:

> But it would be captious criticism and fraudulent reporting to give emphasis to such reservations when the outstanding thing is that a deathless legend came to life again on the Garrick's stage, quickened by the performance of a play that has greatness in it.[59]

Woollcott definitely had reservations about Shaw's abilities. In a posthumously published article he referred to him as "a pedagogue at heart."[60] Woollcott undoubtedly believed that Shaw's pedagogy interfered with his ability to use the theatre as effectively as he might. He also questioned his verbosity and his ability to construct plots and to deal with universal themes. These reservations, however, did not dim Woollcott's appreciation of Shaw's ability to entertain his audiences while displaying keen wit and stimulating them intellectually. As he said of St. Joan, while Shaw sent his audiences home exhausted, he sent them "with an experience to remember all the rest of their lives."[61]

Woollcott was not as comprehensive in his treatment of an earlier socially conscious playwright who drew his attention, Henrik Ibsen.

Henrik Ibsen

Woollcott's commentary on the works of Ibsen, like that on Shakespeare, focuses less on critical remarks on the scripts than on the problems of production. The inferior treatment that Ibsen received was the most frequent comment Woollcott made about the playwright. He lamented a 1920 revival of Hedda Gabler:

> No playwright, living or dead, has suffered such shoddy and generally incompetent production in this country as poor Henrik Ibsen and it is really astonishing that the notion that he could write good plays has nevertheless survived to this day. His most

> fascinating heroine, Hedda Gabler, ... was killed again yesterday afternoon at the Little Theatre.[62]

Woollcott's disenchantment with the quality of Ibsen productions led him to describe the kind of acting they required. Although directed to the acting of Ibsen's plays, the ideas are so elementary that Woollcott could have said them of any number of playwrights. His first observations came in his 1917 book Mrs. Fiske--Her Views on Actors, Acting, and the Problems of Production. He wrote of the "great" Ibsen roles as having "such depths of feeling, such vistas of life as must inspire and exact the best from any player anywhere in the world."[63] In 1926 Woollcott noted that the depth he perceived in Ibsen's plays called for actors to "hold something in reserve":

> Then the Ibsen plays, which unfold like a succession of parting curtains--till the onlooker's vision reaches far, far into the interior of their people's lives--call peculiarly for acting that holds something in reserve, acting that slowly, bit by bit, lets the audience into the secret of the soul.[64]

As with Shakespeare's plays, Woollcott's evaluation of Ibsen's work was quite laudatory, if not always specific in detailing its strengths and weaknesses.[65] In his first review of Ghosts Woollcott referred to it as a "great and oppressive tragedy, ... one of the most austere and lofty plays of our time and one of the greatest tragedies of all literature, ... the first of the great modern plays."[66] Nowhere does Woollcott elucidate what warranted his praise. He described Hedda Gabler as "one of the finest dramatic portraits in all literature and one of the most artful examples of the playmaker's craft in the modern theatre."[67] Rosmersholm was described as "a piece of dramatic craftsmanship" and "a rare and memorable play."[68] But nowhere does he explain in any detail exactly what it was about the structure of these two works that made them so admirable. He considered An Enemy of the People one of the best of Ibsen's plays,[69] and in this instance at least his comments on the play's universality did provide some indication as to the basis for his esteem:

> Dr. Stockman is a universal figure. However much some of the Ibsen plays may have the chill and pinch of Norway about them, "An Enemy of the People" knows no frontier. It happens to be acted at this time by a Russian company for an American

audience. That does not matter. For it is not only as Russian as "The Lower Depths," but also as American as "Lightnin."[70]

Woollcott was somewhat more specific when his criticism was negative. His initial praise of Ghosts in 1917 changed to disfavor, because he was "depressed all evening by the mistiness of this Ibsen play, which has aged visibly and precipitously in the last few years."[71] While Ibsen's craftsmanship was lauded in Hedda Gabler and Rosmersholm, it was found lacking in John Gabriel Borkman, Peer Gynt, and The Master Builder. Of Borkman he wrote: "By the fourth act the dramatic force of the play may have largely spent itself."[72] He found Peer Gynt to be an "undisciplined, unedited play ... with no end of rubbish that fell in by chance as it was being written."[73] He called for the "entire gimcrack fourth act" to be dropped, believing that "all of the beauty" of the play would still be intact.[74] The Master Builder was censured for its "reiteration" and for being "overstrained, arduous."[75]

In his 1923 review of The Lady from the Sea, a play Woollcott didn't like for reasons he didn't specify, he noted that the script had been "shouldered off the stage by the really great plays its author wrote before and after."[76] However, there was little in Woollcott's reviews and commentary on Ibsen that told his readers what informed that greatness. Such phrases applied to Ghosts as "trail-blazing tragedy" and "first of the great naturalistic dramas" reveal a respect for Ibsen's role in opening new subject matters in modern drama, although Woollcott never elaborated on this.[77] To appreciate Woollcott's esteem of Ibsen, one has to look at isolated values praised in individual plays. The quality of universality in Enemy of the People, the fundamental truth in Hedda Gabler, the fine texture of The Wild Duck,[78] and the beauty in Peer Gynt form a compendium of values that Woollcott perceived in Ibsen's work and warranted his praise.

Woollcott is much more explicit in delineating his evaluation of the American playwright who elicited the most commentary from him, Eugene O'Neill.

Eugene O'Neill

No playwright received more praise from Woollcott than Eugene O'Neill. As with John Barrymore, Woollcott seemed to take a special delight in following the development of his career. His reviews and commentary on Beyond the Horizon, the second O'Neill play he reviewed, [79] cite those characteristics of O'Neill's work that he would continue to admire, whatever negative criticism he might later make of other plays. In his initial review, in February 1920, he described O'Neill as "a playwright of real power and imagination."[80] Subsequently he referred to the play's "dramatic force and vitality" as being "extraordinary."[81] When The Emperor Jones opened later in the year Woollcott was moved to say that for strength O'Neill had "no rival among the American writers for the stage."[82] Although he believed The Straw was below the quality of O'Neill's previous work, he wrote in 1921 that it still possessed "enough of his force and quality to make it worth seeing."[83]

There was no aspect of O'Neill that was praised more by Woollcott than his imagination. He believed the "dramatic imagination and the salt of life" in his plays were what gave him a worldwide reputation.[84] In addition to commending O'Neill's imagination in Beyond the Horizon Woollcott also praised it in The Emperor Jones, Anna Christie, and The Hairy Ape.[85] His most extravagant acclamation was in a review of Anna Christie, where he described it as being "as fine an imagination as ever worked in our theatre...."[86]

Woollcott thought Beyond the Horizon was "one of the real plays of our time.... Seldom has an American playwright written for our theatre a piece half so good and true."[87] Along with his imagination O'Neill's ability to construct believable characters and plots was most frequently noted by Woollcott. In addition to Beyond the Horizon he complimented The Emperor Jones, Anna Christie, The Hairy Ape, and Welded for their believability, a quality he valued most highly.[88]

Woollcott was particularly impressed by the believability of O'Neill's secondary characters. He thought the average playwright was often delinquent in this regard. He praised O'Neill for making his secondary characters "original and distinctive ... brought into the theatre with the breath of life in them...."[89]

Woollcott's comments on actors showed him to be attentive to the sounds of theatre as well as its spectacle. This orientation is also seen in the attention he paid to the dialogue of a script. He was impressed by O'Neill's use of language. In Beyond the Horizon he lauded O'Neill's ability to create a feeling for the environment through dialogue:

But a playwright with O'Neill's imagination and dramatic gift can dispense with even such suggested aids [snow flurries out a window], can create with spoken words such effects as make him independent of all the domes, cycloramas and elaborated switchboards in the world. [90]

In his 1920 review of Diff'rent Woollcott was moved to write that "no American playwright can write such dramatic dialogue as his."[91] He defined O'Neill in his review of Anna Christie in 1921 as "a master of dramatic dialogue."[92]

His comments on The Hairy Ape revealed Woollcott's predilection for the use of realistic language on the stage. He seemed to take a particular delight in praising the rough-edged utterances of uncultured characters: O'Neill, he wrote,

holds you while you listen to the rumble of their [the men stoking] discontent, and while you listen, also, to speech more squalid than even an American audience heard before in an American theatre. It is true talk, all of it, and only those who have been so softly bred that they have never really heard the vulgate spoken in all its richness would venture to suggest that he has exaggerated it by so much as a syllable in order to agitate the refined. [93]

Just as no playwright received more praise from Woollcott than did O'Neill, so did none receive more criticism. Woollcott's high esteem for Beyond the Horizon did not prevent him from reproving it. He chided O'Neill for his impracticality in splitting "each of his three acts into two scenes, one outside and one inside the Mayo farmhouse."[94] He believed the breaking of the final act into two scenes was "dissipative" in its effect[95] and voiced his opinion that a more seasoned playwright would have avoided the exterior settings that O'Neill had incorporated into the play:

In the theatre, what you want and what you get are very different. A more shop-wise playwright would have known that for his exteriors, each of them but a portion of an act and therefore certain to be of a hasty and makeshift nature, he could scarcely count on so illusive and charming a vista, so persuasive a creation of the outdoors as glorifies the final act of the Lee Simonson investiture for "The Power of Darkness." The conspicuously

> dinky expanse of nature provided for "Beyond the
> Horizon" must have been a good deal of a shock to
> O'Neill. The wrinkled skies, the portiere-like
> trees, the clouds so close you are in momentary
> expectation that a scrub lady will waddle on and
> wash them--these made doubly futile the dashes in
> and out of the Mayo farmhouse. [96]

Woollcott believed that O'Neill's theatrical naivete
reached its height when he wrote a part with lines and business for a two-year-old girl. [97] Trying to identify the source
of O'Neill's impracticality as he saw it functioning in Beyond
the Horizon, Woollcott pointed to his remoteness from the
theatre. Initially he saw this as a positive factor in O'Neill's
work, noting that he

> has lived so remote from the theatre that he has
> been uncorrupted by the merely theatrical and has
> carried over into his own workshop not one of the
> worn stencils and battered properties which are the
> dust-covered accumulation of years. [98]

Woollcott then continued: "This same remoteness,
which so freshens the air of his play, is probably responsible,
also, for its considerable impracticability." [99] With the appearance of The Hairy Ape two years later Woollcott noted an
improvement in O'Neill's familiarity with the theatre:

> In this piece which is now moving into the Plymouth
> there are new evidences of O'Neill writing not in
> isolation, as has been wont, but on the very stage
> where his work was to be played. The new play
> suggests a greater familiarity with the theatre as
> an instrument, and, as all plays should be, was
> evidently worked out in collaboration with the artists
> who would make it visible and the actors who would
> give it body. [100]

Woollcott did not see O'Neill's improved familiarity
with the theatre serving him in Desire Under the Elms and
Strange Interlude. Again, he faulted O'Neill's craftsmanship.
He thought the climax of Desire Under the Elms ("the young
mother's murder and avowed reason for doing it") "faltered
feebly" and was "most clumsily managed." He further observed that as the playgoer perceives the mother's intentions
"the author of the play becomes almost visible on stage. You
can almost see him working there beside his heroine, breath-

less, shirt-sleeved and more than a little worried."[101]   He
had the same complaint of Strange Interlude, describing the
characters as "store dummies" who were "spouting all too
unmistakably the words of the ventriloquial O'Neill himself."[102]

　　　　Echoing his evaluation of Shaw, Woollcott complained
frequently of the prolixity of O'Neill's dialogue.   The First
Man, The Hairy Ape, Welded, and Strange Interlude were all
faulted for their verbosity.[103]   Additional criticisms of
O'Neill's dialogue were Woollcott's chiding of the "rubbishy
language" in The First Man[104] and "the naive and tasteless
pomposity" of the language in Strange Interlude.[105]   Woollcott
was particularly irritated by O'Neill's communication of the
inner thoughts of the characters:

　　　　　I think that most actors would tell O'Neill with
　　　　　some asperity that such illumination was their busi-
　　　　　ness and none of his, and by thus dispensing with
　　　　　their aid, he would be calmly throwing away his
　　　　　only reason for turning to the dramatic form in the
　　　　　first place.[106]

　　　　Along with prolixity O'Neill's implausability evoked
Woollcott's most frequent criticism of him.   He found believability to be a problem in All God's Chillun Got Wings, Desire Under the Elms, The Fountain, and Strange Interlude.[107]
Woollcott expressed his opinions of All God's Chillun Got
Wings and Strange Interlude after reading the scripts prior
to their being produced.   Believing that "one should judge
the play only on its performance,"[108] he reserved final evaluations until after seeing them in production.   In neither case
did viewing the production alter his opinions of the script.

　　　　Woollcott also criticized a pretentiousness he detected
in Marco Millions and Strange Interlude.   He thought Marco
Millions was "an almost grotesquely elaborate and solemnly
pretentious way of saying a very little and familiar say."[109]
He quarreled with O'Neill's communication of his character's
inner thoughts in Strange Interlude on the ground of its pretentiousness:

　　　　　For such an excursion into the invisible internals
　　　　　of his characters as the author of "Strange Inter-
　　　　　lude" proposes, you do want, I think, a guide who
　　　　　inspires you with the belief that he knows his way.
　　　　　And there were not many moments in all the nine
　　　　　acts of "Strange Interlude" when I did not feel that

its author had undertaken a task calling for a good deal more imagination and even understanding of his own brain-children than he seemed able to bring to it.[110]

As his remarks clearly indicate, Woollcott believed O'Neill was beyond his depth in Strange Interlude. Lest his readers forget he championed O'Neill early in the playwright's career, Woollcott reminded them of the fact and then explained why his admiration had waned:

> This is the lament of one who was a cheer-leader on the sidelines in the days when O'Neill was transmitting the experiences of his roving youth into such plays as "Anna Christie," "Diff'rent," "The Emperor Jones," "The Hairy Ape" and the long succession of beautiful sea-pieces which are still the joy of the college dramatic societies. Thereafter he went out not only beyond my depth, but I think, beyond his own, in such plays as "Welded," "The Great God Brown," and now "Strange Interlude," where he seems to me to be merely floundering.[111]

Here in 1928 we see Woollcott admitting a shift in his attitude toward O'Neill that began with the production of The First Man in 1922. Prior to this production he was a strong supporter of O'Neill. Beginning with The Dreamy Kid in 1918 and continuing through O'Neill's next six plays to The Straw in 1921 Woollcott consistently gave positive reviews to his plays as well as periodically touting his stature as an important American playwright. He included both Beyond the Horizon and The Emperor Jones among the ten best American plays ever written.[112] In 1920 he noted that an opening of an O'Neill play was "an event in the dramatic year."[113] Even when he had reservations about a play during this period, as was the case with Anna Christie, he still made a point of putting O'Neill in a positive light in comparison with his peers. The following demonstrates this as well as Woollcott's penchant for long sentences:

> "Anna Christie" might be described as a work which towers above most of the plays in town, but which falls short of the stature and the perfection reached by Eugene O'Neill in some of his earlier work. The earlier work had established him as the nearest thing to a genius America has yet produced in the way of a playwright, and, though this "Anna

Christie" of his has less directness and more dross and more moments of weak violence than any of its forerunners, it is, nevertheless, a play written with that abundant imagination, that fresh and venturesome mind and that sure instinct for the theatre which set this young author apart--apart from a lot of funny little holiday workers in cardboard and tinsel. [114]

When Woollcott's string of endorsements for O'Neill's plays broke with The First Man in 1922, he still continued to recognize O'Neill's stature. This was true even though only one additional script would win his approval, The Hairy Ape. At the end of the 1922-23 season he cited O'Neill as one of the three best living playwrights. [115] In 1924, while writing of Desire Under the Elms, a play he believed was "essentially unimportant," Woollcott uttered his belief that O'Neill's "work will be read and acted long after most of the contemporary work in the American theatre is forgotten dust. "[116]

Finally in 1932 Woollcott acknowledged that O'Neill was "a master of the theatre as an instrument, and better than most he can make it say what is on his mind." However, he did not always appreciate what was on O'Neill's mind:

> I myself have not much interest in, nor respect for, the contents of that mind as they have been revealed thus far. But when he is not straying off into the dismal swamps which lie on either side of the road he knows so well, the fellow has a magnificent stride. [117]

In the same article Woollcott reiterated his belief that in recent years O'Neill was writing beyond his depth:

> Boldly the author of the first vivid sea-pieces had come ashore and begun the peopling of his stage with characters he himself did not know much about, hardily undertaking, in the succession from "The Great God Brown" onwards, the writing of plays which called (and called in vain) for the touch of one who was both poet and prophet. In the lamentable "Dynamo" and in "Strange Interlude" (that "Abie's Irish Rose" of the pseudo-intelligentsia) he had finally taken on a kind of bombasine pretentiousness. [118]

Despite the change in Woollcott's attitude, his early recognition of O'Neill in his review of <u>Beyond the Horizon</u> as "one of our foremost playwrights, as one of the most spacious men to be both gifted and tempted to write for the theatre in America"[119] undoubtedly helped to establish O'Neill's early reputation. It also testifies to the critical perception of Woollcott himself.

Woollcott's remarks on Shakespeare, Shaw, Ibsen, and O'Neill provide an insight into the qualities he admired in plays and playwriting. Believability was the primary quality he looked for in plays as well as acting. He favored scripts that were written in a realistic style and that presented "truth." He esteemed everyday speech. He hailed plays that possessed an economy of ideas and language. He wanted the playwright to demonstrate a practical knowledge of the physical theatre.

The image of Woollcott projected by his comments on performers is reinforced by his comments on playwrights. His concern for the welfare of the theatre artist as well as the theatre is seen again in his demanding nature. The pattern of initial praise followed by criticism observed in his coverage of Fiske, the Barrymores, and Hayes is repeated with O'Neill.

His perception is best illustrated in his view of O'Neill. In 1925 he wrote:

> O'Neill has yet to see a play of his run as long as any one of several dramas by Samuel Shipman. Probably he will not live to see all his plays put together bring in a sum anything like the royalties that have been gathered by <u>Abie's Irish Rose</u>. But his work will be read and acted long after most of the contemporary work in the American theatre is forgotten dust.[120]

A Nobel Prize, four Pulitzer Prizes, and the continuing popularity of his plays in theatres all over the world testify to O'Neill's staying power. They also testify to Woollcott's critical and prophetic abilities.

Notes

1 "'As You Like It' Agreeably Played," <u>New York Times</u>, March 17, 1914, p. 11.

[2]Ibid.

[3]Ibid.

[4]"'The Merry Wives' at the Criterion," New York Times, March 21, 1916, p. 9.

[5]"Mr. Barker Gives Some Shakespeare," New York Times, February 17, 1915, p. 11.

[6]"Century's 'Tempest,'" New York Times, April 24, 1916, p. 11.

[7]"'As You Like It' Agreeably Played," New York Times, March 17, 1914, p. 11.

[8]"Miss Neilson-Terry in 'Twelfth Night,'" New York Times, November 24, 1914, p. 10.

[9]"Margaret Anglin Splendid as Kate," New York Times, March 20, 1914, p. 11.

[10]"Second Thoughts on First Nights," New York Times, May 7, 1916, Sec. 2, p. 6.

[11]"Sir Herbert Tree in the 'Merchant,'" New York Times, May 9, 1916, p. 9.

[12]See "'The Merry Wives' at the Criterion," March 21, 1916, p. 9; "Shouts and Murmurs," New York Herald, May 16, 1923, p. 10; "Shouts and Murmurs," New York Herald, April 24, 1923, p. 10; and "The Play," New York World, October 26, 1927, p. 15.

[13]"The Play," New York Times, April 20, 1921, p. 11.

[14]"The Stage," New York World, June 6, 1927, p. 11.

[15]"The Stage," New York World, October 12, 1925, p. 13.

[16]"Shouts and Murmurs," New York Herald, March 10, 1923, p. 9.

[17]"The Reviewing Stand," New York Herald, December 3, 1922, Sec. 7, p. 1.

18"The Stage," New York Herald, December 1, 1923, p. 9. The presentation of "the sap of eternal life" aptly describes the particular reward Woollcott could see offered by a revival of an old play. For him a source of pleasure in a revival was its illustration of "the elements common in all ages." As he praised plays for presenting these "elements," so was he critical of plays whose appeal was limited, especially propaganda plays. See "Second Thoughts on First Nights," New York Times, March 26, 1916, Sec. 2, p. 8; "A League as a Patron and a Play of Its Choice," New York Times, April 5, 1914, Sec. 8, p. 6; and "The Play," New York Times, December 11, 1920, p. 11.

19See "Second Thoughts on First Nights," New York Times, October 26, 1919, Sec. 9, p. 2, and "The Play," New York Times, March 17, 1920, p. 14.

20Ibid.

21"The Stage," New York World, October 12, 1925, p. 13.

22"'As You Like It' Agreeably Played," New York Times, March 17, 1914, p. 11.

23"Some Afterthoughts on Miss Anglin's Production," New York Times, March 22, 1914, Sec. 7, p. 6.

24"Second Thoughts on First Nights," New York Times, March 12, 1916, Sec. 2, p. 8.

25Ibid.

26"Century's 'Tempest,'" New York Times, April 24, 1916, p. 11.

27See "The Play," New York Times, August 24, 1921, p. 12, and "The Stage," New York World, March 16, 1926, p. 13.

28"The Play," New York World, October 26, 1927, p. 15. Apparently the separation in time between the Elizabethan period and the twentieth century enabled Woollcott to embrace the modern-dress revivals, for in reviewing Eva Le Gallienne's 1928 modern-dress revival of Hedda Gabler, he wrote that the production "suffered grievously from the unwise decision to play the masterpiece in modern clothes." He explained his opinion saying: "Hedda Gabler, always a singularly parochial play at best, lies just around the corner from our day and it has not yet reached into that universality of distance where costume no longer matters. See "The Stage," New York World, March 27, 1928, p. 13.

29"Plays and Players in These Parts," New York Sun, November 21, 1924, p. 26.

30"The Reviewing Stand," New York Herald, November 17, 1922, p. 8.

31"Shouts and Murmurs," New York Herald, May 16, 1923, p. 10.

32See "The Play," New York Times, February 5, 1921, p. 14.

33"The Play," New York Times, February 28, 1922, p. 17.

34"Shouts and Murmurs," New York Herald, May 21, 1923, p. 6.

35See "Shaw's 'Pygmalion' Has Come to Town," New York Times, October 13, 1914, p. 11; "The Stage," New York World, November 16, 1926, p. 13; "Barker's Season Happily Launched," New York Times, January 18, 1915, p. 9; "Second Thoughts on First Nights," New York Times, April 11, 1915, Sec. 7, p. 6; "Shaw and Dunsany in Grand Street," New York Times, November 15, 1916, p. 9; "Shouts and Murmurs," New York Herald, April 23, 1923, p. 8; and "Shaw's 'Caesar and Cleopatra,'" New York Sun, April 14, 1925, p. 22.

36"Shaw's 'Pygmalion' Has Come to Town," New York Times, October 13, 1914, p. 11.

37"Shaw's 'Caesar and Cleopatra,'" New York Sun, April 14, 1925, p. 22.

38"Second Thoughts on First Nights," New York Times, November 12, 1916, Sec. 2, p. 6.

39See "Second Thoughts on First Nights," New York Times, April 11, 1915, Sec. 7, p. 6, and "'Arms and the Man' Agreeably Revived," New York Times, May 8, 1915, p. 15.

40"Second Thoughts on First Nights," New York Times, December 19, 1915, Sec. 6, p. 8.

41"Second Thoughts on First Nights," New York Times, November 12, 1916, Sec. 2, p. 6.

42"The Play," New York Times, February 28, 1922, p. 17.

43Ibid.

44"Shouts and Murmurs," New York Herald, December 29, 1923, p. 5.

45See reviews of Pygmalion--"The Stage," New York World, November 16, 1926, p. 13; The Doctor's Dilemma--"Mr. Barker Gives Some More Shaw," New York Times, March 27, 1915, p. 11; Major Barbara--"A Shaw Comedy at the Playhouse," New York Times, December 10, 1915, p. 13; Getting Married--"Second Thoughts on First Nights," New York Times, November 12, 1916, Sec. 2, p. 6; The Inca of Persusalem--"Shaw and Dunsany in Grand Street," New York Times, November 15, 1916, p. 9; Heartbreak House--"The Play," New York Times, November 11, 1920, p. 11; "Second Thoughts on First Nights," New York Times, November 21, 1920, Sec. 6, p. 1; Back to Methuselah--"The Play," New York Times, February 28, 1922, p. 17; "Shouts and Murmurs," New York Herald, December 29, 1923, p. 5; "The Wake of the Plays," New York Herald, December 30, 1923, Sec. 7, p. 1; "The Wake of the Plays," New York Herald, January 6, 1924, Sec. 7, p. 1; and Too True to Be Good--"Shouts and Murmurs," New Yorker, March 12, 1932, p. 32. Throughout his career Woollcott was continually faulting plays for requiring cutting. After implausibility it was the most frequent fault he found in scripts.

46"Mr. Barker Gives Some More Shaw," New York Times, March 27, 1915, p. 11. Woollcott's concern for structure was reflected in his comments on the craftsmanship exhibited by playwrights and the degree to which he found plays to be "mechanical," "incredibly clumsy," "not particularly well-written," and "machine made." He was particularly critical of plays he believed to be hastily written. See "Second Thoughts on First Nights," New York Times, April 25, 1915, Sec. 7, p. 4.

47"A Shaw Comedy at the Playhouse," New York Times, December 10, 1915, p. 13.

[48]"Second Thoughts on First Nights, " New York Times, December 19, 1915, Sec. 6, p. 8.

[49]"Second Thoughts on First Nights, " New York Times, November 12, 1916, Sec. 2, p. 6.

[50]"Second Thoughts on First Nights, " New York Times, December 12, 1920, Sec. 6, p. 1.

[51]"Second Thoughts on First Nights, " New York Times, November 12, 1916, Sec. 2, p. 6. Woollcott criticized St. Joan for containing the same defect and in praising The Doctor's Dilemma for its mixture of the "grave and gay, " noted that it was an exception to Shaw's practice. See "The Wake of the Plays, " New York Herald, January 6, 1924, Sec. 7, p. 1, and "Mr. Barker Gives Some More Shaw, " New York Times, March 27, 1915, p. 11.

[52]"Second Thoughts on First Nights, " New York Times, December 12, 1920, Sec. 6, p. 1. Revivals of Arms and the Man and Man of Destiny were both specifically cited for being antiquated. See "The Stage, " New York World, September 15, 1925, p. 18, and "The Stage, " New York World, November 24, 1925, p. 13.

[53]"Shaw's 'Pygmalion' Has Come to Town, " New York Times, October 13, 1914, p. 11.

[54]"The Stage, " New York World, November 16, 1926, p. 13.

[55]"The Stage, " New York World, November 12, 1925, p. 17.

[56]See "'Candida' Revised by Arnold Daly, " New York Times, May 21, 1915, p. 13; "The Play, " New York Times, March 23, 1922, p. 11; and "Richard Bird as Marchbanks, " New York Sun, December 13, 1924, p. 7. This last review illustrates Woollcott's tendency to provide background information on a play at the expense of examining the script and production. Almost half of this review was devoted to comments on the original London and New York productions of Candida.

[57]"Richard Bird as Marchbanks, " New York Sun, December 13, 1924, p. 7.

58"Shouts and Murmurs," New York Herald, December 29, 1923, p. 5.

59Ibid.

60"Mr. Wilder Urges Us On," Atlantic Monthly, March 1943, p. 123.

61"The Wake of the Plays," New York Herald, January 6, 1924, Sec. 7, p. 1.

62"The Play," New York Times, October 5, 1920, p. 12. Another production of Hedda Gabler, as well as productions of John Gabriel Borkman and Little Eyolf, elicited similar commentary. See "The Play," New York Times, September 22, 1919, p. 8; "The Stage," New York World, January 30, 1926, p. 11; and "The Stage," New York World, February 3, 1926, p. 13.

63Woollcott, Mrs. Fiske, p. 59.

64"The Stage," New York World, January 30, 1926, p. 11.

65Of the eleven Ibsen plays that he reviewed Woollcott gave his unqualified praise to three (Hedda Gabler, An Enemy of the People, and Little Eyolf). Five he liked with varying degrees of reservations (Ghosts, Peer Gynt, The Wild Duck, The Master Builder, and Rosmersholm). One, The Lady from the Sea, he disliked, and he expressed no conclusive opinion on two, John Gabriel Borkman and A Doll's House.

66"Satisfying Revival of Ibsen's 'Ghosts,'" New York Times, May 8, 1917, p. 9.

67"'Hedda Gabler' as a Relic," New York Sun, May 26, 1924, p. 18. He also praised the play for possessing "fundamental truth," which reflects the high value Woollcott placed on believability in scripts.

68"'Rosmersholm' in Spite of All," New York Sun, May 6, 1925, p. 22.

69"The Stage," New York Herald, December 4, 1923, p. 9.

70Ibid.

[71]"The Stage," New York World, March 17, 1926, p. 13. Woollcott was particularly conscious of archaic qualities in revivals, as his commentary on Ghosts reveals. On the other hand, plays that failed to show the wear of years were accorded praise. See "The Thirtieth Mrs. Tangueray," Vanity Fair, December 1924, p. 62.

[72]"Reicher Admirable in Ibsen Tragedy," New York Times, April 14, 1915, p. 13.

[73]"Shouts and Murmurs," New York Herald, February 6, 1923, p. 12.

[74]Ibid. As his remarks imply, Woollcott was all in favor of the playwright limiting the amount of material incorporated into a script. Later he was to write: "There is such a thing as leaving a notion out of any play ... leaving it out perhaps with the idea of using it in some later work, perhaps merely to give the ideas left some room to breathe." Consistent with this attitude was Woollcott's belief that the playwright should use as few words as possible to express his ideas. See "The Stage," New York World, November 30, 1927, p. 13, and "A Charming Comedy Gracefully Played," New York Times, September 7, 1914, p. 12.

[75]"The Stage," New York World, November 13, 1925, p. 13.

[76]"The Stage," New York Herald, October 30, 1923, p. 19.

[77]"Satisfying Revival of Ibsen's 'Ghosts,'" New York Times, May 8, 1917, p. 9.

[78]"Ibsen at the Actors' Theatre," New York Sun, February 25, 1925, p. 20.

[79]The Dreamy Kid was the first O'Neill play Woollcott reviewed. He described it as "another good play from Eugene O'Neill" and noted the author's ability to obtain positive reactions for his villainous lead character. See "Second Thoughts on First Nights," New York Times, November 8, 1919, Sec. 8, p. 2.

[80]"The Play," New York Times, February 4, 1920, p. 12.

[81]"The Rise of Eugene O'Neill," Everybody's Magazine, July 1920, p. 49.

[82]"Second Thoughts on First Nights," New York Times, November 7, 1920, Sec. 7, p. 1.

[83]"The Play," New York Times, November 11, 1921, p. 16.

[84]"The Stage," New York World, December 1, 1926, p. 17.

[85]See "The Play," New York Times, November 3, 1921, p. 22; "Second Thoughts on First Nights," New York Times, November 13, 1921, Sec. 6, p. 1; "The Play," New York Times, March 10, 1922, p. 18; and "'The Emperor Jones' Revised," New York Sun, May 8, 1924, p. 20.

[86]"Second Thoughts on First Nights," New York Times, November 13, 1921, Sec. 6, p. 1.

[87]"Second Thoughts on First Nights," New York Times, February 8, 1920, Sec. 8, p. 2.

[88]See "The Rise of Eugene O'Neill," Everybody's Magazine, July 1920, p. 49; "The Stage," New York World, December 1, 1926, p. 17; "'The Emperor Jones' Revised," New York Sun, May 8, 1924, p. 20; "Second Thoughts on First Nights," New York Times, November 13, 1921, Sec. 6, p. 1; "The Play," New York Times, March 10, 1922, p. 18; and "The Stage," New York Herald, March 18, 1924, p. 11.

[89]"Second Thoughts on First Nights," New York Times, April 4, 1920, Sec. 6, p. 6. The frequency with which Woollcott mentioned the presence or absence of originality left no doubt as to the value he placed upon it. Its presence in O'Neill's plays was noted in The Emperor Jones and The First Man and its absence bemoaned in Marco Millions. See "'The Emperor Jones' Revised," New York Sun, May 8, 1924, p. 20; "The Play," New York Times, March 6, 1922, p. 9. He wanted the originality to appear to be natural to the script and abhorred originality for originality's sake. See "The Stage," New York World, April 11, 1928, p. 13; and "'Processional' at the Banick," New York Sun, January 13, 1925, p. 24.

[90]"Second Thoughts on First Nights," New York Times, February 15, 1920, Sec. 8, p. 2.

[91]"The Play," New York Times, December 29, 1920, p. 8.

[92]"Second Thoughts on First Nights," New York Times, November 13, 1921, Sec. 6, p. 1.

[93]"The Play," New York Times, March 10, 1922, p. 18. Woollcott's esteem for realistic language whether crude or not can be seen in a number of his reviews. See "'What Price Glory' Magnificent," New York Sun, September 6, 1924, p. 3; "'Big Jim Garrity' Is All Excitement," New York Times, October 17, 1914, p. 11; and "Shouts and Murmurs," New York Herald, February 6, 1924, p. 9.

[94]"Second Thoughts on First Nights," New York Times, February 8, 1920, Sec. 8, p. 2.

[95]"The Play," New York Times, February 6, 1920, p. 12. Woollcott's disdain for breaking the force of a play by too many intermissions is evident in this comment on Beyond the Horizon. He believed that "something is lost out of any play every time the curtain falls." See "Shouts and Murmurs," New York Herald, November 23, 1923, p. 11. When the third act of Beyond was telescoped into one scene, Woollcott happily noted the change. See "Second Thoughts on First Nights," New York Times, February 8, 1920, Sec. 8, p. 2.

[96]"Second Thoughts on First Nights," New York Times, February 8, 1920, Sec. 8, p. 2.

[97]Ibid.

[98]Ibid.

[99]Ibid.

[100]"Second Thoughts on First Nights," New York Times, April 16, 1922, Sec. 6, p. 1. As early as 1919 Woollcott had expressed his opinion that a playwright had a better chance to write a good play if he was familiar with the theatre, "the instrument he was writing for." He also was cognizant of the need for the playwright to get outside of the theatre and to get to know "intimately the life and ways of people in the remote outside world." See "Second Thoughts on First Nights," New York Times, August 31, 1919, Sec. 4, p. 2, and "An Emerging Masterpiece," Everybody's Magazine, February 1921, p. 54.

101"Through Darkest New England," New York Sun, November 12, 1924, p. 28.

102"Second Thoughts on First Nights," New York World, February 5, 1928, p. 3M.

103See "The Play," New York Times, March 6, 1922, p. 9; The Play," New York Times, March 10, 1922, p. 18; "The Stage," New York Herald, March 18, 1924, p. 11; and "Giving O'Neill Till It Hurts," Vanity Fair, February 1928, p. 48.

104"The Play," New York Times, March 6, 1922, p. 9.

105"Second Thoughts on First Nights," New York World, February 5, 1928, p. 3M.

106"Giving O'Neill Till It Hurts," Vanity Fair, February 1928, p. 48.

107See "All God's Chillun Got Wings," New York Sun, May 16, 1924, p. 24; "Desire Under the Elms," Vanity Fair, January 1925, p. 27; "The Stage," New York World, December 11, 1925, p. 16; and "Giving O'Neill Till It Hurts," Vanity Fair, February 1928, p. 48.

108"O'Neill's New Play 'Welded' a Melancholy Stage Study of Quarrel of Man and Wife," New York Sun, March 22, 1924, p. 4.

109"The Stage," New York World, January 10, 1928, p. 15.

110"Second Thoughts on First Nights," New York World, February 5, 1928, p. 3M.

111Ibid.

112See "The Rise of Eugene O'Neill," Everybody's Magazine, July 1920, p. 49, and "Second Thoughts on First Nights," New York Times, September 11, 1921, Sec. 6, p. 1.

113"The Play," New York Times, December 29, 1920, p. 8.

Woollcott on Playwrights and Playwriting / 103

114"The Play," <u>New York Times</u>, November 3, 1921, p. 22.

115"Shouts and Murmurs," <u>New York Herald</u>, May 21, 1923, p. 6. As noted previously, Shaw and Barrie were the others.

116"Desire Under the Elms," <u>Vanity Fair</u>, January 1925, p. 27.

117"Shouts and Murmurs," <u>New Yorker</u>, March 19, 1932, p. 32.

118Ibid.

119"The Play," <u>New York Times</u>, February 4, 1920, p. 12.

120"Desire Under the Elms," <u>Vanity Fair</u>, January 1925, p. 27.

Chapter 4

WOOLLCOTT ON THEATRE ISSUES

Woollcott did not always limit himself to the evaluation
of plays in his reviews. His remarks on some aspect of a
play or its production might lead him also to comment on the
state of the theatre in general. In addition to his reviews his
non-review newspaper columns and magazine articles also recorded his views on the theatre of his time. The theatrical
issue that drew his greatest attention was censorship.

Censorship

The first production to draw Woollcott's comments on
the topic of censorship was a French comedy, The Beautiful
Adventure. The play opened on September 6, 1914, and received a generally favorable review from Woollcott the next
morning. On September 21, 1914, Anthony Comstock, the
noted vice crusader, filed a complaint with the New York City
District Attorney. Comstock charged that the final scene of
the second act, which contained a discussion of sex, was "immoral, indecent and totally improper."[1] The subsequent in-
vestigation of the play by the District Attorney's office exon-
erated it on September 23, 1914. In his Sunday column on
October 4 Woollcott bemoaned the type of audience the attempted censorship would draw to the play:

> Such criticism may sometimes be welcomed as a
> matter of advertisement, but from the viewpoint of
> "The Beautiful Adventure" is rather to be regretted,
> for surely, with all its delicate and very tender
> charm, the play at the Lyceum will thrive, if thrive
> it does, under a patronage wider than, and splendidly
> different from, the patronage likely to prick up its
> ears just because a play or a book has been made
> the subject of conscientious hostilities by Anthony
> Comstock.[2]

Woollcott's description of Comstock's actions as "conscientious" reflects the attitude he had about many crusaders against allegedly "immoral" dramas: "I feel sure that many of the spokesmen of protest are not fretted by their own possible contamination. Their action is selfless. Their interest in the matter is exclusively their interest in the moral welfare of their neighbors. "3

Woollcott was against censorship, however "noble" its intent. He explained his stand in January 1922, when censorship of the theatre was being discussed in New York. Woollcott's fear of censorship was based on his doubt that the censor could distinguish between vulgarity and art:

> And those of us who are inclined to riot mildly at the very suggestion of a State Censor are not so minded because we cannot bear the thought of certain managers languishing in jail or forced into the hardware business. We are so minded because of an authentic fear that a State Censor will prove unable to stomach anything that is not all sweetness and light, will be unable to distinguish between a beautiful but uncomfortable play like "The Children's Tragedy" and the mere vulgarity of "Getting Gertie's Garter. "
> ... He will smell from afar such didoes as the second act of "Bluebeard's Eighth Wife, " come galloping to town, and then gallantly attack, by mistake, so magnificent a thing as the first act of "Anna Christie, " which, as written, as mounted and as played, belongs among the supreme achievements of the American stage. 4

Woollcott spoke on censorship again the next month. He advised American playwrights to read Bernard Shaw's writings on the subject and particularly recommended Shaw's foreword to The Shewing-up of Blanco Posnet. He quoted an excerpt from the preface, in which Shaw echoed Woollcott's own sentiments:

> What guarantee have I that the new tribunal will not presently resolve into a mere committee to avoid unpleasantness and keep the stage "in good taste"? It is no more possible for me to do my work honestly as a playwright without giving pain than it is for a dentist. The nation's morals are like the teeth: the more decayed they are the more it hurts

to touch them.   Prevent dentists and dramatists
from giving pain, and not only will our morals become as carious as our teeth, but toothache and
the plagues that follow neglected morality will pres-
ently cause more agony than all the dentists and
dramatists at their worst have caused since the
world began. [5]

Woollcott's next discourse on censorship was prompted
by the signing of the Wales Act by Governor Alfred Smith of
New York on April 6, 1927.   The law, popularly known as
the Padlock Law, enabled the Commissioner of Licenses to
close for a year any theatre in which a play judged to be immoral had been produced.   On Sunday, April 17 Woollcott devoted his whole column to the law.   Giving over his Sunday
column to one subject was rare for Woollcott--he usually covered a number of items in that column.   He expressed his
fear that "insurgent pathfinding plays" would now find production in New York impossible.   He further wondered what would
have been the fate of such plays as They Knew What They
Wanted, Goat Song, or What Price Glory? had the new law
been in existence three years earlier and concluded that probably "none would have had a hearing...."[6]

In noting the defect of the law, Woollcott pointed out
that the tastes of a society change:

The Wales Law is the kind of legislation that tends
to swaddle the play of tomorrow in the taste of
yesterday.   It shuts the stage door in the face of
the play (perhaps even now being written in some
hall bedroom) which would mean to 1928 what
"Ghosts" meant to 1893 and "Mrs. Warren's Pro-
fession" to 1906. [7]

Woollcott repeated his reservation about state censorship first
made in 1922:   "For this can be said of those who feel right-
eous enough to cast the first stone.   Their strength, true
enough, is as the strength of ten.   But they are likely to
have a mighty poor aim. "[8]

Realizing that the theatre itself could have avoided the
Wales Act by effectively policing itself, Woollcott criticized
the theatre managers in the closing paragraph of his article:

A roomful of New York theatrical managers contains, among other elements, enough of megalo-

mania, rascality, stupidity, jealousy, short-sighted-
ness and childish vanity to make their united action
on any subject as Utopian a prospect as peace in
Europe. Only the fatuously inexperienced are surprised to find that people as a matter of practice
do not act in their own enlightened self-interest. 9

The first play to be closed by the Wales Act was
Maya, a French drama by Simon Gandillon. In nine scenes
the play revealed the character of Maya, a prostitute. In his
review Woollcott described the play as beautiful, calling it
"an experience that enlarges the heart."10 The production
opened on February 21, 1928, and was closed on the third
of March. In his March 4 Sunday column Woollcott devoted
the whole space to a discussion of Maya's fate. In Woollcott's opinion his fear as to the discriminating ability of the
censor had materialized. He told his readers:

> You must not expect too much consistency from the
> authorities, nor ask rhetorically why, if "Maya"
> must go, so gaudy a tale of bawdy as "The Shang-
> hai-Gesture, " for instance, was left undisturbed,
> and so cheerfully smutty a farce as "The Command
> to Love" did not outrage the official sensitiveness. 11

Woollcott surmised that Maya was a sacrificial "bone"
thrown out to ease and quiet "those worthy citizens who itch
to police their neighbors' morals."12 In June, writing of
Maya's closing, he reiterated his belief: "It may fairly be
assumed that, from time to time, the much badgered authorities will thus squash a play if only to quiet the itching committees of those ravenous societies which are organized to
make the drama behave."13

In May 1937 Woollcott spoke out on the air against
John J. Dunnigan's proposed censorship bill. The bill called
for the revocation of a theatre license for the presentation of
"immoral shows and exhibitions."14 It also "would permit
municipal licensing authorities to refuse a new license for one
year on satisfactory proof of a violation of the penal law."15
In his May 20 Town Crier broadcast Woollcott said: "Up in
Albany right now there awaits the Governor's signature a mischievous censorship bill. If signed, it would turn a local pol-
itician into a theatrical czar."16 Governor Lehman vetoed
the bill on May 19.

In examining Woollcott's pronouncements on censorship,

one can see that he never directly questioned the right to
censor. Only in the Shaw preface that he quoted was the
question of the right to censorship mentioned. Woollcott's
concern was rather with the judicial administration of censorship. He questioned the ability of the would-be censor to
judge what should be censored and found his questioning to
be justified in the case of Maya.

One-Act Plays; Musicals;
Black Dramas--White Audiences

On March 15, 1914, Woollcott noted the failure of the
one-act play to succeed commercially in New York: "It is
rather a pity that the advocates of the one-act play cannot
point with satisfaction to some double bill this season that
made its way to conspicuous financial success."[17] Later
that year he noted that the one-act play was largely depend-
ent upon vaudeville for a hearing. However, even vaudeville's use of one-acts as curtain-raisers was rare. In the
same column Woollcott praised the Princess Theatre for the
hearing it was giving one-acts: "The Princess is doing the
best, not only for the Princess Theatre but for the American
Theatre, when it keeps in mind--its own and ours--the fact
that a play can be vivid, moving and dramatic even if it does
run half an hour."[18] A year later Woollcott again bemoaned
the status of the one-act play while writing on Lord Dunsany's
The Gods of the Mountain:

> Our stage is simply inhospitable to the one-act
> play. Volumes of short stories abound in the land
> and the magazines scream with the pain of the price
> they have to pay for each and every one of them.
> But when the O. Henry or the Rudyard Kipling of
> the theatre comes along, the stage door shuts in
> his face. So "Kismet" was played all over the
> world and made a great deal of money for a great
> many people, but "The Gods of the Mountain" must
> stay in the library because its length is not the con-
> ventional length. Its production by the Comedy Club
> is a fresh reminder of how many short plays hover
> about the theatre like sad, disembodied spirits de-
> nied a hearing and of how good is the work the
> Washington Square Players do just by keeping to
> their program of one-act plays.[19]

Some eleven years later Woollcott was unable to see

any change in the reception being given to the one-act plays:

> We seem hostile to the one-act play hereabouts. The very fact that a play has a curtain raiser (even though it be one by J. M. Barrie) fills the local playgoer with dim forebodings and there is no coaxing him to the box office. 20

The musical, as a form, did not receive the apathetic treatment of the one-act play. Woollcott's concern for it was rather with the lack of originality with which it was usually written. Woollcott referred to this in 1914: "One musical comedy is much like another, and precious seldom does any of them, no matter how well calculated to make an evening pass pleasantly, present material for second thoughts on first nights."21 The lack of originality goaded Woollcott to offer sarcastic advice to Make It Snappy: "Certainly we would spare that song about 'when grandma was a girl.' It is possible that no musical show has ever succeeded without one, but it's worth taking a chance."22

Woollcott was also disenchanted with the characterization of the Negro in American drama, as well as the treatment of the Negro in the theatre. The former was criticized by Woollcott in 1922 in his commentary on Taboo, by Mary Wiborg, a white playwright:

> And, always with the one shining exception [The Emperor Jones], we have never seen a play of negro life and character which was not at least a little condescending. There has always been the most painfully acute consciousness on the part of the playwright that he was on a slumming party. In "Taboo" you could almost visualize the author standing in the wings and murmuring "How quaint these people are!"23

Continuing, Woollcott noted the possible influence of the upper class present at the performance. He then noted the Negroes seated in the balcony and made an implicit criticism of that situation:

> But perhaps this flavor is inevitable. And probably it seeped into "Taboo" not from the author or the players or the producer, but from the audience.

There sat whole rows of matinee ladies, who had
detrained from the Social Register, formed a hollow
square and advanced on the play. They surveyed
through lorgnettes the negro antics and agonies of
which the play was wrought. It would have been
an interesting experiment for some one to have
risen from his seat and inquired loudly by what
coincidence or what device the negroes who had
ventured to come to see this piece about themselves
had all been shunted up into the balcony. Such an
interruption would have been mischievous and grossly
irrelevant. As a gesture it would scarcely have
risen above the plane of disorderly conduct. Yet
it might have given vent to a vague and indefinable
disquiet which Tuesday's enterprise must have bred
in more minds than one. [24]

Woollcott's social consciousness was also evidenced
in his comments on war plays and other social and moral
topics.

War Plays and Other Social and Moral Topics

World War I inspired the writing of a great many war
plays. The writing and producing of these plays continued
well past the armistice. Opening his 1915-16 season of Sunday columns, Woollcott wrote that the war was "too huge,
too near, too overwhelming for the perspective of serious
drama." [25] He became disgusted by the playwrights and producers who used the war simply as an opportunity "to wave
the American flag for profits." [26] One play that obviously
didn't do this, according to Woollcott, was What Price Glory?
He praised the play for containing "the smells of the war as
it was really fought...." [27] Upon returning from the front,
Woollcott would note the plays that presented war unrealis-
tically. Of the marines depicted in What Price Glory? he
was able to write:

Compared with these men, who have their little day
in the three acts of "What Price Glory?," all the
other stage officers and soldiers that have charged
upon us from the embattled dressing rooms of
Broadway have seemed to step glistening from some
magazine cover painted in the thick of a Chicago
studio. [28]

The issue Woollcott most frequently raised in reviewing war plays was their appropriateness to the times. One such play was a 1915 revival of Goethe's Egmont:

> The military atmosphere that pervades it makes it unusually appropriate for presentation at this time. When it is remembered that the action transpires in Brussels, one of the speeches early in the play is remarkably pertinent. A group of citizens are talking of war and boasting of deeds of valor, when one of them proposes a toast to all soldiers and war. "War! War!" responds one of them, "Do you know what you say? It comes easily enough out of your mouth, as is natural, but I can't tell you what a vexatious business it is to us. To have the drum in one's ears the whole year round; to hear of nothing but how one troop was drawn up here and another there; how they came over a hill, and halted near a mill; how many were killed here and how many there; how they rushed on, and one gained and the other lost, without being able to tell, in one's born days, who won and who lost anything, how a town is taken, the citizens murdered, and how it fares with the poor women and innocent children--this is distress and misery indeed! One can't help saying every moment: Here they come! It's our turn next."29

On occasion the war play might motivate Woollcott to comment on the war itself, as What Price Glory? did in 1925. Writing on the play for Vanity Fair, he said there was one speech he could not shake, "a little speech that seems to cover the case completely."30 It was Quirt's, as he rejoined Captain Flagg in battle at the play's end: "What a lot of goddam fools it takes to make a war."31 In 1925 Channing Pollock's The Enemy, which described the stupidities of World War I as seen through the eyes of the Germans, prompted Woollcott to write:

> Nor am I deeply impressed with the profundity of any argument in which the lulls between Wars in Europe are fulsomely referred to as peace, or are regarded as a whit more creditable to humanity than the mere symptomatic outbreaks of physical courage which punctuate them.32

Another social topic that attracted Woollcott's frequent attention was the morality of the 1920s. He saw the period as "a gay, bright, festive revolt against provincialism, pomposities and false sermonizing of all kinds, most especially against hypocritical sex...."[33] In his review of the 1924 revival of Congreve's The Way of the World Woollcott drew a parallel between the world of Congreve's play and New York of 1924:

> Indeed the free, coarse language of Master Congreve is not a patch on the taproom speech that can be heard tonight on more than one stage along Broadway or, for that matter, that can be heard in many an elegant drawing room along Park Avenue. The absence of blushes, goose flesh and other signs of moral agitation in the present day audiences at "The Way of the World" offers a fresh reminder that New York in the year of grace 1924 is strikingly akin to the giddy London which produced and nourished the restoration dramatists.[34]

In his review of the 1925 farce The Cradle Snatchers Woollcott humorously noted that the morality of the plays might catch up with the morality of society:

> Indeed I cannot remember ever having attended a play so sedulously suggestive. In this respect our dramas grow more flagrant every season and if the debauch runs on unchecked they will almost catch up with the house-parties and dinner-parties of the year of grace, 1925.[35]

Woollcott believed that the freedom of the age enabled actresses to play roles they formerly would have abhorred. Of Jane Cowl's 1925 role in Hans Mueller's The Depths he wrote: "Here we have a play on a subject which Miss Cowl would have shunned ten or even five years ago. But in the high tide of the new freedom all the best people are acting prostitutes."[36] In 1926 Ethel Barrymore portrayed Constance Middleton, a wife who leaves her husband for her lover, in Somerset Maugham's The Constant Wife. In his comments on the play Woollcott remarked that twenty years ago Ethel Barrymore "would not have touched its manuscript with a ten foot pole."[37] Woollcott also surmised that the audience's acceptance of the play was partly due "to the shifting customs and standards of the community."[38]

Just as Woollcott might note a new play's reflection of the contemporary morality, so might he point out a new play's failure to reflect current attitudes, as in Grace George's She Had to Know:

> Wherefore when so delicate a comedy as this new venture of Miss George's talks as shyly about sex as Miss Dinsmore and Mr. Trevilla might have done in the Age of Innocence, when the very word "appeal" is not used by the heroine without a slight catch of the breath and when its utterance by her produces something not altogether remote from apoplexy in whatever male character she may be addressing--when all this is unfolded on a Forty-second street stage in the year of grace, 1925, you are troubled by the baleful presence of anachronism....39

At least one play, however, overreached even the roaring twenties in its unmasking of social taboos. In The Depths an unwed pregnant woman commits suicide rather than carry out her pregnancy. Describing the play's plot, Woollcott wrote: "There you have a scenario built around a subject about which most people never speak without a thousand foolish pretenses and seldom even think honestly."40

By November 1925 Woollcott believed playwrights had about reached a saturation point in writing plays that dwelt on the moral attitudes of the age. He implied this opinion in his review of Noel Coward's This Was a Man, which told of a husband who accepted his wife's infidelity with calmness:

> I cannot help wondering, however, if such purely negative drama is not beginning to wear a trifle thin. After the excesses of our dear old, sentimental parents it was well to have a lot of novels and plays written just to suggest that real people do not follow the routine of melodrama in the crises of life. Such corrections were sadly needed. Their effect was tonic, bracing. But that job has about been cleaned up and the first thing you know some playwright is going to realize it.41

Other plays prompted Woollcott to speak on topics including politics, economics, feminism, and psychology. In regard to the latter, in his 1925 review of The Offense he noted the contributions psychoanalysis had made to theatre:

"Psychoanalysis has enlarged our dramatists' vocabulary ... and given some of them a deeper and kindlier penetration which has enriched the theatre."[42] However, Woollcott questioned the value of another influence on the American theatre, the foreign play.

The Foreign Play

Although favoring the exchange of plays between Europe and New York, Woollcott was highly skeptical of the possibility of successfully translating a foreign play into English. Commenting on the Yiddish play The God of Vengeance in February 1923, he wrote: "The play is transmitted to us through the medium of a lumpy, clubfooted translation and deepens a growing conviction that no play can ever be really lifted from one language to another."[43] Later in the same article he went on to say: "Most translations for the American stage seem to be done by men who can read the French or German or Russian original, but who just do not happen to be able to write English."[44]

The 1922 production of Gerhart Hauptmann's Rose Bernd, with translations by Ludwig Lewisohn, prompted Woollcott to offer advice to translators:

> These speeches, fearfully harassing on the printed page, assert themselves even in the performance, tearing their way through the gauze curtain that hangs before every play, clamoring for attention. We are being driven through the years to the conviction that the best refuge of such a translator is a simple, uncolored, unarresting, utterly unlocalized idiom with the task of giving it a pleasant flavor left entirely to the actors, who can manage it better with the slur of speech and the tones of their voices.[45]

In the course of his reviewing career Woollcott did praise translations of foreign plays. The first play to receive such praise was George Egerton's translation from the French of The Beautiful Adventure. Egerton was lauded for preserving "much of the distinguished literary grace and the delightful flavor of the original. He has seen to it that the English words should tell the French story well."[46]

Woollcott's reservations about the foreign play also

included his concern that life depicted in foreign cultures was not in all cases the life to which Americans were accustomed. His attitude on this point was illustrated in his 1919 review of Somerset Maugham's English farce Too Many Husbands, in which he noted that the play

> lies outside the taste and interests of most of us in this neighborhood.
> It requires a knowledge of, and interest in, and a speaking fondness for the English. It will be appreciated most by those who shake with laughter over every number of "Punch."[47]

Woollcott's reservation on the foreign play did not prevent him from welcoming the appearance of foreign actors on the New York stage. In 1928 he did not embrace the movement to prevent English actors from looking for work on the New York stage, noting that had they been prevented in the past, many fine performers would have been missed.[48]

As noted, Woollcott was concerned with the ability of an American audience to relate to the reality depicted in a foreign play; this brings up another topic to which he devoted considerable space in his reviews and elsewhere.

Realism in the Theatre

Woollcott was a firm believer in the necessity of the realistic play to reflect life accurately. He first expressed this belief in admonishing Charles Klein for The Money Maker, which opened on Broadway in October 1914:

> It is not easy, however, to sit through those three acts without experiencing from time to time a keen regret that so competent a craftsman of the theatre should seem a little to forget that after all there is a world outside and that the modern theatregoers enjoy a play which purports to be serious to the degree that it matches up with the world as they see it.
> This is particularly true when the people and things of the play are the people and things of our own time and city; and which we see or read about every day of our lives. When the elements of a play are familiar elements, then what is done and said behind the footlights must appeal in chief to our recognition.[49]

In 1927 Woollcott reaffirmed the value of realism on the stage: "The theatre is at its best when it is journalistic, when it makes its fable and its parable out of the life streaming down its own street...."[50]

As he was quick to praise the reflection of life, so was he quick to criticize the lack of life in plays. Thus he said of Martin C. Flavin's Children of the Moon: "It never quite catches the accent and flavor of life. It never really lives."[51] He described We Moderns, by Israel Zangwill, as "a shallow and sententious play without the accent of life in it."[52] Woollcott demonstrated how accurately he wished a realistic play to reflect life by his comments on Life with Father. Mentioning that the second act of the play was set in 1888, he wrote:

> In the whole play, the only anachronism I detected is the one at the end of the second act, when, to the anguish of the pedantic, Mother gives vent to Sweet Marie, that singularly insipid ballad which swept the country half a century ago and left America incurably addicted to the horrid practice of accenting Marie on the second syllable. But Sweet Mu-ree did not start sweeping until 1892.[53]

Although an admirer of the realistic play and the use of realistic language, Woollcott regretted what he saw as the loss of poetry and romance in plays. He voiced his opinion in writing about John Galsworthy's Justice in 1916:

> It is of course, the sorry limitation of this age in the theatre that there are certain beauties it has lost altogether. It has lost poetry and it has mislaid romance. Run your finger over most of its properties and you find a layer of soot, gray deposit of an industrial age. There is an intended significance in the fact that the school of playwrights of which Galsworthy is foremost is called the Manchester School [Manchester is an important industrial center in Great Britain].[54]

Woollcott was much more intense in expressing his regrets over what he considered another "loss" of his theatrical age, the occasional loss of judgment of the Pulitzer Prize committee.

The Pulitzer Prize

The judgment exercised by the Pulitzer Prize committee incurred Woollcott's wrath on more than one occasion.
Specifically, the awards he disagreed with were Miss Lulu
Bett (1920-21), Ice-Bound (1922-23), Hell Bent for Heaven
(1923-24), They Knew What They Wanted (1924-25), Craig's
Wife (1925-26), and In Abraham's Bosom (1926-27). He believed the awards should have gone to The First Year (1920-
21), The Texas Nightingale (1922-23), The Show-Off (1923-
24), What Price Glory? (1924-25), The Wisdom Tooth (1925-
26), and Saturday's Children or The Road to Rome (1926-27).

In 1929 Woollcott correctly predicted that Elmer
Rice's Street Scene would win the award and used the occasion
to criticize selections of the past: "I would have more con-
fidently predicted its award this year to Mr. Rice if there
were much evidence in the record of the preceding ten years
to suggest that the committee could be counted on to act with
conspicuous intelligence."[55] In the spring of 1930 Woollcott
noted that the award would not be given to The Green Pastures because the play was an adaptation: "Connelly, it seems,
derived his inspiration from a book by Roark Bradford, to
say nothing of a somewhat earlier work called the Old Testa-
ment."[56] Woollcott went on to surmise how the Prize needed
Green Pastures more than Green Pastures needed the Prize:

> Well, it's too bad. Of course with all America
> trying to get into the Mansfield at once, "The Green
> Pastures" does not need the Pulitzer Prize. But
> it fairly staggers one to think how much, for the
> sake of its lost prestige, the Pulitzer Prize needs
> "The Green Pastures."[57]

The committee obviously agreed with Woollcott that
the play deserved the award, and in 1944 Walter Prichard
Eaton, a member of the committee, recalled how they circumvented the fact that the play was an adaptation:

> Before recommending The Green Pastures, which
> was based on Roark Bradford's stories, we con-
> sulted Mr. Pulitzer's son, who said: "Does it add
> something original, making the work a new and per-
> haps larger thing, as Shakespeare added to the sto-
> ries he took?" We said we thought it did. "Then
> give it the prize," said he![58]

Woollcott frequently took issue with the criteria by which the awards were supposedly made. The Prize was to be awarded to "the original American play performed in New York which shall best represent the educational value and power of the stage in raising the standards of good morals, good taste and good manners."[59] To Woollcott this citation was a "meaningless rigmarole of words."[60] In 1926 he wrote:

> But after all, what play performs that service except by virtue of (and in proportion to) its capacity to enlarge the human heart with whatever of truth and beauty its author could bring to it? Indeed, if you study the awards in this and earlier seasons, you will see that this earnest and didactic wording has done nothing to deflect the judges from rewarding the very play they would have named had the instructions merely bidden them fasten on "the best native play produced in New York" in any year.[61]

In 1927 Woollcott continued his crusade, stating what he believed formed the criteria of the award:

> Indeed, I have never been able to see and cannot now see, how a play can ever "represent the educational value of the stage to raise the standard of good morals, good taste and good manners" except as its beauty and its truth may enlarge the human heart. Furthermore, I believe that, knowing this, these judges must consciously or unconsciously forget all the rigmarole of the specifications and decide, in so far as they can reach agreement at all, which of the new native plays seems to have been the truest and the most beautiful. Of course the exigent terms of the award then come in handy to becloud and defend the decision.[62]

Woollcott also disagreed with the awarding of the $1,000 Prize to the playwright alone. He believed that what was really being judged was the produced play, and thus all those who contributed to the production should share in the award and its monetary return. He cited George Kelly's Craig's Wife as an example of the benefit a play may receive from its production team:

> As it happens "Craig's Wife" is a pretty good play --one which flounders and weakly turns false to it-

self in its final act, to be sure, but for all that, a pretty good play. Yet if it had been presented with no greater skill and imagination and wisdom than were the portion of a safe majority of the manuscripts which have been produced in our town this year it would have provided a poor, clumsy, gritty evening in the theatre and long before the examining committee had got around to seeing it its life would have been snuffed out.... 63

   The judges of the Prize themselves were criticized by Woollcott. He was critical of the fact that all three judges for the 1923-24 season had not seen the play they awarded the Prize to, Hell Bent for Heaven. He also questioned the consideration given to quality plays that did not survive on the stage: "There is no evidence to show that they even consider the occasional beautiful play which through stupidity in production or mere incalculable mischance, is sometimes done to death in its cradle."64   In objecting to the Prizes given to Craig's Wife in 1926 and to In Abraham's Bosom in 1927, Woollcott was critical of the judicial abilities of the committees who selected the winners. Owen Davis, A. E. Thomas, and Walter Prichard Eaton made up the committee in 1926. After implying that it was rather improper that Davis and Thomas were judging in a season in which each had a play produced on Broadway, Woollcott wrote: "It would have been easy, I should think, to find a committee of reasonably constant playgoers far more nearly representing what might be called the aristocracy of taste...."65   The 1927 committee remained the same, except for Owen Davis, who was replaced by Clayton Hamilton. Woollcott was quite outspoken in evaluating the committee after their selection of In Abraham's Bosom:

My experience with the minds of these three playwrights, as exhibited in their own critical writings, the plays they themselves have written and the awards they have made in previous years, does not encourage me to expect them to manifest quite so sensitive and informed a taste or so acute a judgement as the Pulitzer award has a right to command. Indeed, I find it difficult to account for the naivete of the annual Maytime surprise they give me. The prestige of the award, which had already suffered by passing blunderingly by such masterpieces as "The Show-Off" and (unforgivably) "What Price Glory?," is, I think diminished still further by the judgement this year. 66

Woollcott's running battle with the Pulitzer Prize committee was not the only campaign he carried out in his life-long war against mediocrity. The star system and other profit-motivated practices that demeaned the theatre, and particularly the actor, drew considerable fire.

The Star System and Selected Issues

Woollcott's desire for quality performances led him to criticize the star system. Reviewing No. 33 Washington Square in his second season as a reviewer, he described its star, May Irwin, as "the most wholesomely and abundantly amusing actress on the American stage."[67] In his comments on the supporting company, however, he noted that its selection was "not inspired."[68] In his column the following Sunday Woollcott voiced his displeasure with the system that nurtured such productions and noted its decline:

> The appearance of the hearty and humorous May Irwin in "No. 33 Washington Square" at the Park Theatre last Monday night was an indictment of the star system and a fresh reminder of how rapidly and how considerably that system has declined in recent years. Broadway feels more and more with every passing August that the mere fact of an actress being a host in herself is no reason why there should be no company.[69]

Woollcott further remarked that the time was quickly passing when performers as competent as Irwin would want to invite comparison with carefully selected companies while she herself was "surrounded for the most part with shoddy support."[70] In addition to his disdain for the star system Woollcott was also against the practice of a performer having a play written for him or herself:

> Those made-to-order plays are almost always bad, not only because that is no way to write a play but because no dramatist who has anything of the artist in him would undertake such a commission unless the Sheriff were at the door or he had some other equally pressing and personal reason.[71]

A primary concern of Woollcott's was the waste of talent he observed. He was highly critical of the lack of management he saw present in the theatre of his day:

As in all human endeavor, there is the question as to what the newcomer will make of his talent. But here, in a special degree, is also the question as to what use the theatre will make of that talent. For it is appallingly true that in our theatre, as at present organized, there is little or no provision made for the deliberate development of the actor-in-the-making. There is not only no dramatic school of established value but no visible design in the development of the oncoming generation of players after they have gone on the stage. There are precious few producers who give any heed whatever to the artistic nurture of the youngsters who pass in and out of their employ. [72]

The appearance of Helen Menken in three inferior productions in 1922 prompted him to write: "The predicament of this young actress named Helen Menken is a caustic commentary on the bungling, haphazard, wasteful manner in which the American theatre is managed--a count in the long indictment of the whole era of mismanagement...."[73] Noting that Menken's appearance in the plays may have been due to her own inability to distinguish between a good play and a bad one, Woollcott charged: "Then surely there should be arms in the theatre strong enough to reach out, take her by the scruff of the neck and plant her firmly where she belongs."[74] In succeeding years Woollcott noted the lack of management in the careers of such actresses as Helen Hayes, Minnie Maddern Fiske, Ethel Barrymore, and Laurette Taylor. In a 1931 article Woollcott wrote of the plight of the actors of that day, using the Russian Eugenie Leontovich as an example:

I do not wish to suggest that from now on her road is clear. Theater Street is not so easy a thoroughfare as that--particularly in our day. In our day, for instance, the paternalistic manager is no longer at work. Time was when an Augustin Daly or a Charles Frohman would fend for a newfound Leontovich, taking pride in nourishing her talent and fashioning opportunities for its exhibition. Of such men David Belasco is the last, and the generation treading on his heels is less generous. The young talents nowadays are left to shift for themselves and take potluck. [75]

While displaying this concern for the management of young performers, Woollcott was critical of the inertia he

saw in them. This came out in his praise of the ambition of
established performers. Upon the death of Sarah Bernhardt
he lauded her "passion and capacity for work," saying: "Even
as a sick and crippled woman of seventy-eight she could do
more work any day than half the inert young people who litter
up the French theater as they do ours."[76] In 1924 he wrote
of Eva Le Gallienne:

> She is that solitary and interesting phenomenon, the
> young person in the American theatre who actually
> works at her job.... And especially is she rare
> in this latter day where the long runs have made
> the players flabby. Most of our younger players,
> at the mere suggestion of such a program as she
> has carried out this season, would have the vapors,
> to say nothing of the fantods.[77]

Woollcott's interest in the opportunities present for
actors to develop themselves moved him to comment on the
plight of the Negro performer in 1922. Although he himself
was against the employment of Negroes in Negro roles "whether
they were actors or not," he noted that: "There has been
everything in our theatre to discourage the development of a
group of negro actors."[78] It wasn't until 1927 that Woollcott
could praise the performance of a company of Negro actors.
The Theatre Guild's cast for Porgy was the recipient:

> Except for the isolated masterpiece "The Em-
> peror Jones," this "Porgy" is the first good job
> the American theatre has done with the Negro, and
> certainly it is the first fine performance of a play
> I have ever seen given by a Negro troupe. For
> with a few exceptions, all the characters in "Porgy"
> are colored folk and the Guild production uses no
> burnt cork.[79]

Woollcott's concern for actors was not limited to their
artistic development. He was also interested in their general
well-being, as his support of the Actor's Fund illustrated.
On Sunday, May 30, 1915, he devoted his entire column to
the Actors' Fund, relating its history and urging his readers
to attend one of the benefit performances it was holding that
week: "For the Actors' Fund is an institution that should
have the loyal and hearty support not only of every player
but of every playgoer in America."[80] In 1925 he lamented
that the tradition of donating 10 percent of benefit proceeds
to the Fund was no longer being consistently honored: "It is,

I fear, a tradition more honored in the breach than in the observance. "[81]

Inasmuch as Woollcott had such a concern for the actor it is somewhat surprising that he did not express in print his opinion of the actors' strike of 1919 while it was in progress. The strike, the first one called by Actors' Equity, lasted one month, from August 6 to September 6. The financial issue that triggered the strike was the theatre managers' refusal to pay the actors for extra matinee performances that might be given on legal holidays or other occasions. Woollcott's only reference to it at the time was to acknowledge its existence. Only in 1928 did he write of it in any detail, noting that after the managers had collaborated with the ticket speculators and had employed false advertising, they were surprised to discover that the public "seemed inclined to sympathize" with the actors during the strike. [82] Woollcott was much more vocal on another issue that held importance for the actor, repertory theatre.

Repertory Theatre

Woollcott first wrote in detail about repertory theatre in 1915: "When all is said and done, the great potential service of the repertory system is the kindly nursing it can give to the beautiful but fragile play which would expire in the jostling competition of the purely commercial theatre." He went on to talk about the cost of repertory, pointing out that it involved "certain financial loss," and he noted that the playwright would not be "content with the meagre repertory returns." Commenting on the variety of plays offered in a repertory situation, Woollcott said that the New York theatre itself comprised a repertory. [83] He did not mention that this type of repertory did not allow the viewer to watch an actor perform in a variety of roles. In an earlier column he had said that this aspect of repertory was "one of the secrets of the hold ... a repertoire company can maintain on the affections of the theatregoers."[84] He concluded his 1915 column by saying: "Repertory is a nice subject for discussion, but it costs too much. It is a sweet topic for Drama League Luncheons, but it won't work."[85]

In April 1917 Woollcott wrote about the repertory theatre's lack of suitability for producing modern drama:

The plays of the old dispensation were written after

a conventional pattern, and could be safely intrusted
to any company that had the usual complement of
leading juvenile, leading heavy, first old woman,
first old man and C. [sic] Not so the modern masterpieces. For them you must seek your actors in
the four corners of the earth. That is one reason
why the stock companies have found life harder
these days and why a repertory theatre cannot hope
to express the best in modern drama. [86]

Later that year Woollcott expressed a different attitude
in his book on Mrs. Fiske: "I am not all sure a well-rounded,
flexible company would not fit any play as well as the special
company its producer might be able to gather together at any
one time in the scramble and hubbub of the Rialto."[87] In
1922 Woollcott reenforced this latter opinion in his last word
on the subject:

Indeed it is so maddeningly difficult to round up the
very actors you would prefer for any one production
that the favorite argument against a repertory theater always sounds a trifle hollow and unconvincing
to us. That argument against a standing, resident
company, of course, is that it is too rigid a thing--
that the producer should be free to cast his nets in
all the seven seas. Well, he is and he does. But
what fish! What fish![88]

Another issue in the repertory debate had to do with
repertory's function as the guardian of fragile plays that
would not survive the competition of the commercial theatre.
During the 1919-20 season Woollcott pointed out that that function was being fulfilled by the special matinee. [89] This was
a practice whereby a play, usually new, was presented in the
afternoon at a theatre that was housing another play in the
evening. Often members of the evening production formed the
cast of the afternoon production.

In January 1922 the revival of The Deluge altered
Woollcott's view of repertory's function as the guardian of
fragile plays. It had been originally produced unsuccessfully
in August 1917, when the country's mind was on World War
I. Woollcott wrote:

The play's career then was so brief that it is a
mere technicality to call its present production a
revival. Yet it is the kind of technicality which is

a bugaboo to most of our managers, and one of the
good reasons why we need repertory companies in
New York today is because a repertory theatre can
steady and comfort a swooning play until it feels
better. We need to have plays like "The Deluge"
done again from time to time, as Mary Garden does
"Pelleas and Melisande." The restoration of "The
Deluge" is so rare a phenomenon in our theatre
that its like has befallen us only once or twice in
the past ten years.[90]

The 1923 visit to the United States by the Moscow Art
Theatre, under the directorship of Constantin Stanislavsky,
reinforced Woollcott's growing appreciation of the advantages
of repertory theatre. At that time Woollcott viewed the company in performances of Tolstoy's Czar Feodor, Gorki's The
Lower Depths, and Chekhov's The Cherry Orchard and The Three
Sisters. He lavished praise on each production, being particularly impressed by The Lower Depths: "Never before had
we seen scenes on the stage so actual, so alive. 'The Lower
Depths' as it was acted last evening at Al Jolson's Theater
in Seventh Avenue was the finest performance of a play within
this reviewer's experience as a playgoer."[91] Woollcott's
admiration for the company after seeing its repertoire led
him to write about the formation of an American "Moscow
Art Theatre" in a Sunday Shouts and Murmurs column for
the Herald. He suggested that the players forming such a
company pledge three years to it. The company would choose
its own director and be governed by a council. Its production
commitment would be at least three plays a season. Woollcott was insistent that the company be housed in a theatre
where it would not be limited by commercial success for
three years. He believed the company needed the freedom
to develop without the strain of having to succeed commercially.

Woollcott went so far as to name a prospective com-
pany: Roland Young, Leslie Howard, George Hassell, Thomas
Mitchell, Walter Abel, Frank Conroy, G. P. Heggie, Ernest
Glendinning, Louise Closser Hale, Ducile Watson, Effie Shan-
non, Alison Skipworth, Winifred Lenivan, Margalo Gillmore,
Eva Le Gallienne, and Katherine Cornell. He also suggested
a possible opening season consisting of Shaw's Caesar and
Cleopatra, Sheridan's The Critic, John Drinkwater's Oliver
Cromwell, and a new play by O'Neill. He went on to tell
his readers:

It should be remembered that if we ever have its

> like in New York the Company will be a thing of
> slow growth, an association of players mostly young
> and all eager, who might be brought together to-
> morrow and who would learn through the year that
> there could be special rewards in such an associa-
> tion to outweigh the larger fortunes and the brighter
> spotlights being enjoyed by other players of like
> ability who were on the loose in the theater. [92]

Woollcott concluded his comments by saying: "Of the
practicability of such a company there may be some question.
Of its desirability there can be none."[93] A month after writing this column in the Herald Woollcott again wrote of the
formation of an American repertory company. In Vanity Fair
he put into words the question the Moscow Art Theatre had
raised:

> The perfection they have achieved is a challenge to
> our own actors and producers and it has caused a
> great searching of hearts in the American theatre.
> When the last curtain falls after so vivid, sym-
> phonic and richly orchestrated a transcript from
> life as their performance of Gorky's defiant Lower
> Depths, the baffled American playgoer mutters:
> "Now why can't we have something like that in this
> country?"[94]

A month later he was still urging the idea:

> There are certain men in this town ... who must
> feel that they would like to see as much done for
> the stage in this country as has already been done
> for orchestrated music and grand opera. A fine
> model can now be studied under the roof of Mr.
> Jolson's playhouse near the park.[95]

Woollcott believed "that the best plays and the best
performances of the next few years will not come from shoe-
string stars and temporarily assembled casts but from companies rooted each in its own theater and left there to work
out its destiny."[96] The work of the Theatre Guild and Eva
Le Gallienne's Civic Repertory Company during the next six
years further reinforced Woollcott's confidence in the perman-
ent theatre concept and repertory. In 1928 he wrote:

> A hundred and one portents in the rapidly shifting

economic tensions of the American theatre all point
to the fact that with the Guild as a mark to shoot
at, the next few seasons will witness the establishment of several theatres in this town similar, that
is in scheme and intention and even better, we may
hope, in product. Indeed, I think, that most of the
plays and performances worth talking about in the
next five years will be found in those theatres. [97]

Indeed, when the Moscow Art Theatre returned to New
York in 1924 Woollcott dismissed one of his original complaints
against repertory theatre--its cost. He made his comments
in February after viewing their production of a Russian comedy entitled The Death of Pazukkim:

And all those who protest that just such a repertory
company enlisted on our stage would be too expensive
for this city to support are urged to contemplate this
production. They can scarcely help noting how utterly negligible in its effect on the performance is
the fact that the comedy has been revived without
any scenery worth mentioning. [98]

In May of that same year Woollcott pointed out the
readiness of America for a repertory theatre and its probable
need of endowment. After noting that capable actors were
available he went on to say:

With such playwrights as Eugene O'Neill, George
Kaufman, Marc Connelly, Mr. George Kelly, Mr.
Frank Craven, and not a few others, with such
sorcerers of light and color as Norman Geddes and
Robert E. Jones, everything--the impulse, the material, the need--is ready for the establishment of
such a theater as wisdom and devotion wrought in
Moscow. Unless a lucky leader comes up out of
some side street to create it by man's force such
a New York art theater would need endowment for
its first few seasons. [99]

The Moscow Art Theatre was most influential in shap-
ing Woollcott's attitude toward repertory theatre. It also presented him with opportunities to praise a type of acting he
esteemed highly.

Ensemble Acting

The element of the Moscow Art Theatre Company's performances that Woollcott acclaimed the most was its ensemble acting. Of the crowd scenes in its 1923 production of Ibsen's An Enemy of the People he wrote:

> And of course this company imparts an extraordinary life and truth to the town meeting scene which constitutes the fourth act of the play. All the winds of doctrine blow across that meeting and you can see them blow as clearly as you can see a field of wheat swirl and sway in a summer's breeze.
> We are all too used to seeing such scenes either penuriously or dully staged. Sometimes three young nondescripts are compelled by some thrifty management to constitute a mob....
> Or a large but singularly wooden crowd sits in full view, their eyes roaming about the theater, their thoughts all a thousand miles from the speeches to which they are supposed to be listening avidly. But in "An Enemy of the People" as it was staged last evening, the very crowd was protagonistic, every atom of it participating with a thoroughness and liveliness that would have warmed Mr. [David] Belasco's heart had he been there to see.[100]

Writing about the productions the company presented in New York in 1923, he was prompted to speak of the importance of ensemble acting: "It is a company made up not merely of good actors trained to play well but of good actors trained through the years to play well together, which is something else and something more."[101] After viewing their performance of Czar Feodor he commented on the contribution of the ensemble playing to the company:

> The secret of the power which spread the name of Stanislavsky's company all over the world and packed to eager standing room a theatre in an alien city thousands of miles from Moscow lies in the fact that ... the members of this close knit company work together in a way that makes the play a complete and living thing.[102]

This contribution was noted again during the company's visit:

> As the rich, lovingly wrought repertoire of the Mos-

cow Art Theater unfolds week by week at Master
Jolson's Playhouse it becomes increasingly apparent
that it has derived its strength from two sources.
One is the presence at its head of a director of
genius, gifted not only as an artist but as a leader.
The other is the mere fact of its long, close as-
sociation--the mere fact that these players who work
together in "The Lower Depths" for instance, have
for the most part been working together in "The
Lower Depths" off and on for twenty years. 103

In addition to having Woollcott's respect for its ensemble playing the Moscow Art Theatre represented the type
of theatre organization that Woollcott esteemed--a company
whose raison d'être was more than the achievement of mone-
tary success. The American companies that drew most of
his commentary in this regard were the Washington Square
Players and its successor, The Theatre Guild.

The Washington Square Players
and the Theatre Guild

Woollcott was a constant supporter of the Washington
Square Players from the evening of their debut with a bill of
one-act plays in February 1915. Of special appeal to him,
in fact, was precisely this devotion to one-act plays, a policy
that he strongly encouraged and that the players continued,
producing sixty-two before their demise in 1918. Summing
up their experiment in 1921, he called it "the most richly
productive theatrical venture of this generation." 104 In support of this extravagant praise he cited their contribution to
the American theatre of such actors as Roland Young, Edward
J. Ballantine, Jose Ruben, Frank Conroy, and Glenn Hunter;
their introduction of designers Lee Simonson and Rollo Peters
and their championship of Robert E. Jones's early work;
their staging of the first New York productions of plays by
Zöe Akins, Philip Moeller, Zona Gale, and Susan Glaspell;
and above all, their function as the genesis of the Theatre
Guild.

When the Theatre Guild's first production opened on
April 19, 1919, Woollcott was still in the Army. However,
he was on hand for the opening of its third production, which
launched its second season, and soon became one of its
staunchest supporters and most pungent critics.

As a Guild supporter, Woollcott voluntarily paid for his tickets during its first five years and frequently pointed out the importance of his darling to the theatre world. His first evaluation of its status came prior to the start of its fourth season in the fall of 1922. He devoted an entire Sunday article to the Guild, noting that in its first three years it had "become the most important, the most interesting and, to the watchers overseas, the most celebrated theatre in what is still quaintly called the Anglo-Saxon world."[105] He then proceeded to go to bat for the Guild with its public, urging endowed support and citing its pressing needs: a fully equipped modern theatre, a little theatre for experimental productions and training programs, and more money for better actors. Hailing the Guild again in March 1923, he wrote: "Indisputable ... is the fact that as Maecenas roams the town seeking whom he might endow there is no producer among the producers now at work in the American Theatre who inspires his confidence as fully as does the Theatre Guild."[106] By July 1923 Woollcott could discuss with some satisfaction a successfully concluded bond drive on behalf of the Guild's new theatre and modestly attribute its success to the Guild's own record of "bold, intelligent, resourceful productions," e.g., John Ferguson, Jane Clegg, Mr. Pim Passes By, Heartbreak House, He Who Gets Slapped, Liliom, and The Devil's Disciple. He praised the Guild's willingness to mount difficult productions that would most probably lose money, citing Peer Gynt and Back to Methuselah as examples, surmising that the attitude the Guild displayed in producing Methuselah "fired a good many playgoers to the subscription point when finally the hat was passed."[107]

Woollcott's support of the Guild did not blind him to its failings, one of the more glaring of which in its early years was the apparent indifference to American plays. In its first four seasons only two of the twenty plays produced were by American playwrights: The Rise of Silas Lapham, by Lillian Sabine, and Ambush, by Arthur Richman. Woollcott registered his first complaint in a review of the Guild's 1920 production of Jane Clegg:

> While applauding vigorously the production of Jane Clegg, one may still feel considerable regret that the Theatre Guild has accomplished so little in the way of finding new material and new playwrights in this country, has indeed found no worthwhile plays by native authors which would have really given roots to its still wobbly organization.[108]

The Rise of Silas Lapham, which had been produced earlier in the season, he rejected for its failure to preserve any of those qualities of Howells's novel that might have made it at least an interesting adaptation. [109]

A year later Woollcott offered a reason for the Guild's continuing failure to receive plays from established American dramatists:

> It seems probable that none of our established playwrights has been pressing masterpieces on the Guild's directors, not because of any fear that they would not do them well, but because of the fear that the Guild's grim determination to do five plays a year would curtail their royalties far below the reasonable expectations held out by the confessedly commercial theatre. [110]

Although this problem was alleviated somewhat in the mid-twenties, [111] by 1930 he was still hurling verbal barbs at the Guild's directorate for scouring Europe "looking everywhere for American manuscripts." [112]

Woollcott was also critical of the Guild's apparent infatuation with the new for its own sake regardless of quality:

> Indeed if the Theatre Guild would take some of the time it spends raking Europe for new plays and devote it to quickening some of the beautiful old works that lie mute in the library it would, we think, be serving the theatre better and reinforcing more solidly the bulwarks of its public. [113]

Woollcott's criticism of the Guild increased after the opening of the Guild Theatre in 1925. In reviewing Merchants of Glory, he noted a degree of complacency about the organization:

> The Guild, I think, is lolling too comfortably on the ample bosom of its subscription list, putting forth plays half ready in the hope that they will be ready by the time the advance sale has run its course. The Guild, I think, is doing more this season than it can do well, scattering its forces, confusing itself with the whilom Klaw and Erlanger. The Guild, I think, is not quite deserving the lovely new theatre its fond subscribers built. [114]

In 1929 he did a take-off on the New York Times's One Hundred Neediest Cases. His ninety-second case was the Theatre Guild. After noting that the Guild had always been "too proud to ask for anything, except subscriptions to its performances, or to its building programs," he cited its needs: "a new play-reader, just a dash of personal charm for use as an emollient, and a Columbus to assist the Guild in discovering America."[115] Indeed, with the critic's perennial advantage of hindsight, he eventually came to criticize even the location of the Guild Theatre on West Fifty-Second Street:

> I think it may have already dawned on the Guild's directorate that what their enterprise needs is just a dash of wilderness, that they were lacking in sagacity and imagination when they cravenly built their playhouse in the theatrical district, that theirs has progressively lost character and distinction by being merely one of sixty theatres nestled sheeplike in the most grotesquely congested quarter of Manhattan.[116]

By 1931 Woollcott was able to balance this view with unabashed admiration of an important contribution the Guild was making to theatre-goers across the country. He pointed out that, profit not being its primary concern, the Guild, unlike the more commercial companies, was willing to close a money-making production such as Elizabeth the Queen and tour it to subscription cities as promised on date due. The importance of this contribution derived from the pitiful status of the "road" generally. As Woollcott himself pointed out, there were "three grades" of productions that usually toured: (1) "a bored performance of a play given by a troupe that has already acted it for two seasons on Broadway," (2) "a makeshift performance of a play given by a troupe that is only a blurred carbon copy of the one even then acting it on Braodway," (3) "a discouraged performance of a play that is touring only because no one in New York would go to see it at all."[117] Such productions did nothing to build an audience for the road, of course, and there was serious question whether the entire country could be fed from one center anyway. In 1925 Woollcott had predicted that in the next twenty-five years two new "Broadways" would develop to alleviate the problem, one in Los Angeles and one in Chicago. However, this had not happened by 1931, so he called for other managers to follow the Guild's touring practice: "I think the road can be reclaimed only if the managers, not singly, but in groups, will follow the Guild's example."[118]

Woollcott's last evaluation of the Guild as a newspaper reviewer came in his final month of writing for the World. In a Sunday column he noted that the Guild had "grown into a theatrical producer with more prestige than any other theatre in the English-speaking world enjoys. Probably with more prestige than any other theatre enjoys anywhere."[119] He also wryly remarked that he had been described as the Theatre Guild's "journalistic lackey." He did not take the trouble to defend himself. He didn't have to. His praises of the Guild were indeed a matter of record, but so too were his criticisms--a balanced history of continued support of the best kind, offering praise when it was deserved, chastizing when it seemed necessary, but always supportive, always demanding excellence, and always confident that the object of his affection was capable of achieving the high goals he set for it.

As noted earlier, Woollcott had praised the Guild's predecessor, the Washington Square Players, for using some of Robert Edmond Jones's early designs. Jones proved to be the designer who drew most of Woollcott's attention.

Robert Edmond Jones

Woollcott reviewed the production in which Jones made his debut as a professional designer, Anatole France's The Man Who Married a Dumb Wife. However, he made no mention of Jones being the designer in his review of the play on January 28, 1915. He did, though, praise the setting, as well as the one for Shaw's Androcles and the Lion, which followed it on the evening's program: "The outstanding features of the investiture prepared for the two plays at Wallack's are its simplicity, its great decorative beauty, and its economy in space and time."[120] Woollcott concluded his remarks on the scenery by saying that it provided "for the player a simple, pretty, suggestive and appropriate background."[121] Beauty proved to be the quality most praised in settings in Woollcott's reviews and Jones the most consistent recipient of his praise in regard to this quality. Woollcott praised the beauty of Jones's designs more frequently than anything else. Of the forty-five Jones sets that Woollcott reviewed, nineteen of them were cited for their beauty.[122] As was his wont, Woollcott was quick to use superlatives. The Happy Ending in 1916 was the third Jones show Woollcott reviewed. He wrote that its "final scene has probably never been surpassed in beauty on the American stage."[123] He de-

scribed his design for Arthur Hopkins's 1920 production of
Shakespeare's Richard III as "the most beautiful Shakespearean
investiture this country has known."[124] By 1924 beauty was
an expected attribute of a Jones design, as Woollcott's comments on Stark Young's The Saint illustrated: "The settings
are by Mr. Jones, of course, which means this time, as
usual, that they are beautiful...."[125]

Woollcott's reaction to Jones's second Broadway design, The Devil's Garden, is not noteworthy for what Woll-
cott specifically said about the design, which he thought possessed beauty and was a good example of the new stagecraft.[126]
In writing of the production in a Sunday column, however,
Woollcott was moved to praise Jones's work in general and
write of the designer's function:

> Robert E. Jones is one of those working in a day
> that marks the advent of the authentic artist in the
> service of the theatre. The word service is used
> advisedly, for it is of the essence of his creed that
> his part in the proceedings should be suffered at
> all only in so far as it assists play and players.
> ... He knows that the place for the background
> is not in the foreground but in the background. He
> reduces the elements of his picture to the barest
> necessities and not only keeps solicitously out of
> the player's way, but so deftly arranges the lines,
> colors, lights, and shadows as to concentrate atten-
> tion on the player as completely as ever the green
> spotlight did in the stagecraft of the old dispensa-
> tion.
> Of course, the scenic artist cannot make a bad
> play nor unmake a good one. The play's the thing.
> He can only help. Indeed it is the tragedy of Mr.
> Jones' art that never for a moment can it exist for
> itself. The finer it is, the more subservient the
> role it plays.[127]

Woollcott was quick to praise Jones when he functioned
with an awareness of the designer's subservient nature. The
word "appropriate" conveyed this praise for Jones's designs
for The Man Who Married a Dumb Wife and Samson and Delilah[128] and "unobtrusive" for A Successful Calamity.[129] He
described the designs for Richard III as "rich and right."[130]
Woollcott criticized Jones most severely for his 1921 designs
for Macbeth, when he thought Jones usurped the designer's
role. He was shocked "that Mr. Jones, for all the three or

four high moments of great beauty that he achieves should
have indulged in such antics of decoration as to become the
star of 'Macbeth.'..."131

The Macbeth design represented one of the two times
when Woollcott thought Jones's work was inappropriate. His
main complaint was that the "cubistic" features of the Inver-
ness castle clashed with the "conventionally drawn and literal"
Macbeth of Lionel Barrymore. He was further disenchanted
by Jones's mixing his unreal setting with "quite actual can-
dles."132 Atypically, Woollcott offered descriptions of some
of the settings. He sarcastically described the castle as "a
giant molar tooth pitched rakishly in space" and the heath as
"the lodge room of the Ku Klux Klan, Poughkeepsie Chapter."133 Writing, less amorphously, of the heath scene,
Woollcott described the three five-foot suspended masks that
dominated the environment as being "startling," "decorative,"
and "memorable" but did not think they projected the appropriate atmosphere "of supernatural soliciting, of storm and
portent and dread...."134 Woollcott believed the scene called
for "night and wind and banshee wailing and an unearthly light,"
none of which was projected by the "three giant metal
masks."135

The other Jones design that Woollcott initially thought
was inappropriate was the one for Desire Under the Elms in
1924. As with the Macbeth design, Woollcott did not think
Jones's work for Desire served the play well. He was greatly
disturbed by the lack of believability of the farmhouse with
the removable walls:

> Then, as it becomes necessary to reveal first the
> kitchen, then the bedrooms above, and finally the
> musty, funeral parlor, these sections are bared and
> lighted up and the characters move from one to the
> other.
>   There are even times when one of the members
> of this afflicted household may be astroll in the
> garden. Mr. O'Neill permits such a one to observe
> how "purty" the sky is and to say as much quite
> often. But the same character is not permitted to
> notice also that a large hunk of the wall of his home
> has been neatly cut away for the benefit of some
> Peeping Toms out in the audience. Thus an en-
> tirely fresh set of terms in the standing "Let's
> Pretend" agreement is abruptly added by this some-
> what high standard playwright. The strain on the

illusion is painful. The setting becomes a mechanical toy, not unsuited to farce, but disastrous when used as the background for so dour and grave a play.[136]

Writing of the design two months after his review, Woollcott reiterated his displeasure: "To me this structure never seemed more than a disturbing mechanical toy."[137] However, he now admitted that it allowed for the juxtaposition of contrasting emotional tones:

> It was a heavy price to pay, but it bought something. It bought, for instance, the intensely dramatic juxtaposition of the two bedrooms--the candle-lit chamber of the gabby, troubled old farmer and his young, scheming bride on one side of the wall and, on the other, the smouldering stepson tossing restless on the bed on which he had thrown himself, now and again sitting up and cocking his ear for what sounds would come to him through the lath and plaster which the hot coals of his eyes seemed likely to kindle into a flame that would consume the house. It bought, too, the picture of that jeering crowd of neighbors drinking to the new baby in the kitchen below, while the still ailing mother rocks moodily in the corner. And at the same time held in suspense as an essential part of the same picture, you could see the silhouette of the cradle against the candle light in her bedroom above and, in the adjoining bedroom, the mute father of that baby twisting tormented in the lonely silence enforced upon him. You may remember that scene when you have forgotten much that seemed weak and raucous and untrue in Desire Under the Elms.[138]

The value Woollcott placed on imagination in the work of the actor and playwright is echoed in his praise of this quality in the work of Jones. His design for Richard III prompted Woollcott to refer to his imagination as "boundless."[139] Although he rejected the design concept for Macbeth, Woollcott was still moved to write: "Anything he does or may yet do is sure to be done with imagination and courage and honesty."[140] He marveled at what Jones and his co-designer, Cleon Throckmorton, achieved in the physical space they had to work with for O'Neill's The Hairy Ape:

That preposterous little theatre [the Provincetown Playhouse] has one of the most cramped stages New York has ever known, and yet on it the artists have created the illusion of vast spaces and endless perspectives. They drive one to the conclusion that when a stage seems pinched and little, it is the mind of the producer that is pinched and little. This time O'Neill, unbridled, set them a merry pace in the eccentric gait of his imaginings. They kept up with him. [141]

Woollcott was in favor of designers enhancing productions through the ingenious, economic use of their craft. His praise of the "economy in space and time" in Jones's design for The Man Who Married a Dumb Wife alluded to this. He was more explicit in expressing this attitude in evaluating the design for Richard III:

The Robert Edmond Jones settings for "Richard III," ... are ingeniously thrifty of time and money. A single, towering massive background, as of gray stone, serves for every scene, with such shifting disguises of lights, tapestries, and iron work as each demands. This is as it should be, for the greatest beauty and appropriateness of stage decoration is far too dearly bought if it encumbers the stage, slackens the pace of the performance or loads with needless and discouraging expense the initial cost of production. There should be a good deal of craft in stagecraft. [142]

The only negative aspect of the design confusingly seems to address the same issue, as Woollcott faults the time required for scene shifts: "One may still regret that Mr. Jones' plans did not, after the continental fashion, make use of the forestage, but rather called for more than a dozen illusion-dispelling intervals for the shifting of scenery."[143]

Woollcott was quick to recognize the ability of Jones. After reviewing his first two Broadway designs, he prophesied in January 1916 that Jones's work would "live on indefinitely as a manner to be remembered, as a style to be imitated in many a production to come."[144] Later that year he noted that "none of the new artists who have come from overseas to decorate our plays have done better work than this young

American...."[145] In May 1917 Woollcott saluted Jones as
one of the stars of the 1916-17 Broadway season:

> ROBERT E. JONES had attracted attention with
> investiture of "A Man Who Married a Dumb Wife"
> during the Barker season at Wallack's two years
> ago but this year he has shown his adaptability to
> the varying demands of widely different plays, put-
> ting beauty into 1917 backgrounds, and so giving
> promise of tremendous usefulness and influence in
> the theatre of tomorrow and the day after. His
> settings for the three Hopkins productions, for the
> Torrence plays, and for the brave "Till Eulenspiegel"
> of Mr. Nijinski, represent a splendid year's work
> and a new reputation achieved. [146]

Woollcott's continuing esteem for Jones was evident
in his 1919 comments on Arthur Hornblow's newly published
A History of the Theatre in America: "His work may be
briefly described as a two-volumed history of the American
Theatre, which contains no reference to one of the rare ge-
niuses produced by that institution--Robert Edmond Jones."[147]
Even in decrying his design of Macbeth in 1921, Woollcott
described Jones as "unquestionably the foremost conjurer of
light and color in the history of the American theater...."[148]

In the fall of 1925 Theatre Arts, Inc., published
Drawings for the Theatre, a collection of thirty-five plates
depicting Jones's designs. The book's publication prompted
Woollcott to describe the identifying characteristics of Jones's
best designs:

> At its best, Jones' work in the theatre has a greatly
> enhancing effect upon the scene being played within
> it, a heightening of that scene's spiritual momentu-
> ousness, an intensification of its emotion akin to
> the same service that may sometimes be rendered
> a player's speech by the throb of sound from strings
> invisible. [149]

Woollcott's own evaluation of the power of Jones's designs to enhance the spiritual and emotional values of a scene
seems to have foreshadowed Jones's own pronouncement of
what a set should do. In his book The Dramatic Imagination,
published in 1941, Jones wrote:

> A setting is not just a beautiful thing, a collection

of beautiful things. It is a presence, a mood, a
wind fanning the drama to flame. It echoes, it en-
hances, it animates. It is an expectancy, a fore-
boding, a tension. It says nothing but gives everything.... The designer creates an environment in
which all noble emotions are possible. Then he
retires. The actor enters. If the designer's work
has been good, it disappears from our consciousness at that moment.... The actor has taken the
stage; and the designer's only reward lies in the
praise bestowed on the actor. 150

Jones's belief in the subordinate nature of the designer
echoed Woollcott's own belief. The detail of Woollcott's design commentary on such productions as Macbeth and Desire
Under the Elms is atypical of his evaluations of Jones, and
other designers for that matter. Of the forty-five Jones-
designed productions that he reviewed, he neglected to evaluate the designs of twenty-one. 151 The sparsity of Woollcott's
evaluations of Jones's work is a reflection of his general
treatment of design and technical matters in his reviews.
Comments of this nature are found in fewer than 16 percent
of his reviews. Woollcott simply placed a much greater
value on the actor and the play, viewing the scenic and technical dimensions of a production as subservient elements.
This point of view is also reflected in his commentary on
the new stagecraft.

The New Stagecraft

At first Woollcott was quite receptive to the new stagecraft movement, praising its lighting effects, settings, use of
the stage, and what he interpreted to be an economical use
of money. This praise was given between 1914 and 1917.
In 1917 he first muttered his two major complaints against
the new stagecraft: a failure to light the stage adequately
and a placing of the emphasis on the scenery rather than on
the actor. He registered his complaints in his review of a
play entitled Nju, by the Russian playwright Ossip Dymow:

The settings by Mr. Joseph Urban are always pleasing to the eye and occasionally admirable for the
ingenuity with which, by the shifting of a few flats
on a cramped stage, he has made the scenes var-
iously intimate, spacious, luxurious, and bleak.
But they are all dim-lit and gloomy until the per-

formance becomes little more than "a mournful
rustling in the dark." It is Mr. Urban's besetting
sin that he has a composition which delights the
eye, but ignores the actors and their needs.

It is all very well to scorn the footlights and
spotlights of the old dispensation, but the Urbanites
carry the rebellion too far. As like as not he will
throw a footstool or an inkwell into brilliant relief
and leave the actors wailing in outer darkness.[152]

Later reviews saw Woollcott registering his opposition
to the new stagecraft by praising productions that were well
lighted and thus placed the proper emphasis on the actors.
His comments on the Theatre Guild's production of The Power
of Darkness in 1920 illustrates this theme in his reviewing
during the 1920s:

> Though there is present in the play every oppor-
> tunity to induce the sombre mood by mantling the
> stage in darkness according to the new tradition,
> the Theatre Guild foregoes this temptation to be
> merely suggestive in favor of the old routine of
> interpreting the author's intent by visible actors.[153]

In his Sunday column of April 18, 1920, commenting
once again on the problem of stage lighting, Woollcott expanded his complaint against the new stagecraft:

> There would really be no need of keeping an eye on
> the lighting of plays were it not often involved in a
> larger tendency characteristic of our modern pro-
> ducers to reduce the actors to mere vaguely de-
> scried puppets in an impressionistic group. This
> tendency is kin to the Urban stagecraft which in
> seasons past has often seemed to regard the actor
> as a nuisance in a play, much as Gilbert barked at
> music as the curse of an opera. It is kin--distant
> but recognizable kin--to the Gordon Craig reduction
> of the actors to the level of a marionette. Against
> this degrading heresy we bitterly rebel. It is a
> denial of an elemental force in the drama, some-
> thing that was in drama before there was a theatre,
> something in drama that brought theatres into ex-
> istence. This heresy was a natural reaction against
> the pompous and protruding actor of the palmy days.
> It was the weakness of the fine upstanding man who
> falls over backward. Against it we shall be carried
> screaming to our grave.[154]

In Woollcott's eyes it was the director's responsibility to coordinate the production elements into a harmonious whole and thus prevent the distortion that the critic occasionally saw in the new stagecraft.

The Director

Woollcott discussed his conception of the director's role in commentary on the final scene of the 1916 production of Jean and La Macpherson's The Happy Ending: "And for this final moment the work of playwright, players, decorator, and composer was brought into that perfect harmony which is the director's finest achievement--his very reason for existence."[155] The only other theoretical pronouncement on directing was made in his comments on the 1916 production of Treasure Island. He found great fault in the casting of Charles Hopkins for the two roles of Ben Gunn and Pew. In voicing his criticism he made a parenthetical comment on directing:

> To suggest to the director of the Punch & Judy producing organization (who remembers, of course, that it is a director's first business to guard jealously the interests of the play) that he might cast more satisfactorily these two important and tempting roles would be a more delicate task if it were not for the convenient fact that the director and the actor who plays both Ben Gunn and Pew are the one and same person.[156]

Woollcott's scant attention to directing is seen again in the fact that in fewer than 8 percent of his reviews did he discuss the direction. In his comments Woollcott exhibited a concern for the necessity of a director being able to control the actor. When he came upon a production in which it appeared to him that the actors had gained the upper hand he let his opinion be bluntly known. Such was the case in H. Austin Adams's Curiosity, which was directed by Edgar Selwyn:

> It seems likely that Mr. Selwyn was feeling entirely too affable and avuncular to show a director's necessary sternness. He let the play run on and on unchecked and he let such well known and experienced actors as Cyril Knightley, Irene Fenwick, and Ramsey Wallace run wild from scene to scene.[157]

Woollcott was obviously being sarcastic in describing the performers mentioned as "well known and experienced." None
of these people fit that description in 1919, the year of the
play's production.

Woollcott praised and faulted directors for a variety
of reasons in addition to the already cited points. Among
the qualities he extolled were intelligence, imagination, deft-
ness and quickness of touch, competency, and the ability to
hear well and instill the proper pacing into a production.
Among the faults he noted were rigidity, tactlessness, lack
of intelligence and imagination, the inability to correct over-
acting, false dialects, faulty delivery of speeches, and the
failure to instill the proper pacing into a production.

Woollcott's commentary on directing, as well as on
such theatrical issues as censorship, repertory theatre, and
the star system, reinforce the image he projected in his remarks on performers and playwrights. His primary concern
was the welfare of the theatre artist and the theatre itself.
He praised and encouraged those forces that enhanced the
creative environment of the theatre artist and was quick to
denounce those that might damage it.

Notes

1"Assails Frohman Play," New York Times, September 22, 1914, p. 11.

2"Second Thoughts on First Nights," New York Times,
October 4, 1914, Sec. 6, p. 9.

3"Second Thoughts on First Nights," New York World,
January 23, 1927, p. 3M.

4"Second Thoughts on First Nights," New York Times,
January 1, 1922, Sec. 6, p. 1.

5"Second Thoughts on First Nights," New York Times,
February 19, 1922, Sec. 6, p. 1.

6"Second Thoughts on First Nights," New York World,
April 17, 1927, p. 3M.

7Ibid.

[8]Ibid.

[9]Ibid.

[10]"The Stage, " New York World, February 22, 1928, p. 11. The "artist's business," as Woollcott saw it, was to present the truth, and in so doing afford the consumer of his art an experience that has the potential at least to "enlarge his heart" and "quicken his imagination. " See "Shouts and Murmurs, " New York Herald, May 26, 1924, p. 18; "Ernest Truex in 'The Fall Guy, '" New York Sun, March 11, 1925, p. 16; "The Stage, " New York World, February 22, 1928, p. 11; and "Lest We Forget," Collier's, June 8, 1929, p. 50.

[11]"Second Thoughts on First Nights, " New York World, March 4, 1928, p. 3M.

[12]Ibid.

[13]"Other Times, Other Morals, " Vanity Fair, June 1928, p. 80.

[14]"Senate Passes Theatre Curb, " New York Times, May 6, 1937, p. 26.

[15]Ibid.

[16]Script for Town Crier radio broadcast of May 13, 1937, Alexander Woollcott Collection, Hamilton College, Clinton, New York.

[17]"The One-Act Play Not Yet an Institution in America, " New York Times, March 15, 1914, Sec. 8, p. 12.

[18]"Second Thoughts on First Nights, " New York Times, November 29, 1914, Sec. 7, p. 8.

[19]"Second Thoughts on First Nights, " New York Times, December 26, 1915, Sec. 6, p. 6.

[20]"The Stage, " New York World, January 13, 1927, p. 15.

[21]"Second Thoughts on First Nights, " New York Times, November 8, 1914, Sec. 7, p. 8.

[22]"The Play, " New York Times, April 14, 1922, p. 20.

23"Second Thoughts on First Nights," New York Times, April 9, 1922, Sec. 8, p. 1.

24Ibid.

25"Second Thoughts on First Nights," New York Times, August 15, 1915, Sec. 6, p. 2.

26"The Play," New York Times, December 11, 1919, p. 11.

27"'What Price Glory' Magnificent," New York Sun, September 6, 1924, p. 3.

28Ibid.

29"German Farewell in Goethe Drama," New York Times, April 21, 1915, p. 13.

30"Hard Boiled Drama," Vanity Fair, November 1924, p. 110.

31Ibid.

32"Second Thoughts on First Nights," New York World, November 1, 1925, p. 2M.

33Emory Lewis, Stages, the Fifty Year Childhood of the American Theatre (Englewood, N.J.; Prentice-Hall, 1969), p. 31.

34"Plays and Players in These Parts," New York Sun, November 29, 1924, p. 7.

35"The Stage," New York World, September 8, 1925, p. 14.

36"Jane Cowl at the Broadhurst," New York Sun, January 28, 1925, p. 12.

37"Second Thoughts on First Nights," New York World, December 5, 1926, p. 3M.

38Ibid.

39"Grace George in Fine Fettle," New York Sun, February 4, 1925, p. 12.

40"Jane Cowl at the Broadhurst," New York Sun, January 28, 1925, p. 12.

41"The Stage," New York World, November 24, 1926, p. 15.

42"The Stage," New York World, November 16, 1925, p. 13.

43"Shouts and Murmurs," New York Herald, February 24, 1923, p. 9.

44Ibid.

45"Second Thoughts on First Nights," New York Times, October 1, 1922, Sec. 7, p. 1.

46"A Charming Comedy Gracefully Played," New York Times, September 7, 1914, p. 12.

47"The Play," New York Times, October 9, 1919, p. 6. This concern is also seen in his comments on Eugene Brieux's The American in Paris and John Galsworthy's The Skin Game. See "The Play," New York Times, August 4, 1920, p. 14, and "The Play," New York Times, October 21, 1920, p. 11.

48"Second Thoughts on First Nights," New York World, April 29, 1928, p. 3M. Woollcott's own positive re-actions to American performances by the Moscow Art Company and Max Reinhardt's Company among others document his stand. See "Shouts and Murmurs," New York Herald, January 16, 1923, p. 12; "Weekly Log of the Navigator Among the Reefs of Broadway," New York Sun, May 31, 1924, p. 4; "Shouts and Murmurs," New York Herald, January 14, 1923, Sec. 7, p. 1; "The Stage," New York World, November 18, 1927, p. 13; "The Stage," New York World, December 8, 1927, p. 13; and "Second Thoughts on First Nights," New York World, January 29, 1928, p. 3M.

49"New Klein Drama Is Short," New York Times, October 6, 1914, p. 11.

50"The Stage," New York World, February 14, 1927, p. 11.

51"Shouts and Murmurs," New York Herald, August 18, 1923, p. 8.

52"Shouts and Murmurs," New York Herald, March 12, 1924, p. 9.

53"What the Doctor Ordered," Ladies Home Journal, May 1941, p. 55.

54"Second Thoughts on First Nights," New York Times, April 9, 1916, Sec. 2, p. 8.

55"Elmer, the Unexpected," Collier's, May 4, 1929, p. 15.

56"Shouts and Murmurs," New Yorker, March 22, 1930, p. 34.

57Ibid.

58John Peter Toohey, The Pultizer Prize Play (New York: Citadel, 1969), p. 86.

59Ibid.

60"Plays and Players in These Parts," New York Sun, April 27, 1925, p. 12.

61"Second Thoughts on First Nights," New York World, May 9, 1926, p. 3M.

62"Second Thoughts on First Nights," New York World, May 8, 1927, p. 3M.

63"Second Thoughts on First Nights," New York World, May 9, 1926, p. 3M. Woollcott's comments reveal his belief that theatre was a collaborative art form, a view he stated on several occasions. See "'As You Like It' Agreeably Played," New York Times, March 17, 1914, p. 11; "A Passing Salutation to Some Players of Parts," New York Times, March 1, 1914, Sec. 7, p. 6; "The Reviewing Stand," December 17, 1922, Sec. 7, p. 1; "The Leak in the Sieve," Vanity Fair, March 1927, p. 54; and "Staged in Moscow," Collier's, December 16, 1933, p. 46.

64"Second Thoughts on First Nights," New York World, February 28, 1926, p. 3M.

65"Second Thoughts on First Nights," New York World, May 9, 1926, p. 3M.

66"Second Thoughts on First Nights, " New York World, May 8, 1927, p. 3M.

67"May Irwin Shines in Her New Face, " New York Times, August 24, 1915, p. 11.

68Ibid.

69"Second Thoughts on First Nights, " New York Times, August 29, 1915, Sec. 6, p. 5.

70Ibid.

71"Second Thoughts on First Nights, " New York Times, August 20, 1916, Sec. 2, p. 7.

72"Second Thoughts on First Nights, " New York Times, December 17, 1916, Sec. 2, p. 6.

73"Second Thoughts on First Nights, " New York Times, January 22, 1922, Sec. 6, p. 1.

74Ibid.

75"A Ship Comes In, " Collier's, April 11, 1931, p. 56.

76"Shouts and Murmurs, " New York Herald, April 11, 1923, Sec. 7, p. 1.

77"Mademoiselle Eva Le Gallienne, " New York Sun, March 24, 1924, p. 18.

78"Second Thoughts on First Nights, " New York Times, April 9, 1922, Sec. 8, p. 1.

79"The Stage, " New York World, October 11, 1927, p. 11.

80"Second Thoughts on First Nights, " New York Times, May 30, 1915, Sec. 7, p. 8.

81"Plays and Players in These Parts, " New York Sun, January 26, 1925, p. 16.

82"Second Thoughts on First Nights, " New York World, May 6, 1928, p. 3M.

83"Second Thoughts on First Nights," New York Times, October 10, 1915, Sec. 6, p. 6.

84"Second Thoughts on First Nights," New York Times, November 29, 1914, Sec. 7, p. 8.

85"Second Thoughts on First Nights," New York Times, October 10, 1915, Sec. 6, p. 6.

86"Second Thoughts on First Nights," New York Times, April 1, 1917, Sec. 8, p. 5.

87Woollcott, Mrs. Fiske, p. 145.

88"The Reviewing Stand," New York Herald, October 29, 1922, Sec. 7, p. 1.

89See "Second Thoughts on First Nights," New York Times, March 14, 1920, Sec. 5, p. 5.

90"The Play," New York Times, January 28, 1922, p. 14.

91"Shouts and Murmurs," New York Herald, January 16, 1923, p. 12.

92"Shouts and Murmurs," New York Herald, February 4, 1923, Sec. 7, p. 1.

93Ibid.

94"The New York Art Theatre," Vanity Fair, March 1923, p. 36.

95"Shouts and Murmurs," New York Herald, January 14, 1923, Sec. 7, p. 1.

96Ibid.

97"Second Thoughts on First Nights," New York World, February 19, 1928, p. 3M.

98"Shouts and Murmurs," New York Herald, February 12, 1924, p. 9.

99"Weekly Log of the Navigator Among the Reefs of Broadway," New York Sun, May 31, 1924, p. 4.

100"The Stage," New York Herald, December 4, 1923, p. 9.

101"Shouts and Murmurs," New York Herald, January 14, 1923, Sec. 7, p. 1.

102"Shouts and Murmurs," New York Herald, January 9, 1923, p. 14.

103"Shouts and Murmurs," New York Herald, January 28, 1923, Sec. 7, p. 1.

104"Second Thoughts on First Nights," New York Times, March 6, 1921, Sec. 6, p. 1.

105"Second Thoughts on First Nights," New York Times, September 17, 1922, Sec. 6, p. 1.

106"Shouts and Murmurs," New York Herald, March 11, 1923, Sec. 7, p. 1.

107"The New York Playgoer Erects a Theater," Vanity Fair, July 1930, p. 39.

108"Second Thoughts on First Nights," New York Times, March 28, 1920, Sec. 5, p. 6.

109"The Play," New York Times, November 26, 1919, p. 11.

110"Second Thoughts on First Nights," New York Times, January 30, 1921, Sec. 6, p. 1.

111"Plays and Players in These Parts," New York Sun, March 28, 1925, p. 5.

112"Shouts and Murmurs," New Yorker, July 26, 1930, p. 28.

113"Shouts and Murmurs," New York Herald, April 23, 1923, p. 8.

114"The Stage," New York World, December 15, 1925, p. 15.

115"Shouts and Murmurs," New Yorker, December 14, 1929, p. 42.

116"Shouts and Murmurs," New Yorker, July 26, 1930, p. 28.

117"The Dollar After Next," Collier's, February 7, 1931, p. 10.

118Ibid.

119"Second Thoughts on First Nights," New York World, May 20, 1928, p. 3M.

120"Barker's Season Happily Launched," New York Times, p. 9.

121Ibid.

122The settings for the following productions were praised for their beauty: Androcles and the Lion--"Barker's Season Happily Launched," New York Times, January 28, 1915, p. 9; The Devil's Garden--"'Devil's Garden' a Sombre Drama," New York Times, December 29, 1915, p. 11; The Happy Ending--"Many Beauties in 'The Happy Ending,'" New York Times, August 22, 1916, p. 7; "Second Thoughts on First Nights," New York Times, August 27, 1916, Sec. 2, p. 8; A Successful Calamity--"Gillette Returns in a Brilliant Play," New York Times, February 6, 1917, p. 10; Richard III--"The Play," New York Times, March 8, 1920, p. 7; "Second Thoughts on First Nights," New York Times, March 21, 1920, Sec. 6, p. 6; Macbeth--"The Play," New York Times, February 18, 1921, p. 16; Daddy's Gone A-Hunting--"The Play," New York Times, August 31, 1921, p. 8; Swords --"The Play," New York Times, September 2, 1921, p. 9; The S.S. Tenacity--"The Play," New York Times, December 21, 1921, p. 26; Voltaire--"The Play," New York Times, March 21, 1922, p. 17; Hamlet--"The Reviewing Stand," New York Herald, November 17, 1922, p. 8; "The Reviewing Stand," New York Herald, December 3, 1922, Sec. 7, p. 1; Romeo and Juliet--"The Reviewing Stand," New York Herald, December 28, 1922, p. 6; The Spook Sonata--"The Reviewing Stand," New York Herald, January 7, 1924, p. 9; Henry IV --"Shouts and Murmurs," New York Herald, January 22, 1924, p. 9; The Saint--"Stark Young Submits 'The Saint,'" New York Sun, October 13, 1924, p. 18; Beyond--"'Beyond' in Macdougal Street," New York Sun, January 29, 1925, p. 18; The Buccaneer--"The Stage," New York World, October 3, 1925, p. 11; In a Garden--"The Stage," New York World, November 17, 1925, p. 13; and The Fountain--"The Stage," New York World, December 11, 1925, p. 16.

123"Many Beauties in 'The Happy Ending,'" New York Times, August 22, 1916, p. 7.

124"Second Thoughts on First Nights," New York Times, February 27, 1921, Sec. 6, p. 1.

125"Stark Young Submits 'The Saint,'" New York Sun, October 13, 1924, p. 18.

126"'Devil's Garden' a Sombre Drama," New York Times, December 29, 1915, p. 11.

127"Second Thoughts on First Nights," New York Times, January 9, 1916, Sec. 6, p. 2. In these comments Woollcott was echoing sentiments he expressed in his first year of reviewing when he wrote: "The role of the designer of stage decoration is like the role of the composer of incidental music, a subservient one...." See "Second Thoughts on First Nights," New York Times, December 6, 1914, Sec. 9, p. 2.

128See "Barker's Season Happily Launched," New York Times, January 28, 1915, p. 9, and "The Play," New York Times, November 18, 1920, p. 18.

129"Gillette Returns in a Brilliant Play," New York Times, February 6, 1917, p. 10.

130"The Play," New York Times, March 8, 1920, p. 7.

131"The Play," New York Times, February 18, 1921, p. 16.

132"Second Thoughts on First Nights," New York Times, February 27, 1921, Sec. 6, p. 1.

133"The Play," New York Times, February 18, 1921, p. 16. It is interesting to note that Woollcott's use of sarcasm underwent an evolutionary process during the course of his newspaper career. While his first four seasons of reviews do contain certain examples of sarcasm, there is a notable increase in its use when he resumes reviewing after his return from World War I. From this first post-war theatre season of 1919-20 at the Times through the 1925-26 season, when he joined The World, the increase in his use of sarcasm eventually earned him a reputation that he did not really deserve. The great body of his reviewing is completely free of sarcasm and often enthusiastic in its praise of worthy efforts. See his review of Tolstoy's The Power of Darkness-- "The Play," New York Times, January 22, 1920, p. 22.

134Ibid.

135"Second Thoughts on First Nights," New York Times, February 27, 1921, Sec. 6, p. 1.

136"Through Darkest New England," New York Sun, November 12, 1924, p. 28.

137"Desire Under the Elms," Vanity Fair, January 1925, p. 27.

138Ibid.

139"The Play," New York Times, March 8, 1920, p. 7.

140"Second Thoughts on First Nights," New York Times, February 27, 1921, Sec. 6, p. 1.

141"The Play," New York Times, March 10, 1922, p. 18.

142"Second Thoughts on First Nights," New York Times, March 21, 1920, Sec. 6, p. 6.

143Ibid.

144"Second Thoughts on First Nights," New York Times, January 9, 1916, Sec. 6, p. 2.

145"Many Beauties in 'The Happy Ending,'" New York Times, August 22, 1916, p. 7.

146"Second Thoughts on First Nights," New York Times, May 13, 1917, Sec. 8, p. 7.

147"Second Thoughts on First Nights," New York Times, December 28, 1919, Sec. 8, p. 2.

148"Second Thoughts on First Nights," New York Times, February 27, 1921, Sec. 6, p. 1.

[149]"The Stage," New York World, October 2, 1925, p. 14.

[150](New York: Theatre Arts Books, 1941), pp. 26-7.

[151]The twenty-one were The Merry Death, Good Gracious Annabelle, Three One-Act Plays for a Negro Theatre, George Washington: The Man Who Made Us, The Claw, Anna Christie, The Mountain Man, Deluge, Rose Bernd, The Laughing Lady, Launzi, A Royal Fandango, Fashion or Life in New York, Welded, George Dandin or the Husband Confounded, The Ancient Mariner, Love for Love, The Great God Brown, The Jest, Paris Bound, and Salvation.

[152]"Darkest Russia at the Bandbox," New York Times, March 23, 1917, p. 7.

[153]"Second Thoughts on First Nights," New York Times, January 25, 1920, Sec. 8, p. 2.

[154]"Second Thoughts on First Nights," New York Times, April 18, 1920, Sec. 6, p. 2.

[155]"Second Thoughts on First Nights," New York Times, August 27, 1916, Sec. 2, p. 8.

[156]"Second Thoughts on First Nights," New York Times, October 29, 1916, Sec. 2, p. 6.

[157]"The Play," New York Times, December 19, 1919, p. 13.

Chapter 5

POSTSCRIPT

What was Alexander Woollcott's contribution to the American theatre? Certainly one thing that this study has documented in some detail is that Woollcott was not a critic in any but a rather general sense of the term. He never produced any detailed, analytical criticism; indeed, it was rare that he bothered to offer support for the opinions expressed even in his reviews. Whatever body of theory guided his judgments was not shared with his readers. What he did share with them, however, was the excitement and glitter of Broadway in its heyday, as seen by one of its own. Reporter, publicist, playwright, actor, broadcast columnist, man-about-town, famous wit, member of the fabled Algonquin Club--but preeminently and most memorably a reviewer who loved the theatre and who loved writing about it--Woollcott was one of the most widely read and influential theatrical personalities of his time.

And he did have impact. It was young Alec Woollcott who, in May 1915, noting that the Washington Square Players were not committed to a program for the following season, urged them to continue their production of one-act plays. Encouraged by Woollcott, the Washington Square Players produced a total of sixty-two short plays during their five seasons of existence, rescuing the form from vaudeville and assuring its continued existence as a viable genre in the legitimate theatre. In 1920 Woollcott twice called for John Barrymore to play Hamlet. In December of that year Barrymore gave the American theatre one of the finest Hamlets of the century. Woollcott continually supported and encouraged young talent, such as O'Neill, Helen Hayes, and the Lunts; and he chastized them in print when they wasted their talents on worthless material or performed below his ambitious expectations for them.

Woollcott opened his welcoming arms to foreign com-

154

panies, like the Moscow Art Theatre, and performers, like Sarah Bernhardt. He was an ardent champion of the new stagecraft and a tireless supporter of the Theatre Guild. He struggled for years on behalf of repertory theatre in this country and fought pitched battles time and again against censorship and the star system, constantly campaigning on behalf of a theatre whose welfare was his chief concern.

Profound theorist Woollcott certainly was not, but ardent dilettante in the most positive sense of that word he certainly was. Whatever he may have thought about New York, he loved its theatre and devoted his life to it. He made valuable contributions to it while he lived, and now his writings about it constitute one of the important legacies of the Golden Age of American theatre.

BIBLIOGRAPHY

The bibliographical material relevant to the preparation of this study is organized in the following manner: Section I lists the published works written and edited by Alexander Woollcott. The first subsection contains Woollcott's newspaper articles arranged chronologically according to the newspaper in which they appeared. Articles bearing an asterisk are unsigned but attributable to Woollcott. The remaining subsections list magazine articles and books written by Woollcott and books edited by him. Section II lists works about Woollcott, and Section III contains unpublished materials relevant to this study.

I. PUBLISHED WORKS WRITTEN OR EDITED BY ALEXANDER WOOLLCOTT

A. NEWSPAPERS

1. New York Times

"Baby Makes a Hit in Wilson's New Play." December 28, 1909, p. 6.*

"A Passing Salutation to Some Players of Parts." March 1, 1914, Sec. 7, p. 6.*

"The One-Act Play Not Yet an Institution in America." March 15, 1914, Sec. 8, p. 12.*

"'As You Like It' Agreeably Played." March 17, 1914, p. 11.*

"Margaret Anglin Splendid as Kate." March 20, 1914, p. 11.*

New York Times (cont.)

"Some Afterthoughts on Miss Anglin's Production."
March 22, 1914, Sec. 7, p. 6.*

"A League as a Patron and a Play of Its Choice." April
5, 1914, Sec. 8, p. 6.*

"A Scrap of Paper Yellow with Age." May 12, 1914,
p. 11.*

"A Charming Comedy Gracefully Played." September 7,
1914, p. 12.*

"Mrs. Drew Appears in a Patchy Play." September 8,
1914, p. 11.*

"Assails Frohman Play." September 22, 1914, p. 11.*

"Second Thoughts on First Nights." October 4, 1914,
Sec. 6, p. 9.*

"New Klein Drama Is Short." October 6, 1914, p. 11.*

"Joy of New Play an Aged Actress." October 8, 1914,
p. 11.*

"Shaw's 'Pygmalion' Has Come to Town." October 13,
1914, p. 11.*

"'Big Jim Garrity' Is All Excitement." October 17,
1914, p. 11.*

"Good Melodrama at the Longacre." October 20, 1914,
p. 13.*

"Second Thoughts on First Nights." November 8, 1914,
Sec. 7, p. 8.*

"Miss Neilson-Terry in 'Twelfth Night.'" November 24,
1914, p. 10.*

"Second Thoughts on First Nights." November 29, 1914,
Sec. 7, p. 8.*

"Second Thoughts on First Nights." December 6, 1914,
Sec. 9, p. 2.*

"Ethel Barrymore in a Fine Play." January 26, 1915,
p. 11.*

"Barker's Season Happily Launched." January 28, 1915,
p. 9.*

"Mr. Barker Gives Some Shakespeare." February 17,
1915, p. 11.*

"Lou-Tellegen in a German Farce." March 18, 1915,
p. 11.*

"Mr. Barker Gives Some More Shaw." March 27, 1915,
p. 11.*

"An All-Star 'Trilby.'" April 4, 1915, Sec. 2, p. 5.

"Second Thoughts on First Nights." April 11, 1915,
Sec. 7, p. 6.*

"Reicher Admirable in Ibsen Tragedy." April 14, 1915,
p. 13.*

"Second Thoughts on First Nights." April 15, 1915,
Sec. 7, p. 6.*

"German Farewell in Goethe Drama." April 21, 1915,
p. 13.*

"Second Thoughts on First Nights." April 25, 1915,
Sec. 7, p. 4.*

"'Arms and the Man' Agreeably Revived." May 8, 1915,
p. 15.*

"'Candida' Revised by Arnold Daly." May 21, 1915,
p. 13.*

"Second Thoughts on First Nights." May 30, 1915, Sec.
7, p. 8.*

"Second Thoughts on First Nights." August 15, 1915,
Sec. 6, p. 2.*

"May Irwin Shines in Her New Face." August 24, 1915,
p. 11.*

New York Times (cont.)

"Second Thoughts on First Nights." August 29, 1915,
Sec. 6, p. 5.*

"'Young America' Has Wide Appeal." August 30, 1915,
p. 7.*

"Second Thoughts on First Nights." October 10, 1915,
Sec. 6, p. 6.*

"Emma McChesney Goes on the Stage." October 20,
1915, p. 11.*

"Second Thoughts on First Nights." October 24, 1915,
Sec. 6, p. 6.*

"Second Thoughts on First Nights." December 5, 1915,
Sec. 6, p. 6.*

"Second Thoughts on First Nights." December 9, 1915,
Sec. 6, p. 8.*

"A Shaw Comedy at the Playhouse." December 10,
1915, p. 13.*

"Reicher Presents Hauptmann Play." December 15,
1915, p. 15.*

"Second Thoughts on First Nights." December 19, 1915,
Sec. 6, p. 8.*

"Second Thoughts on First Nights." December 26, 1915,
Sec. 6, p. 6.*

"'Devil's Garden' a Sombre Drama." December 29,
1915, p. 11.*

"Second Thoughts on First Nights." January 9, 1916,
Sec. 6, p. 2.*

"Mrs. Fiske Returns in Delightful Role." January 19,
1916, p. 12.*

"Second Thoughts on First Nights." January 23, 1916,
Sec. 6, p. 6.*

"Second Thoughts on First Nights." February 27, 1916, Sec. 2, p. 7.

"Second Thoughts on First Nights." March 12, 1916, Sec. 2, p. 8.

"'The Merry Wives' at the Criterion." March 21, 1916, p. 9.*

"Second Thoughts on First Nights." March 26, 1916, Sec. 2, p. 8.

"'Justice' Done Here with Superb Cast." April 4, 1916, p. 11.*

"Second Thoughts on First Nights." April 9, 1916, Sec. 2, p. 8.

"Second Thoughts on First Nights." April 23, 1916, Sec. 2, p. 8.

"Century's 'Tempest.'" April 24, 1916, p. 11.*

"Second Thoughts on First Nights." May 7, 1916, Sec. 2, p. 6.

"Sir Herbert Tree in the 'Merchant.'" May 9, 1916, p. 9.*

"Second Thoughts on First Nights." August 20, 1916, Sec. 2, p. 7.

"Many Beauties in 'The Happy Ending.'" August 22, 1916, p. 7.*

"Second Thoughts on First Nights." August 27, 1916, Sec. 2, p. 8.

"Second Thoughts on First Nights." October 29, 1916, Sec. 2, p. 6.

"Second Thoughts on First Nights." November 12, 1916, Sec. 2, p. 6.

"Shaw and Dunsany in Grand Street." November 15, 1916, p. 9.*

New York Times (cont.)

"Beauty and Truth in 'The Harp of Life.'" November 28, 1916, p. 11.*

"Second Thoughts on First Nights." December 17, 1916, Sec. 2, p. 6.

"Gillette Returns in a Brilliant Play." February 6, 1917, p. 10.*

"Darkest Russia at the Bandbox." March 23, 1917, p. 7.*

" 'Out There' Power Most Appealing." March 28, 1917, p. 11.*

"Second Thoughts on First Nights." April 1, 1917, Sec. 8, p. 5.

"Three Negro Plays Played by Negroes." April 6, 1917, p. 11.*

"Second Thoughts on First Nights." April 8, 1917, Sec. 8, p. 5.

"An Acting Edition of 'Peter Ibbetson.'" April 19, 1917, p. 13.*

"Second Thoughts on First Nights." April 22, 1917, Sec. 9, p. 3.

"Satisfying Revival of Ibsen's 'Ghosts.'" May 8, 1917, p. 9.*

"Second Thoughts on First Nights." May 13, 1917, Sec. 8, p. 7.

"Ethel Barrymore Returns." May 26, 1917, p. 11.*

"The Play." August 6, 1919, p. 7.

"Second Thoughts on First Nights." August 31, 1919, Sec. 4, p. 2.

"Second Thoughts on First Nights." September 7, 1919, Sec. 4, p. 2.

"The Play." September 20, 1919, p. 14.

"The Play." September 22, 1919, p. 8.

"Second Thoughts on First Nights." October 5, 1919, Sec. 4, p. 2.

"The Play." October 7, 1919, p. 22.

"The Play." October 9, 1919, p. 6.

"The Play." October 17, 1919, p. 22.

"Second Thoughts on First Nights." October 26, 1919, Sec. 9, p. 2.

"Second Thoughts on First Nights." November 8, 1919, Sec. 8, p. 2.

"Second Thoughts on First Nights." November 23, 1919, Sec. 9, p. 2.

"The Play." November 26, 1919, p. 11.

"The Play." December 11, 1919, p. 11.

"The Play." December 19, 1919, p. 13.

"Second Thoughts on First Nights." December 28, 1919, Sec. 8, p. 2.

"The Play." January 22, 1920, p. 22.

"Second Thoughts on First Nights." January 25, 1920, Sec. 8, p. 2.

"The Play." February 4, 1920, p. 12.

"Second Thoughts on First Nights." February 8, 1920, Sec. 8, p. 2.

"Second Thoughts on First Nights." February 15, 1920, Sec. 8, p. 2.

"The Play." February 24, 1920, p. 11.

"The Play." March 8, 1920, p. 7.

"Second Thoughts on First Nights." March 14, 1920, Sec. 5, p. 5.

New York Times (cont.)

"The Play." March 17, 1920, p. 14.

"Second Thoughts on First Nights." March 21, 1920, Sec. 6, p. 6.

"Second Thoughts on First Nights." March 28, 1920, Sec. 5, p. 6.

"Second Thoughts on First Nights." April 4, 1920, Sec. 6, p. 6.

"Second Thoughts on First Nights." April 18, 1920, Sec. 6, p. 2.

"The Play." August 4, 1920, p. 14.

"Second Thoughts on First Nights." August 22, 1920, Sec. 6, p. 1.

"Second Thoughts on First Nights." September 26, 1920, Sec. 6, p. 1.

"The Play." October 5, 1920, p. 12.

"Second Thoughts on First Nights." October 10, 1920, Sec. 6, p. 1.

"The Play." October 19, 1920, p. 12.

"The Play." October 21, 1920, p. 11.

"Second Thoughts on First Nights." October 24, 1920, Sec. 6, p. 1.

"Second Thoughts on First Nights." November 7, 1920, Sec. 7, p. 1.

"The Play." November 11, 1920, p. 11.

"The Play." November 18, 1920, p. 18.

"Second Thoughts on First Nights." November 21, 1920, Sec. 6, p. 1.

"The Play." December 11, 1920, p. 11.

"Second Thoughts on First Nights." December 12, 1920, Sec. 6, p. 1.

"The Play." December 29, 1920, p. 8.

"The Play." January 18, 1921, p. 14.

"Second Thoughts on First Nights." January 30, 1921, Sec. 6, p. 1.

"The Play." February 5, 1921, p. 14.

"The Play." February 18, 1921, p. 16.

"Second Thoughts on First Nights." February 27, 1921, Sec. 6, p. 1.

"Second Thoughts on First Nights." March 6, 1921, Sec. 6, p. 1.

"The Play." April 19, 1921, p. 15.

"The Play." April 20, 1921, p. 11.

"Second Thoughts on First Nights." April 24, 1921, Sec. 6, p. 1.

"The Play." August 15, 1921, p. 14.

"Second Thoughts on First Nights." August 21, 1921, Sec. 6, p. 1.

"The Play." August 24, 1921, p. 12.

"The Play." August 31, 1921, p. 8.

"The Play." September 2, 1921, p. 9.

"Second Thoughts on First Nights." September 11, 1921, Sec. 6, p. 1.

"The Play." October 11, 1921, p. 22.

"The Play." October 18, 1921, p. 20.

"The Play." November 2, 1921, p. 20.

"The Play." November 3, 1921, p. 22.

New York Times (cont.)

"Second Thoughts on First Nights." November 6, 1921, Sec. 6, p. 1.

"The Play." November 8, 1921, p. 8.

"The Play." November 11, 1921, p. 16.

"Second Thoughts on First Nights." November 13, 1921, Sec. 6, p. 1.

"The Play." December 21, 1921, p. 26.

"Second Thoughts on First Nights." January 1, 1922, Sec. 6, p. 1.

"Second Thoughts on First Nights." January 22, 1922, Sec. 6, p. 1.

"The Play." January 28, 1922, p. 14.

"Second Thoughts on First Nights." February 19, 1922, Sec. 6, p. 1.

"The Play." February 21, 1922, p. 20.

"The Play." February 28, 1922, p. 17.

"The Play." March 6, 1922, p. 9.

"The Play." March 10, 1922, p. 18.

"Second Thoughts on First Nights." March 12, 1922, Sec. 6, p. 1.

"The Play." March 21, 1922, p. 17.

"The Play." March 23, 1922, p. 11.

"Second Thoughts on First Nights." April 9, 1922, Sec. 8, p. 1.

"The Play." April 14, 1922, p. 20.

"Second Thoughts on First Nights." April 16, 1922, Sec. 6, p. 1.

"Second Thoughts on First Nights." September 17, 1922, Sec. 6, p. 1.

"The Play." September 21, 1922, p. 18.

"Second Thoughts on First Nights." October 1, 1922, Sec. 7, p. 1.

"Second Thoughts on First Nights." October 8, 1922, Sec. 6, p. 1.

"That Benign Demon, George S. Kaufman." December 3, 1933, Sec. 9, p. 5.

2. <u>New York Herald</u>

"The Reviewing Stand." October 25, 1922, p. 8.

"The Reviewing Stand." October 29, 1922, Sec. 7, p. 1.

"The Reviewing Stand." November 17, 1922, p. 8.

"The Reviewing Stand." November 19, 1922, Sec. 7, p. 1.

"The Reviewing Stand." December 3, 1922, Sec. 7, p. 1.

"The Reviewing Stand." December 17, 1922, Sec. 7, p. 1.

"The Reviewing Stand." December 28, 1922, p. 6.

"Shouts and Murmurs." January 9, 1923, p. 14.

"Shouts and Murmurs." January 14, 1923, Sec. 7, p. 1.

"Shouts and Murmurs." January 16, 1923, p. 12.

"Shouts and Murmurs." January 28, 1923, Sec. 7, p. 1.

"Shouts and Murmurs." February 2, 1923, p. 12.

New York Herald (cont.)

    "Shouts and Murmurs." February 4, 1923, Sec. 7, p. 1.

    "Shouts and Murmurs." February 6, 1923, p. 12.

    "Shouts and Murmurs." February 13, 1923, p. 10.

    "Shouts and Murmurs." February 24, 1923, p. 9.

    "Shouts and Murmurs." March 10, 1923, p. 9.

    "Shouts and Murmurs." March 11, 1923, Sec. 7, p. 1.

    "Shouts and Murmurs." April 6, 1923, p. 12.

    "Shouts and Murmurs." April 11, 1923, Sec. 7, p. 1.

    "Shouts and Murmurs." April 22, 1923, Sec. 7, p. 1.

    "Shouts and Murmurs." April 23, 1923, p. 8.

    "Shouts and Murmurs." April 24, 1923, p. 10.

    "Shouts and Murmurs." May 16, 1923, p. 10.

    "Shouts and Murmurs." May 19, 1923, p. 7.

    "Shouts and Murmurs." May 21, 1923, p. 6.

    "Shouts and Murmurs." August 7, 1923, p. 8.

    "Shouts and Murmurs." August 18, 1923, p. 8.

    "Shouts and Murmurs." September 12, 1923, p. 8.

    "Shouts and Murmurs." October 7, 1923, Sec. 7, p. 1.

    "The Stage." October 30, 1923, p. 9.

    "Shouts and Murmurs." November 13, 1923, p. 9.

    "Shouts and Murmurs." November 23, 1923, p. 11.

    "The Stage." November 29, 1923, p. 15.

"The Stage." December 1, 1923, p. 9.

"The Stage." December 4, 1923, p. 9.

"Shouts and Murmurs." December 29, 1923, p. 5.

"The Wake of the Plays." December 30, 1923, Sec. 7, p. 1.

"The Wake of the Plays." January 6, 1924, Sec. 7, p. 1.

"The Reviewing Stand." January 7, 1924, p. 9.

"The Stage." January 8, 1924, p. 9.

"Shouts and Murmurs." January 22, 1924, p. 9.

"Shouts and Murmurs." February 6, 1924, p. 9.

"Shouts and Murmurs." February 12, 1924, p. 9.

"Shouts and Murmurs." March 12, 1924, p. 9.

"The Stage." March 18, 1924, p. 11.

3. New York Sun

"Harpo Marx and Some Brothers." March 20, 1924, p. 18.

"O'Neill's New Play 'Welded' a Melancholy Stage Study of Quarrel of Man and Wife." March 22, 1924, p. 4.

"Mademoiselle Eva Le Gallienne." March 24, 1924, p. 18.

"Shouts and Murmurs." March 29, 1924, p. 4.

"Mrs. Fiske in 'Helena's Boys.'" April 8, 1924, p. 24.

"Leah Kleschna After Twenty Years." April 22, 1924, p. 18.

"'The Emperor Jones' Revised." May 8, 1924, p. 20.

New York Sun (cont.)

"All God's Chillun Got Wings." May 16, 1924, p. 24.

"Shouts and Murmurs." May 26, 1924, p. 18.

"Weekly Log of the Navigator Among the Reefs of Broadway." May 31, 1924, p. 4.

"'What Price Glory' Magnificent." September 6, 1924, p. 3.

"Stark Young Submits 'The Saint.'" October 13, 1924, p. 18.

"Gayety in Thirty-fifth Street." October 14, 1924, p. 28.

"Through Darkest New England." November 12, 1924, p. 28.

"Plays and Players in These Parts." November 21, 1924, p. 26.

"Plays and Players in These Parts." November 29, 1924, p. 7.

"Richard Bird as Marchbanks." December 13, 1924, p. 7.

"Helen Hayes in 'Quarantine.'" December 17, 1924, p. 30.

"'Processional' at the Banick." January 13, 1925, p. 24.

"Lionel Barrymore Returns." January 16, 1925, p. 20.

"Plays and Players in These Parts." January 21, 1925, p. 14.

"Plays and Players in These Parts." January 26, 1925, p. 16.

"Jane Cowl at the Broadhurst." January 28, 1925, p. 12.

"Beyond in Macdougal Street." January 29, 1925, p. 18.

"Grace George in Fine Fettle." February 4, 1925, p. 12.

"Ibsen at the Actor's Theatre." February 25, 1925, p. 20.

"Ernest Truex in 'The Fall Guy.'" March 11, 1925, p. 16.

"Plays and Players in These Parts." March 14, 1925, p. 5.

"Plays and Players in These Parts." March 28, 1925, p. 5.

"Shaw's 'Caesar and Cleopatra.'" April 14, 1925, p. 22.

"Plays and Players in These Parts." April 27, 1925, p. 12.

"'Rosmersholm' in Spite of All." May 6, 1925, p. 22.

"Lionel Barrymore Once More." May 22, 1925, p. 4.

4. New York World

"The Stage." September 8, 1925, p. 14.

"The Stage." September 15, 1925, p. 18.

"The Stage." October 2, 1925, p. 14.

"The Stage." October 3, 1925, p. 11.

"The Stage." October 12, 1925, p. 13.

"Second Thoughts on First Nights." November 1, 1925, p. 2M.

"The Stage." November 12, 1925, p. 17.

"The Stage." November 13, 1925, p. 13.

"The Stage." November 16, 1925, p. 13.

"The Stage." November 17, 1925, p. 13.

New York World (cont.)

 "The Stage." November 24, 1925, p. 13.

 "The Stage." December 11, 1925, p. 16.

 "The Stage." December 15, 1925, p. 15.

 "Second Thoughts on First Nights." December 27, 1925, p. 2M.

 "The Stage." December 28, 1925, p. 11.

 "The Stage." January 30, 1926, p. 11.

 "The Stage." February 1, 1926, p. 11.

 "The Stage." February 3, 1926, p. 13.

 "Second Thoughts on First Nights." February 28, 1926, p. 3M.

 "The Stage." March 16, 1926, p. 13.

 "The Stage." March 17, 1926, p. 13.

 "The Stage." April 14, 1926, p. 17.

 "Second Thoughts on First Nights." May 9, 1926, p. 3M.

 "The Stage." August 26, 1926, p. 13.

 "The Stage." October 12, 1926, p. 15.

 "Second Thoughts on First Nights." November 14, 1926, p. 3M.

 "The Stage." November 16, 1926, p. 13.

 "The Stage." November 24, 1926, p. 15.

 "The Stage." November 26, p. 13.

 "The Stage." December 1, 1926, p. 17.

 "Second Thoughts on First Nights." December 5, 1926, p. 3M.

"The Stage. " January 4, 1927, p. 4.

"The Play. " January 11, 1927, p. 17.

"The Stage. " January 13, 1927, p. 15.

"Second Thoughts on First Nights. " January 23, 1927, p. 3M.

"The Stage. " February 14, 1927, p. 11.

"Second Thoughts on First Nights. " April 17, 1927, p. 3M.

"Second Thoughts on First Nights. " May 8, 1927, p. 3M.

"The Stage. " June 6, 1927, p. 11.

"The Stage. " October 11, 1927, p. 11.

"The Play. " October 26, 1927, p. 15.

"The Stage. " November 9, 1927, p. 13.

"The Stage. " November 18, 1927, p. 13.

"The Stage. " November 30, 1927, p. 13.

"The Stage. " December 8, 1927, p. 13.

"The Stage. " January 10, 1928, p. 15.

"Second Thoughts on First Nights. " January 29, 1928, p. 3M.

"Second Thoughts on First Nights. " February 5, 1928, p. 3M.

"Second Thoughts on First Nights. " February 19, 1928, p. 3M.

"The Stage. " February 22, 1928, p. 11.

"Second Thoughts on First Nights. " March 4, 1928, p. 3M.

174 / Bibliography

New York World (cont.)

"The Stage." March 20, 1928, p. 13.

"The Stage." March 27, 1928, p. 13.

"The Stage." April 11, 1928, p. 13.

"Second Thoughts on First Nights." April 29, 1928, p. 3M.

"Second Thoughts on First Nights." May 6, 1928, p. 3M.

"Second Thoughts on First Nights." May 20, 1928, p. 3M.

B. MAGAZINES

1. "Are We Out of the Woods?" Vanity Fair, January 1923, p. 35.

2. "The Child-Actor Grows Up." Everybody's Magazine, February 1920, p. 57.

3. "Desire Under the Elms." Vanity Fair, January 1925, p. 27.

4. "The Dollar After Next." Collier's, February 7, 1931, p. 10.

5. "Elmer, the Unexpected." Collier's, May 4, 1929, p. 15.

6. "An Emerging Masterpiece." Everybody's Magazine, February 1921, pp. 54-5.

7. "The Exclusive Managers." Vanity Fair, May 1929, p. 58.

8. "Excursions with Mr. Hackett." Bookman 53 (June 1921):361-2.

9. "Giving O'Neill Till It Hurts." Vanity Fair, February 1928, p. 48.

10. "Hamlet in Mufto." Vanity Fair, January 1926, p. 70.

11. "Hard Boiled Drama." Vanity Fair, November 1924, p. 38.

12. "The Haunted House of Lunt." Vanity Fair, March 1929, p. 60.

13. "The House of the Second Chance." Vanity Fair, December 1924, p. 41.

14. "How a Critic Gets That Way." Collier's, February 25, 1928, p. 12.

15. "I'm Glad I'm Absent-Minded." American Magazine, July 1932, p. 59.

16. "In Memoriam: Rose Field." Atlantic Monthly, May 1939, pp. 643-8.

17. "The Leak in the Sieve." Vanity Fair, March 1927, p. 54.

18. "Lest We Forget." Collier's, June 8, 1929, p. 7.

19. "The Long Run as a Curse." Everybody's Magazine, May 1921, pp. 26-7.

20. "Luck and Mr. Lunt." Cosmopolitan, April 1933, p. 56.

21. "Miss Kitty Takes to the Road." Saturday Evening Post, August 18, 1934, p. 14.

22. "Mr. Wilder Urges Us On." Atlantic Monthly, March 1943, pp. 121-3.

23. "Murder at 8:30 Sharp." Collier's, March 17, 1928, pp. 22-49.

24. "The New York Art Theatre." Vanity Fair, March 1923, p. 36.

25. "The New York Playgoer Erects a Theater." Vanity Fair, July 1923, p. 39.

26. "Other Times, Other Morals." _Vanity Fair_, June 1928, p. 80.

27. "Richard Mansfield." _Hamilton Literary Magazine_ 42 (November 1907):100-3.

28. "The Rise of Eugene O'Neill." _Everybody's Magazine_, July 1920, p. 49.

29. "A Ship Comes In." _Collier's_, April 11, 1931, p. 19.

30. "Shouts and Murmurs." _New Yorker_, February 16, 1929, p. 40.

31. "Shouts and Murmurs." _New Yorker_, December 14, 1929, p. 42.

32. "Shouts and Murmurs." _New Yorker_, March 22, 1930, p. 34.

33. "Shouts and Murmurs." _New Yorker_, July 26, 1930, p. 28.

34. "Shouts and Murmurs." _New Yorker_, March 12, 1932, p. 32.

35. "Shouts and Murmurs." _New Yorker_, March 19, 1932, p. 32.

36. "Staged in Moscow." _Collier's_, December 16, 1933, p. 22.

37. "The Story of Irving Berlin." _Saturday Evening Post_, February 21, 1925, p. 34.

38. "The Story of Mrs. Fiske." _Collier's_, November 21, 1925, p. 20.

39. "The Success of the Season." _Century_, July 1920, pp. 412-18.

40. "The Thirtieth Mrs. Tangueray." _Vanity Fair_, December 1924, p. 62.

41. "Walt Whitman--Dramatic Critic." _Bookman_ 53 (March 1921):75-7.

42. "What the Doctor Ordered." <u>Ladies Home Journal</u>, May 1941, p. 20.

43. "Who Is the Best Young American Actress?" <u>Pictorial Review</u>, April 1931, p. 2.

C. BOOKS WRITTEN BY ALEXANDER WOOLLCOTT

1. <u>The Command Is Forward</u>. New York: Century, 1919.

2. <u>Enchanted Aisles</u>. New York: Putnam's, 1924.

3. <u>Going to Pieces</u>. New York: Putnam's, 1928.

4. <u>The Letters of Alexander Woollcott</u>. Edited by Beatrice Kaufman and Joseph Hennessey. New York: Viking, 1944.

5. <u>Long, Long Ago</u>. New York: Viking, 1943.

6. <u>Mr. Dickens Goes to the Play</u>. New York: Putnam's, 1922.

7. <u>Mrs. Fiske--Her Views on Actors, Acting, and the Problems of Production</u>. New York: Century, 1917.

8. <u>The Portable Woollcott</u>. Edited by Joseph Hennessey. New York: Viking, 1946.

9. <u>Shouts and Murmurs</u>. New York: Century, 1922.

10. <u>The Story of Irving Berlin</u>. New York: Putnam's, 1925.

11. <u>While Romes Burns</u>. New York: Viking, 1934.

D. BOOKS EDITED BY ALEXANDER WOOLLCOTT

1. <u>As You Were</u>. New York: Viking, 1943.

2. <u>Two Gentlemen and a Lady</u>. New York: Coward-McCann, 1928.

3. The Woollcott Reader. New York: Viking, 1935.

4. Woollcott's Second Reader. New York: Viking, 1937.

II. PUBLISHED WORKS DEALING
WITH ALEXANDER WOOLLCOTT

A. NEWSPAPER ARTICLES

1. "Actors Vote on Critics." New York Times, August 3, 1927, p. 29.

2. "Alex. Woollcott Home." New York Times, June 3, 1919, p. 12.

3. "Alexander Woollcott to Lecture." New York Times, October 29, 1925, p. 28.

4. Atkinson, Brooks. "The Play." New York Times, October 18, 1929, p. 24.

5. _____. "The Play." New York Times, November 10, 1931, p. 28.

6. _____. "The Play." New York Times, November 27, 1933, p. 20.

7. _____. "The Play." New York Times, February 22, 1938, p. 18.

8. _____. "The Play." New York Times, October 17, 1939, p. 31.

9. _____. "Town Crier on Stage." New York Times, March 23, 1941, Sec. 9, p. 1.

10. Brown, John Mason. "The Play." New York Evening Post, November 10, 1931, p. 14.

11. Eustis, Morton. "'I'm Not an Actor' Says Mr. Woollcott." New York Post, November 14, 1931, Sec. D, p. 4.

12. Hall, Mordaunt. "Two Merry Pictorial Musical Comedies." New York Times, May 6, 1934, Sec. 9, p. 3.

13. Hutchens, John K. "The Late Town Crier." New York Times, January 31, 1943, Sec. 2, p. 9.

14. Lewis, Lloyd. "Woollcott Speaking." Chicago Daily News, December 29, 1937, p. 17.

15. Loos, Anita. "Miss Loos Pays a Call on a Rising Young Actor." New York Times, November 15, 1931, Sec. 8, p. 1.

16. Morehouse, Ward. "Broadway After Dark." The Sun, December 9, 1933, p. 10.

17. "Senate Passes Theatre Curb." New York Times, May 6, 1937, p. 26.

18. Sennwald, Andre. "The Screen." New York Times, May 8, 1935, p. 23.

19. Taylor, Laurette. "Actress Gets Back at the Critics." New York Times, May 1, 1922, p. 20.

20. "Woollcott Takes Lindbergh to Task." New York Times, May 26, 1941, p. 12.

B. MAGAZINE ARTICLES

1. Bellamy, Francis. "The Theatre." The Outlook and Independent, November 6, 1929, p. 389.

2. Gibbs, Wolcott. "Big Nemo-II." New Yorker, March 25, 1939, pp. 24-9.

3. _____. "Big Nemo-III." New Yorker, April 1, 1939, pp. 22-7.

4. Hutchens, John. "In Many Moods." Theatre Arts Monthly 13(December 1929):875-90.

5. Isaacs, Edith J. R. "The Critical Arena, the Theatre of Alexander Woollcott." Theatre Arts 26 (March 1942):191-6.

6. _____. "Fresh Fields, Broadway in Review." Theatre Arts Monthly 22(April 1938):247-55.

7. Kronenberger, Louis. "Down with Woollcott." Nation, December 18, 1935, pp. 720-1.

8. Krutch, Joseph Wood. "Drama." Nation, March 5, 1938, pp. 280-1.

9. _____. "Drama." Nation, October 28, 1939, pp. 474-5.

10. _____. "Drama, the Kinds of Comedy." Nation, December 2, 1931, pp. 621-2.

11. "New Trustees." Hamilton Alumni Review 1(January 1936):34-36.

12. "Summer Theatre." Life, September 1, 1941, pp. 53-7.

13. "The Theatre." Time, October 30, 1939, pp. 42-3.

14. "Town Crier." Newsweek, February 1, 1943, p. 63.

15. Troy, William. "Films." Nation, May 22, 1935, pp. 610-12.

16. Wilson, Edmund. "Woollcott and Fourier." Nation, February 6, 1943, pp. 194-6.

17. Young, Stark. "Theatre Guild Fore and Aft." New Republic, March 9, 1938, p. 132.

18. _____. "Three More Plays." New Republic, December 2, 1931, pp. 69-71.

C. BOOKS

1. Adams, Samuel Hopkins. A. Woollcott, His Life and His World. New York: Reynal and Hitchcock, 1945.

2. Atkinson, Brooks. Broadway. New York: Macmillan, 1970.

3. Behrman, S. N. Brief Moment. New York: Farrar & Rinehart, 1931.

4. Chaplin, Charlie. My Autobiography. New York: Simon and Schuster, 1964.

5. Chatterton, Wayne. Alexander Woollcott. Boston: Twayne, 1978.

6. Drennan, Robert E. The Algonquin Wits. New York: Citadel, 1968.

7. Hewitt, Barnard. Theatre U.S.A. New York: McGraw-Hill, 1959.

8. Hoyt, Edwin P. Alexander Woollcott: The Man Who Came to Dinner. New York: Abelard-Schuman, 1968.

9. Jones, Robert Edmond. The Dramatic Imagination. New York: Theatre Arts Books, 1941.

10. Krutch, Joseph Wood. American Drama Since 1918. New York: Braziller, 1957.

11. Langner, Lawrence. The Magic Curtain. New York: Dutton, 1951.

12. Lewis, Emory. Stages, the Fifty Year Childhood of the American Theatre. Englewood, N.J.: Prentice-Hall, 1969.

13. Teichmann, Howard. Smart Aleck, the Wit, World and Life of Alexander Woollcott. New York: William Morrow, 1976.

14. Toohey, John Peter. The Pulitzer Prize Play. New York: Citadel, 1967.

15. Zolotow, Maurice. Stagestruck: The Romance of Alfred Lunt and Lynn Fontanne. New York: Harcourt, Brace and World, 1965.

III. UNPUBLISHED MATERIALS

A. MANUSCRIPT COLLECTIONS

1. Cambridge, Massachusetts. Harvard University. Alexander Woollcott Collection.

2. Clinton, New York. Hamilton College. Alexander Woollcott Collection.

B. THESES

1. Walters, Henry. "Representative Trends in American Theatrical Criticism from 1900 to 1940." Ph.D. dissertation, Western Reserve, 1950.

APPENDIX:
Plays Reviewed by Alexander Woollcott

(Title, author, newspaper, date, page)

Abraham Lincoln, by John Drinkwater
        Times, 16/12/19, p. 18

Accused, by George Middleton
        World, 30/9/25, p. 16

Across the Border, by Beulah Marie Dix
        Times, 25/11/14, p. 11

Across the Street, by Richard A. Purdy
        Sun, 25/3/24, p. 22

Adam and Eve, by Guy Bolton and George Middleton
        Times, 15/9/19, p. 16

Adding Machine, The, by Elmer Rice
        Herald, 20/3/23, p. 8

Admiral, The, by Charles R. Kennedy
        Sun, 25/4/24, p. 22

Adventure of Lady Ursula, The, by Anthony Hope
        Times, 2/3/15, p. 9

Adventurous Age, The, by Frederick Witney
        World, 8/2/27, p. 13

Advertising of Kate, The, by Annie N. Meyer
        Times, 9/5/22, p. 22

Aglavaine and Selysette, by Maurice Maeterlinck
        Times, 8/5/16, p. 9; Times, 4/1/22, p. 11

Albert Carroll's Vanities of 1927, by Agnes Morgan (book and
    lyrics) and Max Ewing (music)
        World, 20/5/27, p. 11

Ali Baba and the Forty Thieves, by Knowles Entrikin
        World, 23/12/26, p. 13

Alias Jimmy Valentine, by Paul Armstrong
        Times, 9/12/21, p. 20

Alice in Wonderland, by Alice Gerstenberg
        Times, 24/3/15, p. 11

All God's Chilluns Got Wings, by Eugene O'Neill
        Sun, 16/5/24, p. 24

Along Came Ruth, by Holman Day
        Times, 24/12/14, p. 12

Altruism, by Karl Ettlinger
        Times, 14/11/16, p. 8

Amber Empress, by Marcus Connelly (book and lyrics) and
    Zoel Partenau (music)
        Times, 20/9/16, p. 7

American Born, by George M. Cohan
        World, 6/10/25, p. 15

American in France, The, by Eugene Brieux
        Times, 4/8/20, p. 14

American Tragedy, An, by Patrick Kearney
        World, 25/10/26, p. 13

Anathema, by Leonid Andreyev
        Herald, 11/4/23, p. 10

Ancient Mariner, The, by Eugene O'Neill
        Sun, 7/4/24, p. 20

And So to Bed, by James B. Fagen
        World, 10/11/27, p. 13

Androcles and the Lion, by George B. Shaw
        Times, 28/1/15, p. 9

Angel Face, by Harry B. Smith (book), Robert R. Smith (lyrics), and Victor Herbert (music)
Times, 30/12/19, p. 18

Angel in the House, by Eden Phillpotts and Basil M. Hastings
Times, 9/11/15, p. 13

Anna Ascends, by Harry C. Ford
Times, 23/9/20, p. 14

Anna Christie, by Eugene O'Neill
Times, 6/11/21, Sec. 6, p. 1

Annie Dear, by Clare Kremmer, Sigmund Romberg, Florenz Ziegfeld, and others
Sun, 5/11/24, p. 28

Another Comedy, by J. C. Nugent and Elliott Nugent
Sun, 28/4/25, p. 18

Another Way Out, by Lawrence Langner
Times, 14/11/16, p. 8

Antick, The, by Percey Mackaye
Times, 5/10/15, p. 11

Antony and Cleopatra, by William Shakespeare
Herald, 20/2/24, p. 11

Any House, by Owen Davis and Robert H. Davis
Times, 15/2/16, p. 9

Anything Might Happen, by Edgar Selwyn
Herald, 21/2/23, p. 8

Aphrodite, by P. Frondale and G. C. Hazelton (book) and Fevrier and A. Goetzl (music)
Times, 7/12/19, Sec. 9, p. 2

Apple Blossom, by William Le Baron (books and lyrics) and Fritz Kreisler and Victor Jacobi (music)
Times, 8/10/19, p. 22

Arabesque, by Cloyd Head and Eunice Tietjens
World, 21/10/25, p. 15

Aria da Capo, by Edna St. Vincent Millay
    Times, 14/12/19, Sec. 8, p. 2

Ariadne, by A. A. Milne
    Sun, 24/2/25, p. 20

Arms and the Girl, by Grant Stewart and Robert Baker
    Times, 28/9/16, p. 7

Arms and the Man, by G. B. Shaw
    Times, 4/5/15, p. 15; World, 15/9/25, p. 18

Artists and Models, by Harry Albert and M. Rubens (music)
    and Benny Davis and J. K. Brennan (lyrics)
        World, 16/11/27, p. 13

As It Was in the Beginning, by Arturo Giovanitti
    Times, 29/1/17, p. 9

As You Like It, by William Shakespeare
    Times, 17/3/14, p. 11; Herald, 24/4/23, p. 10

As You Were, by Arthur Wernperia (book and lyrics) and
    H. Darewski and R. R. Goetz (music)
        Times, 28/1/20, p. 22

Assumption of Hannele, by Gerhart Hauptmann
    Herald, 16/2/23, p. 11

At Mrs. Beam's, by C. K. Munro
    World, 26/4/26, p. 11

At 9:45, by Owen Davis
    Times, 16/8/19, p. 10

At the Barn, by Anthony P. Wharton
    Times, 1/12/14, p. 13

Aucassin and Nicolete, by Andrew Lang
    Times, 9/4/21, p. 9

Awakening of Spring, The, by Frank Wedekind
    Times, 31/3/17, p. 9

Awful Truth, The, by Arthur Richman
    Times, 19/9/22, p. 14

Battle Cry, The, by Anonymous
    Times, 2/11/14, p. 9

Be Yourself, by George S. Kaufman and Marc Connelly (book)
    and Lewin Gensler, Milton Schwarzwald, and Ira Gershwin
    (music)
        Sun, 4/9/24, p. 16

Bear, A, by Anton Tchekhov
    Times, 25/5/15, p. 15

Beaten Track, The, by J. O. Francis
    World, 9/2/26, p. 11

Beau Brummell, by Clyde Fitch
    Times, 26/4/16, p. 11

Beautiful Adventure, The, by George Egerton
    Times, 9/7/14, p. 12

Because of Helen, by Alan Brook
    Times, 14/11/20, Sec. 6, p. 1

Beggar on Horseback, by George S. Kaufman and Marc Con-
    nelly
        Herald, 13/2/24, p. 9

Beggar's Opera, The, by John Gay
    World, 29/3/28, p. 15

Behavior of Mrs. Crane, The, by Harry Segall
    World, 21/3/28, p. 13

Behold the Bridegroom, by George Kelly
    World, 27/12/27, p. 11

Behold This Dreamer, by Fulton Ousler and Aubrey Kennedy
    World, 7/11/27, p. 13

Belt, The, by Paul Sifton
    World, 20/10/27, p. 11

Best People, The, by David Gray and Avery Hopwood
    Sun, 20/8/24, p. 13

Betty, by Frederick Lonsdale and Gladys Unger (book and lyr-
    ics) and Paul A. Rubens (music)
        Times, 22/10/16, Sec. 2, p. 6

Beverly's Balance by Paul Kester
    Times, 13/4/15, p. 11

Bewitched, by Edward Sheldon and Sidney Howard
    Sun, 2/10/24, p. 26

Beyond, by Walter Hasenclever
    Sun, 29/1/25, p. 18

Beyond the Horizon, by Eugene O'Neill
    Times, 4/2/20, p. 12; Times, 10/3/20, p. 9; World,
    1/12/26, p. 17

Big Boy, by Harold Atteridge and Others
    Sun, 8/1/25, p. 28

Big Game, by Willard Robinson and Kilbourn Gordon
    Times, 25/1/20, Sec. 8, p. 2

Big Idea, The, by A. E. Thomas and Clayton Hamilton
    Times, 17/11/14, p. 13

Big Jim Garrity, by Owen Davis
    Times, 17/10/14, p. 11

Big Show, The, by John L. Golden (lyrics) and Raymond
    Hubbell (music)
    Times, 1/9/16, p. 7

Bill of Divorcement, by Clemence Dane
    Times, 16/10/21, Sec. 6, p. 1

Bit O' Love, A, by John Galsworthy
    Sun, 13/5/25, p. 22

Black Boy, by Jim Tully and Frank Dazey
    World, 7/10/26, p. 15

Blackbirds of 1928, by Dorothy Fields (lyrics) and Jimmy
    McHugh (music)
    World, 10/5/28, p. 15

Blond Beast, The, by Henry Meyers
    Herald, 3/3/23, p. 13

Blood and Sand, by Toth Cushing
    Times, 21/9/21, p. 16

Blue Bird, The, by Anonymous (Revue)
    Sun, 29/12/24, p. 18

Blue Bonnet, by George Scarborough
    Times, 30/8/20, p. 12

Blue Envelope, by Frank Hatch and Robert E. Homans
    Times, 14/3/16, p. 9

Blue Eyes, by Leon Gordon and LeRoy Clemens (book),
    I. B. Kornblum (music) and Z. Meyers (lyrics)
    Times, 22/2/21, p. 11

Blue Flame, The, by George V. Hobart and John Willard
    Times, 16/3/20, p. 18

Blue Kitten, The, by Otto Harbach and W. E. Duncan (book)
    and Rudolf Friml (music)
    Times, 14/1/22, p. 9

Blue Lagoon, The, by Norman MacOwan and Charleton Mann
    Times, 15/9/21, p. 16

Blue Peter, The, by E. J. Thurston
    Sun, 25/3/25, p. 18

Bluebeard's Eighth Wife, by Clariton Andrews
    Times, 20/9/21, p. 12

Bon-Bon, by Edgar Allan Poe
    Times, 1/3/20, p. 12

Bonbouroche, by George Courtline
    Times, 29/11/21, p. 20

Bonehead, by Arnold Kummer
    Times, 13/4/20, p. 12

Book of Charm, The, by John Kirkpatrick
    World, 4/9/25, p. 14

Boomerang, The, by Winchell Smith and Victor Mapes
    Times, 11/8/15, p. 9

Bottled, by Anne Collins and Alice Timoney
    World, 11/4/28, p. 13

Bought and Paid For, by George Broadhurst
    Times, 8/12/21, p. 17

Box Seats, by Edward Massey
    World, 20/4/28, p. 13

Breakfast in Bed, by Georges Feydeau
    Times, 4/2/20, p. 12

Breaking Point, The, by Mary R. Rinehart
    Herald, 17/9/23, p. 4

Breaks, The, by J. C. Nugent and Elliott Nugent
    World, 17/4/28, p. 13

Bride, The, by Stuart Oliver
    Sun, 6/5/24, p. 18

Bride of the Land, by William Hurlbut
    World, 31/3/26, p. 13

Broadway, by Philip Dunning and George Abbott
    World, 17/9/26, p. 15

Broadway and Buttermilk, by Willard Mack
    Times, 16/8/16, p. 5

Broken Wing, The, by Paul Dickey and Charles W. Goddard
    Times, 5/12/20, Sec. 7, p. 1

Brook, by Thomas P. Robinson
    Herald, 20/8/23, p. 8

Brother Ellis, by Larry Johnson
    World, 15/9/23, p. 18

Brothers Karamazoff, The, by Fydor Dostoievsky
    Herald, 27/2/23, p. 14; Herald, 20/11/23, p. 11

Brothers Karamazov, by Jacques Copeau and Jean Croue
    World, 4/1/27, p. 11

Bronx Express, by Owen Davis
    Times, 27/4/22, p. 12

Bubble, The, by Edward Locke
    Times, 6/4/15, p. 11

Buccaneer, by Maxwell Anderson and Laurence Stallings
    World, 3/10/25, p. 11

Buddies, by George V. Hobart (book) and B. C. Hilliam
  (music and lyrics)
        Times, 29/10/19, p. 11

Bully, The, by Julie H. Percival and Calvin Clark
    Sun, 27/12/24, p. 3

Bulldog Drummond, by Cyril McNeill
    Times, 8/1/22, Sec. 6, p. 1

Bunker Bean, by Lee Wilson Dodd
    Times, 3/10/16, p. 9

Bunny, by Austin Strong
    Times, 5/1/16, p. 13

Burlesque, by George M. Watters
    World, 2/9/27, p. 11

Bushido, by M. C. Marcus
    Times, 14/11/16, p. 8

Business Window, The, by Gladys Unger
    Herald, 11/12/23, p. 9

Butter and Egg Man, The, by George S. Kaufman
    World, 24/9/25, p. 16

Buzzard, The, by Courtenay Savage
    World, 15/3/28, p. 13

Caesar and Cleopatra, by G. B. Shaw
    Sun, 14/4/25, p. 22

Caesar's Wife, by W. Somerset Maugham
    Times, 25/11/19, p. 9

Caliban, by Percy Mackaye (book) and Arthur Farwell
  (music and lyrics)
        Times, 25/5/16, p. 11

Call of Life, The, by Arthur Schnitzler
    World, 10/10/25, p. 14

Call the Doctor, by Jean Archibald
    Times, 1/9/20, p. 14

Camel's Back, The, by Somerset Maugham
    Herald, 14/11/23, p. 9

Camille, by Alexandre Dumas fils
    Herald, 16/11/22, p. 12

Canary Cottage, by Oliver Morosco and Elmer Harris (book)
    and Earl Carroll (music and lyrics)
    Times, 5/2/17, p. 9

Canary Dutch, by Willard Mack
    World, 9/9/25, p. 14

Candida, by G. B. Shaw
    Times, 21/5/15, p. 13; Times, 23/3/22, p. 11; Sun,
    13/12/24, p. 7; World, 12/11/25, p. 17

Cape Smoke, by Walter A. Frost
    Sun, 17/2/25, p. 18

Captain Applejack, by Walter Hackett
    Times, 31/12/21, p. 14

Captain Brassbound's Conversion, by G. B. Shaw
    Times, 30/3/16, p. 11

Captain Kidd, Jr., by Rita J. Young
    Times, 19/11/16, Sec. 2, p. 6

Captive, The, by Arthur Hornblow, Jr.
    World, 30/9/26, p. 15

Care of Lady Camber, by Horace A. Vachell
    Times, 27/3/17, p. 9

Carnival, by C. M. Hardinge and Matherson Lang
    Times, 25/12/19, p. 20

Carnival, by Ferenc Molnar
    Sun, 30/12/24, p. 8

Caroline, by Harry B. Smith and Edward D. Dunn (book) and
    Edward Kunneke and Edward Rideamus (music)
    Herald, 1/2/23, p. 6

Challenge, The, by Eugene Walter
    Times, 6/8/19, p. 7

Champion, The, by A. E. Thomas and Thomas Louden
    Times, 9/1/21, Sec. 6, p. 1

Changelings, The, by Lee W. Dodd
    Herald, 18/9/23, p. 17

Charlatan, The, by Leonard Praskins and Ernest Pascal
    Times, 30/4/22, Sec. 7, p. 1

Charlot Revue of 1926, The, by Anonymous (A Revue)
    World, 11/11/25, p. 16

Charm School, The, by Alice D. Miller
    Times, 3/8/20, p. 12

Chastening, The, by Charles R. Kennedy
    Herald, 17/2/23, p. 9

Chauve Souris, by Anonymous
    Sun, 15/1/25, p. 20

Cheaper to Marry, by Samuel Shipman
    Sun, 16/4/24, p. 26

Cheating Cheaters, by Max Marcin
    Times, 10/8/16, p. 7

Checkerboard, by Frederic and Fanny Hottan
    Times, 20/8/20, p. 7

Cherry Orchard, The, by Anton Chekhov
    Herald, 24/1/23, p. 9; World, 6/3/28, p. 13

Chicago, by Maurine Watkins
    World, 31/12/26, p. 9

Chief, The, by H. A. Vachell
    Times, 23/11/15, p. 13

Chief Thing, by Nicolas Evreinoff
    World, 23/3/26, p. 11

Children of Earth, by Alice Brown
    Times, 13/1/15, p. 9

Children of the Moon, by Martin C. Flavin
    Herald, 18/8/23, p. 8

Children's Tragedy, The, by Benjamin Glazer
    Times, 12/10/21, p. 18

China Rose, by Harry L. Court and George E. Stoddard
    (book) and A. B. Sloanne (music)
        Sun, 20/1/25, p. 20

Chinese Love, by Clare Kummer
    Times, 1/3/21, p. 18

Chip Woman's Fortune, The, by Willis Richardson
    Herald, 9/5/23, p. 12

Chocolate Soldier, by Rudolph Bernauer and Leopold Jacobson
    (libretto) and Oscar Strauss (music)
        Times, 18/12/21, Sec. 6, p. 1

Choir Rehearsal, The, by Clare Kummer
    Times, 1/3/21, p. 18

Cinderella Man, The, by Edward C. Carpenter
    Times, 23/1/16, Sec. 6, p. 6

Cinders, by Rudolf Friml (music) and Edward Clark (lyrics)
    Herald, 4/4/23, p. 12

Circle, The, by Somerset Maugham
    Times, 13/9/21, p. 12

Circus Princess, The, by Julius Brummer, Alfred Grunwald,
    and Harry B. Smith (book and lyrics) and Emmerich Kal-
    man (music)
        World, 26/4/27, p. 15

Civilian Clothes, by Thompson Buchannan
    Times, 13/9/19, p. 9

Clare de Lune, by Michael Strange
    Times, 19/4/21, p. 15

Clarence, by Booth Tarkington
    Times, 22/9/19, p. 8

Claw, The, by Edward D. Dunn and Louis Walheim
    Times, 18/10/21, p. 20

Claw, The, by Georges Renavent
World, 13/1/27, p. 15

Clever Ones, The, by Alfred Sutro
Times, 29/1/15, p. 9

Clinging Vine, The, by Zelda Sears (book and lyrics) and
Harold Levy (music)
Herald, 25/12/22, p. 8

Close Harmony, by Dorothy Parker and Elmer Rice
Sun, 1/12/24, p. 20

Clouds, by Helen Brown
World, 3/9/25, p. 14

Clutching Claw, The, by Ralph T. Kettering
World, 15/2/28, p. 13

Coat-Tales, by Edward Clark
Times, 1/8/16, p. 7

Cobra, by Martin Brown
Sun, 23/4/24, p. 24

Cock O' the Walk, by Henry Arthur Jones
Times, 28/12/15, p. 11

Cock Robin, by Philip Barry
World, 13/1/28, p. 13

Cocoanuts, by George S. Kaufman (book) and Irving Berlin
(music and lyrics)
World, 9/12/25, p. 17

Cohan Review 1916, The, by George M. Cohan
Times, 10/2/16, p. 9

Come Out of the Kitchen, by A. E. Thomas
Times, 24/10/16, p. 14

Comedian, The, by David Belasco
Herald, 14/3/23, p. 8

Comedy of Errors, The, by William Shakespeare
Herald, 16/5/23, p. 10

Comic, The, by Lajoa Luria
World, 20/4/27, p. 13

Command to Love, The, by Rudolph Lothan and Fritz Gottwald
World, 21/9/27, p. 13

Common Clay, by Cleves Kinkead
Times, 27/8/15, p. 9

Connecticut Yankee, A, by Herbert Fields (book), Richard
Rodgers (music) and Lorenz Hart (lyrics)
World, 4/11/27, p. 13

Connie Goes Home, by Edward Childs
Herald, 7/9/23, p. 16

Conscience, by Don Mullally
Sun, 12/9/24, p. 26

Consequences, by H. F. Rubinstein
Times, 2/10/14, p. 11

Constant Nymph, The, by Margaret Kennedy and Basil Dean
World, 10/12/26, p. 11

Constant Wife, The, by W. Somerset Maugham
World, 30/11/26, p. 13

Coquette, by George Abbott and Ann P. Bridgess
World, 9/11/27, p. 13

Cordelia Blossom, by George Randolph Chester and Lillian
Chester
Times 9/12/20, p. 18

Cornered, by Dodson Mitchell
Times, 1/9/14, p. 9

Cosi Sia, by Tommaso G. Scotti
Herald, 17/11/23, p. 7

Countess Maritza, by Julius Brammer and Alfred Grunwald
(books and lyrics) and Emmerich Kalman (music)
World, 20/9/26, p. 13

Courting, by A. K. Matthews
World, 14/9/25, p. 16

Cousin Lucy, by Charles Klein
    Times, 28/8/15, p. 7

Cradle Snatchers, by Russell G. Medcroft and Norma
    Mitchell
        World, 8/9/25, p. 14

Cradle Song, The, by Gregorio and Maria Martinez
    World, 25/1/27, p. 11

Craig's Wife, by George Kelly
    World, 13/10/25, p. 15

Creaking Chair, The, by Allene T. Wilkes
    World, 23/2/26, p. 13

Creoles, by Samuel Shipman
    World, 23/9/27, p. 17

Crime, by Samuel Shipman
    World, 23/2/27, p. 13

Crime in the Whistler Room, The, by Edmund Wilson
    Sun, 10/10/24, p. 24

Critic, The, by Richard Sheridan
    Times, 31/1/15, Sec. 7, p. 6; Sun, 9/5/25, p. 4

Crooked Friday, The, by Monekton Hoffe
    World, 9/10/25, p. 14

Crooked Square, The, by Samuel Shipman
    Herald, 16/9/23, Sec. 7, p. 1

Crown Prince, The, by Zöe Akins
    World, 24/13/27, p. 13

Cup, The, by William Hurlbut
    Herald, 15/11/23, p. 9

Curiosity, by H. Austin Adams
    Times, 19/12/19, p. 13

Cymbeline, by William Shakespeare
    Herald, 3/10/23, p. 16

Cyrano de Bergerac, by Edmond Rostand
    Herald, 2/11/23, p. 9; Herald, 18/12/23, p. 11

Czar Feodor, by Leo Tolstoy
Herald, 9/1/23, p. 14

Czarina, The, by Melchior Lengyel and Lajor Biro
Times, 1/2/22, p. 22

Daddy Long Legs, by Jean Webster
Times, 4/10/14, Sec. 6, p. 9

Daddy's Gone a Hunting, by Zöe Akins
Times, 1/9/21, p. 18; Times, 25/9/21, Sec. 6, p. 1

Dagger, The, by Marian Wrightman
World, 10/9/25, p. 16

Daisy Mayme, by George Kelly
World, 26/10/26, p. 17

Damn the Tears, by William Gaston
World, 22/1/27, p. 11

Dancer, The, by Edward Locke
Times, 2/10/19, p. 20

Dancers, The, by Sir Gerald Bennett
Herald, 18/10/23, p. 9

Dancing Duchess, The, by C. V. Kerr and R. H. Burnside
(book and lyrics) and Milton Lusk (music)
Times, 21/8/14, p. 9

Dancing Mothers, by Edgar Selwyn and Edmund Goulding
Sun, 12/8/24, p. 10

Danger, by Cosmo Hamilton
Times, 23/12/21, p. 18

Danton's Tod, by Georg Buchner
World, 21/12/27, p. 14

Dark, The, by Martin Brown
World, 2/2/27, p. 13

Dark Angel, by Guy Arlen
Sun, 11/2/25, p. 32

Diversion, by John Van Druten
World, 12/1/28, p. 15

Doctor David's Dad, by Carrington North and Joseph J. Green
Sun, 14/8/24, p. 10

Doctor's Dilemma, The, by G. B. Shaw
Times, 27/3/15, p. 11; World, 22/11/27, p. 13

Doll's House, A, by Henrik Ibsen
Herald, 22/2/24, p. 9

Dolly Jordan, by B. Iden Payne
Times, 4/10/22, p. 26

Don Juan, by Henry Bastille
Times, 8/9/21, p. 14

Don Q. Jr., by Bernard S. Hubert
World, 28/1/26, p. 13

Donovan Affair, The, by Owen Davis
World, 31/8/26, p. 11

Don't Tell, by Graham Moffat
Times, 29/9/20, p. 12

Doormat, The, by H. S. Sheldon
Herald, 8/12/22, p. 8

Dope, by Hermann Lieb
World, 4/1/26, p. 11

Doubles, by Frank Stayton
World, 27/4/27, p. 15

Dove, The, by Willard Mack
Sun, 12/2/25, p. 14

Dover Road, by A. A. Milne
Times, 24/12/21, p. 7

Down Stream, by A. G. Herman and Leslie P. Eichhler
World, 12/1/26, p. 17

Dracula, by Bram Stoker
World, 26/10/27, p. 13

Dragon, The, by Lady Gregory
        Herald, 27/12/22, p. 12

Dragon's Claw, by Austin Strong
        Times, 15/9/14, p. 11

Dream Girl, The, by Rita J. Young and Harold Atteridge
    (book) and Victor Herbert (music)
        Sun, 21/8/24, p. 15

Dream Maker, The, by William Gillette
        Times, 22/11/21, p. 17

Dream Play, The, by August Strindberg
        World, 21/1/26, p. 13

Dreams for Sale, by Owen Davis
        Times, 14/4/22, p. 24

Dreamy Kid, The, by Eugene O'Neill
        Times, 9/11/19, Sec. 8, p. 2

Driven, by E. Temple Thurston
        Times, 15/12/14, p. 13

Duke of Killicrankie, by Robert Marshall
        Times, 7/9/15, p. 13

Dulcy, by George S. Kaufman and Marc Connelly
        Times, 15/8/21, p. 14

Dumb and the Blind, The, by Harold Chapin
        Times, 14/12/14, p. 13

Dumb Bell, by J. C. Nugent and Elliott Nugent
        Herald, 27/11/23, p. 11

Dummy, The, by Harvey J. O'Higgins
        Times, 14/4/14, p. 11

Dunce Boy, The, by Lula Vollmer
        Sun, 4/4/25, p. 5

Dust Heap, The, by Paul Dickey and Bernard J. McOwen
        Sun, 25/4/24, p. 22

Dybbuk, by S. Ansky
        World, 16/12/25, p. 15; World, 6/1/26, p. 13; World
        14/12/26, p. 13

Earl Carroll Vanities, by George Henry and Morris Hamilton (lyrics and music) and Stanley Rauh and William A. Grew (sketches)
    World, 25/8/26, p. 13

Earth, by Em Jo Basshe
    World, 10/3/27, p. 15

Earth, The, by James B. Fagan
    Times, 16/2/16, p. 9

Easiest Way, The, by Eugene Walter
    Times, 7/9/21, p. 14

East Lynne, by Mrs. Henry Wood
    World, 11/3/26, p. 13

East of Suez, by Somerset Maugham
    Times, 23/9/22, p. 16

Easy Mark, The, by Jack Larrie
    Sun, 27/8/24, p. 12

Easy Street, by Ralph T. Kettering
    Sun, 15/8/24, p. 5

Easy Virtue, by Noel Coward
    World, 8/12/25, p. 17

Egmont, by Johann Goethe
    Times, 21/4/15, p. 13

Egotist, by Ben Hecht
    Herald, 4/1/23, p. 12

Eight Thirty O'Clock Revue
    Herald, 10/1/24, p. 9

Eighteenth Chair, The, by Bayard Veiller
    Times, 21/11/16, p. 9

Eileen, by Henry Blossom (libretto) and Victor Herbert (score)
    Times, 25/3/17, Sec. 8, p. 5

Electra, by Sophocles
    World, 4/5/27, p. 17

Elga, by Gerhart Hauptmann
    Times, 24/2/15, p. 9

Fast and Grow Fat, by George Broadhurst
    Times, 2/9/16, p. 5

Fata Morgana, by Ernest Vajda
    Herald, 4/3/24, p. 11

Fedora, by Victorien Sardou
    Times, 2/11/22, p. 18; Herald, 24/1/24, p. 9

Fifty-Seven Bowery, by Edward Locke
    World, 27/1/28, p. 13

Fire and Water, by Harvey White
    Times, 5/10/15, p. 11

Firebrand, by Edwin J. Mayer
    Sun, 16/10/24, p. 26

First Fifty Years, The, by Henry Myers
    Times, 14/3/22, p. 11

First Flight, by Maxwell Anderson and Laurence Stallings
    World, 18/9/25, p. 12

First Is Last, by Samuel Shipman and Percival Wilde
    Times, 18/9/19, p. 14

First Love, by Zöe Akins
    World, 9/11/26, p. 15

First Man, The, by Eugene O'Neill
    Times, 6/3/22, p. 9

First Stone, The, by Walter Ferris
    World, 14/1/28, p. 11

First Year, The, by Frank Craven
    Times, 27/11/21, Sec. 6, p. 1

Five O'Clock, by Frank Bacon
    Times, 19/10/19, Sec. 8, p. 2

Fixing Sister, by Lawrence Whitman
    Times, 5/10/16, p. 9

Flame, The, by Richard W. Tully
    Times, 5/9/16, p. 7

Flesh, by A. J. Lamb
    Sun, 8/5/25, p. 24

Floradoa, by Owen Hall (book), E. B. Jones and Paul Rubens
    (lyrics) and Leslie Stuart (music)
    Times, 6/4/20, p. 18

Floriani's Wife, by Luigi Pirandello
    Herald, 1/10/23, p. 8

Fog, The, by Frederick Truesdell
    Times, 25/11/14, p. 11

Fog-Bound, by Hugh Stanislaus
    World, 2/4/27, p. 13

Fool, The, by Channing Pollock
    Herald, 25/10/22, p. 8

Fools Errant, by Louis E. Shipman
    Times, 22/8/22, p. 12

Foot Loose, by George C. Taylor
    Times, 15/8/20, Sec. 6, p. 1

Forbidden, by Dorothy Donnelly
    Times, 22/12/19, p. 19

Forbidden Fruit, by George Jay Smith
    Times, 8/5/15, p. 15

Forty Niners, by Ring Lardner, F. P. Adams, George S.
    Kaufman and Others
    Herald, 7/11/22, p. 10

Fountain, The, by Eugene O'Neill
    World, 11/12/25, p. 15

Fourth Music Box Revue, by Irving Berlin
    Sun, 2/12/24, p. 32

French Lady, The, by Samuel Shipman and Neil Twomey
    World, 16/3/27, p. 13

French Leave, by Reginald Berkeley
    Times, 9/11/20, p. 13

Frivolities of 1920, by William A. Maguire (book) and William
   B. Friedlander, Harry Auracher, and Tom Johnstone
   (music and lyrics)
      Times, 9/1/20, p. 22

Fugitive, The, by John Galsworthy
      Times, 20/3/17, p. 9

Full House, A, by Fred Jackson
      Times, 11/5/15, p. 15

Funny Face, by Fred Thompson and Paul G. Smith (book),
   George Gershwin (music) and Ira Gershwin (lyrics)
      World, 23/11/27, p. 13

Furies, The, by Zöe Akins
      World, 8/3/28, p. 13

Garden of Eden, The, by Avery Hopwood
      World, 28/9/27, p. 13

Garden of Paradise, The, by Edward Sheldon
      Times, 30/11/14, p. 9

Garden of Weeds, by Leon Gordon
      Sun, 29/4/24, p. 18

Garrick Gaities, by Richard Rodgers (music) and Lorenz
   Hart (lyrics)
      World, 11/5/26, p. 19

Gay Paree, by Harold Atteridge (book), Clifford Grey (lyrics)
   and Alfred Goodman, Maurie Rubenc, and J. F. Coats
   (music)
      World, 19/8/25, p. 13

Genius and the Crowd, by John T. McIntyre
      Times, 7/9/20, p. 20

Gentle Grafters, by Owen Davis
      World, 28/10/26, p. 15

Gentlemen Prefer Blondes, by Anita Loos and John Emerson
      World, 29/7/26, p. 15

George Dandin, by Moliere
      Sun, 7/4/24, p. 20

Go to It, by John L. Golden, John E. Hazzard, and Anne Caldwell
Times, 25/10/16, p. 9

Goat Song, The, by Franz Werfel
World, 26/1/26, p. 13; World, 1/2/26, p. 11

God Loves Us, by J. J. McEvoy
World, 20/10/26, p. 13

God of Vengeance, The, by Sholom Asch
Herald, 20/12/22, p. 14

Gold Diggers, The, by David Belasco
Times, 1/10/19, p. 20

Golden Age, The, by Lester Lonergap and Charlton Andrews
World, 25/4/28, p. 13

Golden Days, by Sidney Taylor and Marvin Short
Times, 6/11/21, Sec. 6, p. 1

Goldfish, The, by Gladys Unger
Times, 18/4/22, p. 15

Gondoliers, The, by William S. Gilbert and Arthur Sullivan
Times, 9/12/19, p. 15

Good Fellow, The, by George S. Kaufman and Herman J. Mankiewicz
World, 6/10/26, p. 15

Good Gracious Annabelle, by Clare Kummer
Times, 1/11/16, p. 9

Good Hope, The, by Herman Heijermans
World, 19/10/27, p. 13

Good News, by Laurence Schwab and B. G. De Sylva (book) and Ray Henderson and Lew Brown (music)
World, 7/9/27, p. 13

Good Old-Days, The, by Aaron Hoffman
Herald, 15/8/23, p. 16

Goose Hangs High, The, by James Forbes
Herald, 30/1/24, p. 9

Gorilla, The, by Ralph Spence
    Sun, 29/4/25, p. 22

Grab Bag, The, by Ed Wynn
    Sun, 24/10/24, p. 28

Grand Duchess and the Waiter, The, by Alfred Savoir
    World, 14/10/25, p. 11

Grand Duke, The, by Sacha Guitry
    Times, 2/11/21, p. 20; Times, 27/11/21, Sec. 6,
    p. 1

Granny Maumee, by Ridgely Torrence
    Times, 6/4/17, p. 11

Grasshopper, by Padraic Colum and Mrs. F. E. Washburn
    Times, 9/4/17, p. 11

Great Adventure, The, by Arnold Bennett
    Times, 26/2/21, p. 9

Great Broxopp, The, by A. A. Milne
    Times, 27/11/21, Sec. 6, p. 1

Great Catherine, by G. B. Shaw
    Times, 15/11/16, p. 9

Great Divide, The, by William V. Moody
    Times, 11/2/17, Sec. 3, p. 2

Great Gatsby, The, by Owen Davis
    World, 3/2/26, p. 13

Great God Brown, by Eugene O'Neill
    World, 25/1/26, p. 15

Great Lover, The, by Leo Ditrichstein and Frederic and
    Fanny Hutton
        Times, 15/11/15, p. 13

Great Necker, The, by Elmer Harris
    World, 7/3/28, p. 13

Great Way, The, by Helen Freeman and Horace Fish
    Times, 13/11/4, Sec. 6, p. 1

Green Goddess, The, by William Asher
    Times, 24/1/21, p. 14

Green Hat, The, by Michael Arlen
    Sun, 25/4/25, p. 4; World, 16/9/25, p. 18

Green Ring, The, by Zinaida Hippuis
    Times, 5/4/22, p. 22

Greenwich Village Follies, by George V. Hobart (book),
    Louis A. Hirsh (music) and Irving Caesar and John M.
    Anderson (lyrics)
    Times, 13/9/22, p. 18

Greenwich Village Follies, by Cole Porter (music) and Cole
    Porter, John M. Anderson, and Irving Caesar (lyrics)
    Sun, 17/9/24, p. 24

Greenwich Village Follies, The, by Harold Levey and Owen
    Murphy (lyrics and music)
    World, 25/12/25, p. 17

Gringo, by Sophie Treadwell
    Herald, 15/12/22, p. 14

Grounds for Divorce, by Guy Bolton
    Sun, 24/9/24, p. 26

Guardsman, The, by Ferenc Molnar
    Sun, 14/10/24, p. 28

Guilty Man, The, by Ruth H. Davis and Charles Klein
    Times, 19/8/16, p. 7

Guilty One, The, by Michael Morton and Peter Traill
    Herald, 21/3/23, p. 8

Gypsy Jim, by Oscar Hammerstein II and Milton H. Cropper
    Herald, 15/1/24, p. 7

H.M.S. Pinafore, by William S. Gilbert and Arthur Sullivan
    Times, 26/10/19, Sec. 9, p. 2; World, 12/4/26, p. 13

Habitual Husband, The, by Dana Burnet
    Sun, 26/12/24, p. 20

Hairy Ape, The, by Eugene O'Neill
    Times, 10/3/22, p. 18

Half Caste, The, by Jack McClellah
    World, 30/3/26, p. 13

Hamlet, by William Shakespeare
    Times, 26/10/19, Sec. 9, p. 2; Times, 17/3/20, p.
    14; Herald, 17/11/22, p. 8; Herald, 3/12/22, Sec. 7,
    p. 1; Herald, 1/12/23, p. 9; Herald, 2/2/23, p. 12;
    World, 12/10/25, p. 13; World, 10/11/25, p. 15

Hangman's House, by Willard Mack
    World, 17/12/26, p. 13

Happiness, by J. Hartley Manners
    Times, 7/3/14, p. 11

Happy Days, by R. H. Burnside (book) and Raymond Hubbell
    (music)
    Times, 25/8/19, p. 8

Happy Ending, The, by Jean and La du Roche Macpherson
    Times, 22/8/16, p. 7

Happy-Go Lucky, by Ian Hay
    Times, 25/8/20, p. 6

Happy Husband, The, by Harrison Owen
    World, 8/5/28, p. 15

Harem, by Avery Hopwood
    Sun, 3/12/24, p. 30

Harp of Life, The, by J. Hartley Manners
    Times, 28/11/16, p. 11

Hassan, by James E. Flecker
    Sun, 23/9/24, p. 20

Haunted House, The, by Owen Davis
    Sun, 3/9/24, p. 18

Have a Heart, by Guy Bolton and P. G. Wodehouse (book
    and lyrics) and Jerome Kern (music)
    Times, 12/1/17, p. 11

Hello Broadway, by George M. Cohan
    Times, 26/12/14, p. 7

Hello Lola, by Dorothy Donnelly (book and lyrics) and William
    M. Kernell (music)
    World, 13/1/26, p. 15

Henry IV, by Luigi Pirandello
    Herald, 22/1/24, p. 9

Henry's Harem, by Fred Ballard and Arthur Stern
    World, 14/9/26, p. 15

Her Cardboard Lover, by Jacques Deval
    World, 22/3/27, p. 13

Her Contemporary Husband, by Edward A. Paulton
    Times, 1/9/22, p. 16

Her Husband's Wife, by A. E. Thomas
    Times, 21/1/17, Sec. 2, p. 4

Her Soldier Boy, by Rita J. Young (libretto) and Emmer
    Kalman (score)
    Times, 7/12/16, p. 11

Here's Howie, by Fred Thompson and Paul G. Smith (book),
    Roger W. Kahn and Joseph Meyer (music), and Irving
    Caesar (lyrics)
    World, 2/5/28, p. 15

Hero, The, by Emery Pottle
    Times, 15/3/21, p. 14

Hero of Santa Maria, The, by Kenneth Goodman and Ben
    Hecht
    Times, 14/2/17, p. 7

Hidden, by William Hurlbut
    World, 5/10/27, p. 13

High Cost of Living, The, by Frank Mandel and Lew Fields
    Times, 26/8/14, p. 9

High Hatters, The, by Louis Sobol
    World, 11/5/28, p. 11

High Stakes, by Willard Mack
    Sun, 10/9/24, p. 24

Highway of Life, The, by Louis N. Parker
    Times, 27/10/14, p. 11

Him, by E. E. Cummings
    World, 19/4/28, p. 13

Hip Hip Hooray, by John J. Golden (lyrics) and Raymond
    Hubbell (music)
    Times, 1/10/15, p. 11

His Bridal Night, by Laurence Rising
    Times, 17/8/16, p. 9

His Honor Are Potash, Montague Glass and Jules E. Goodman
    Times, 15/10/19, p. 20

His Little Windows, by Rita J. Young and William C. Duncan
    (book and lyrics) and William Schroder (music)
    Times, 1/5/17, p. 11

Hit-the-Trail Holiday, by George M. Cohan
    Times, 14/9/15, p. 11

Hoboken Blues, by Marshall Gold
    World, 18/2/28, p. 11

Hole in the Wall, The, by Fred Jackson
    Times, 27/3/20, p. 11

Holy Terror, A, by Wendell Smith and George Abbott
    World, 29/9/25, p. 16

Home Fires, by Owen Davis
    Herald, 21/8/23, p. 16

Home Towners, by George M. Cohan
    World, 24/8/26, p. 11

Honeymooning, by Hatcher Hughes
    World, 18/3/27, p. 13

Honor of the Family, The, by Paul M. Potter
    World, 27/12/26, p. 11

and Harry Tierney (music)
Times, 19/11/19, p. 11

Irving Berlin's Music Box Review, by Frances Nordstrom,
William Collier, Thomas J. Gray, George V. Hobart, and
Others (book) and Irving Berlin (music and lyrics)
Times, 23/9/21, p. 18

Irving Berlin's Music Box Revue, by Irving Berlin (music and
lyrics) and Irving Berlin and Others (book)
The Combined New York Morning Paper, 24/9/23, p. 4

Isabel, by Arthur Richman
Sun, 14/1/25, p. 24

It Is the Law, by Elmer Rice
Herald, 30/11/22, p. 18

It's Up to You, by Augustin MacHugh and Douglas Leavitt
(book), Harry Clarke and Edward Paulton (lyrics), and
Manuel Klein, John McManus and Ray Perkins (music)
Times, 29/3/21, p. 20

Iz Zat So?, by James Gleason
Sun, 31/1/25, p. 5

Jack and Jill, by Frederic Isham and Otto Harbach (book),
and John Murry Anderson, Otto Harbach, and Augustus
Barratt (lyrics)
Herald, 23/3/23, p. 12

Jack in the Pulpit, by Gordon Morris
Sun, 7/1/25, p. 14

Jane Clegg, by St. John Ervine
Times, 25/2/20, p. 14

Jedermann, by Hugo von Hoffmannsthal
World, 8/12/27, p. 13

Jest, The, by Sam Benelli
Times, 20/9/19, p. 14; World, 5/2/26, p. 13

Jitta's Atonement, by Siegfried Trebitsch
Herald, 22/1/23, p. 8

Joannes Kreisler, by Carl Meinhard and Rudolph Bernauer
        Herald, 25/12/22, p. 8

John, by Philip Barry
        World, 5/11/27, p. 11

John Gabriel Borkman, by Henrik Ibsen
        Times, 14/4/15, p. 13; World, 30/1/26, p. 11

John Hawthorne, by David Lebovitz
        Times, 24/1/21, p. 16

Johnny Get Your Gun, by Dorothy Donnelly
        Times, 18/2/17, Sec. 2, p. 6

Jolly Roger, The, by A. E. Thomas
        Herald, 31/8/23, p. 8

Juarez and Maximilian, by Franz Werfel
        World, 12/10/26, p. 15

Julius Caesar, by William Shakespeare
        Times, 29/3/16, p. 9; World, 7/6/27, p. 13

June Love, by Otto Harbach and W. H. Post (book), Rudolf
    Friml (music), and Brian Hooker (lyrics)
        Times, 26/4/21, p. 20

Junk, by Edwin B. Shelf
        World, 6/1/27, p. 13

Juno and the Paycock, by Sean O'Casey
        World, 16/3/26, p. 13

Just a Woman, by Eugene Walter
        Times, 18/1/16, p. 12

Just as Well, by J. Hartley Manners
        Times, 7/3/14, p. 11

Just Herself, by Edward Sheldon
        Times, 24/12/14, p. 9

Just Life, by John Bowie
        World, 15/9/26, p. 17

Just Married, by Adelaide Mathews and Ann Nicholas
        Times, 27/4/21, p. 21

King Lear, by William Shakespeare
Herald, 10/3/23, p. 9

King Saul, by Paul Heyse
World, 19/9/23, p. 7

Kiss for Cinderella, A, by J. M. Barrie
Times, 26/12/16, p. 9

Kiss in a Taxi, by Clifford Gery
World, 26/8/25, p. 11

Kitty's Kisses, by Philip Bartholomue and Otto Harbach (book),
Con Conrad (music), and Gus Kahn (lyrics)
World, 7/5/26, p. 15

Knife, The, by Eugene Walter
Times, 13/4/17, p. 11

Kreutzer Sonata, The, by Langden Mitchell
Sun, 15/5/24, p. 24

La Belle Aventure, by G. A. de Caillavet, Robert de Flers,
and Etienne Rey
Times, 19/7/14, Sec. 7, p. 8

La Courturiere de Luneville, by Alfred Savoir
Sun, 26/3/24, p. 24

La Gringa, by Tom Cusing
World, 2/2/28, p. 11

La Passe, by Georges de Porto-Riche
Sun, 28/3/24, p. 28

La Porta Chiusa, by Marco Praga
Herald, 21/11/23, p. 11

La Tendreese, by Henri Batille
Times, 26/9/22, p. 18

Ladder, The, by J. F. Davis
World, 23/10/26, p. 13

Ladies Night, by Avery Hopwood and Charlton Andrews
Times, 10/8/20, p. 10

Last Waltz, The, by Oscar Strauss (score) and Harold Atteridge and Edward D. Dunn (book)
    Times, 11/5/21, p. 20

Laugh, Clown, Laugh, by David Belasco and Tom Cushing
    Herald, 29/11/23, p. 15

Laughing Lady, The, by Alfred Sutro
    Herald, 2/13/23, p. 10

Launzi, by Ferenc Molnar
    Herald, 11/10/23, p. 9

L'Avare, by Moliere
    Herald, 13/3/24, p. 7

Lawbreaker, The, by Jules E. Goodman
    Times, 7/2/22, p. 12

Lawful Larceny, by Samuel Shipman
    Times, 3/1/22, p. 20

Law of the Land, by George Broadhurst
    Times, 1/10/14, p. 11

Lazybones: A Chronicle of a Country Town, by Owen Davis
    Sun, 27/9/24, p. 5

Le Bourgeois Gentilhomme, by Moliere
    Sun, 20/11/24, p. 28

Le Misanthrope, by Moliere
    Herald, 22/11/22, p. 12

Le Monde on l'on s Ennuie, by Edouard Palleron
    Times, 18/4/16, p. 11

Le Poilu, by Pierre Veber, Maurice Hennequin, and
H. Maurice Jacquet
    Times, 10/10/16, p. 12

Le Poussin, by Edmond Giraud
    Times, 25/1/16, p. 9

Lea Lyon, by Alexander Brody
    Times, 3/2/16, p. 7

Love Call, The, by Edward Locke (book), Sigmund Romberg
(music) and Harry B. Smith (lyrics)
World, 25/10/27, p. 13

Love Child, The, by Martin Brow
Herald, 19/11/22, Sec. 7, p. 1

Love Em and Leave Em, by George Abbott and John V. A.
Weaver
World, 4/2/26, p. 13

Love for Love, by William Congreve
Sun, 1/4/25, p. 26

Love in a Mist, by Amelie Rives and Gilbert Emery
World, 13/4/26, p. 13

Love Is Like That, by S. N. Behrman and Kenyon Nicholson
World, 19/4/27, p. 15

Love of Mike, by Thomas Sydney (book), Harry B. Smith
(lyrics) and Jerome Kern (music)
Times, 16/1/17, p. 10

Love Nest, The, by Robert E. Sherwood
World, 23/12/27, p. 11

Lovely Lady, by James L. Williams
World, 15/10/25, p. 13

Love's Call, by Joe Byron
World, 11/9/25, p. 16

Loves of Lulu, by Frank Wedekind
Sun, 12/4/25, p. 24

Lovers and Enemies, by Michael Artrzybachelff
World, 21/9/27, p. 13

Lover's Luck, by Georges de Porto-Riche
Times, 8/10/16, Sec. 2, p. 6

Lower Depths, The, by Maxim Gorki
Herald, 16/1/23, p. 12

Loyalties, by John Galsworthy
Times, 28/9/22, p. 18

Levey (music)
    Sun, 26/11/24, p. 14

Maid in America, by Harold Atteridge, Sigmund Romberg,
    and Harry Carroll
    Times, 19/2/15, p. 9

Maid of All Work, by Dermont Derby
    World, 13/1/27, p. 15

Main Street, by Harvey O'Higgins and Harriet Ford
    Times, 6/10/21, p. 21

Major Barbara, by G. B. Shaw
    Times, 10/12/15, p. 13

Major Pendennair, by Langdon Mitchell
    Times, 27/10/16, p. 7

Make It Snappy, by Harold Atteridge (book and lyrics) and
    Jean Schwartz (music)
    Times, 14/4/22, p. 20

Malia, by Luigi Capuana
    Times, 10/9/21, p. 12

Malvaloca, by Serafin and Joaquin A. Quintero
    Times, 3/10/22, p. 22

Mama's Affair, by Rachel B. Butler
    Times, 20/1/20, p. 10

Mam'zelle Nitouche, by Meilhac and Milland (libretto) and
    Herve (music)
    Times, 27/4/15, p. 13

Man and Superman (Scene in Hell), by G. B. Shaw
    Times, 21/2/22, p. 20

Man and the Masses, by Ernst Toller
    Sun, 15/4/24, p. 22

Man in Enemy Clothes, The, by Andre Picard and Yves
    Mirande
    Sun, 6/12/24, p. 7

Man of Destiny, by G. B. Shaw
    World, 24/11/25, p. 13

Man or Devil, by Jerome K. Jerome
    Sun, 22/5/25, p. 24

Man Who Came Back, by Jules E. Goodman
    Times, 4/9/16, p. 5

Man Who Married a Dumb Wife, The, by Anatole France
    Times, 28/1/15, p. 9

Man with a Load of Mischief, The, by Ashley Duke
    World, 27/10/25, p. 15

Mandarin, The, by Herman Bernstein
    Times, 10/11/20, p. 18

Manhattan, by Leighton Osmum and Henry Hull
    Times, 16/8/22, p. 7

Man's Name, The, by Eugene Walter and Marjorie Claire
    Times, 16/11/21, p. 22

March Hares, by Harry W. Gribble
    Times, 12/8/21, p. 8; Herald, 13/3/23, p. 12; World,
    3/4/28, p. 13

Marco Millions, by Eugene O'Neill
    World, 10/1/28, p. 15

Margaret Schiller, by Hall Caine
    Times, 1/2/16, p. 9

Marie Antoinette, by Edymar
    Times, 23/11/21, p. 16

Marie-Odile, by Edward Knoblauch
    Times, 27/1/15, p. 9

Mariners, by Clemence Dane
    World, 29/3/27, p. 15

Marriage of Columbine, The, by Harold Chapin
    Times, 11/11/14, p. 13

Marriage of Kitty, The, by Cosmo Gordon Lennox
    Times, 19/12/14, p. 13

Married Woman, The, by Chester B. Fenald
    Times, 26/12/21, p. 21

Milady's Boudoir, by J. C. Drum
    Times, 30/10/14, p. 9

Mile a Minute Kendall, by Owen Davis
    Times, 29/11/16, p. 9

Mimick, by George S. Kaufman and Edna Ferber
    Sun, 25/9/24, p. 26

Miracle, The, by Vollmoeller
    Herald, 26/1/24, p. 9

Miracle Man, A, by George M. Cohan
    Times, 22/9/14, p. 11

Miracle of St. Anthony, A, by Maurice Maeterlinck
    Times, 8/5/15, p. 15

Mirage, The, by Edger Selwyn
    Times, 1/10/20, p. 14

Mirrors, by Milton H. Grooper
    World, 19/1/28, p. 11

Miss Information, by Paul Dickey and Charles N. Goddard
    Times, 6/10/15, p. 11

Miss Lulu Bett, by Zona Gale
    Times, 28/12/20, p. 9; Times, 23/1/21, Sec. 6, p. 1

Miss Springtime, by Emmerick Kalmen
    Times, 26/9/16, p. 9

Mister Antonio, by Booth Tarkington
    Times, 19/9/16, p. 9

Mister Pitt, by Zona Gale
    Herald, 23/1/24, p. 7

Mistress of the Inn, The, by Carlo Goldoni
    Herald, 22/11/23, p. 11

Mix-Up, A, by Parker A. Hord
    Times, 29/12/14, p. 11

Mob, The, by John Galsworthy
    Times, 11/10/20, p. 18

Morris Dance, The, by Granville Barker
    Times, 12/2/17, p. 7

Mountain Man, The, by Clare Kummer
    Times, 13/12/21, p. 24

Move On, by Charles B. Hoyt
    World, 19/1/26, p. 13

Mozart, by Sasha Guitry
    World, 28/12/26, p. 11

Mr. Lazarus, by Harvey O'Higgins and Harriet Ford
    Times, 6/9/16, p. 7

Mr. Merton of the Movies, by George S. Kaufman and Marc
    Connelly
        Herald, 14/11/22, p. 8; Herald, 13/4/23, p. 12

Mr. Pim Passes By, A. A. Milne
    Times, 1/3/21, p. 18

Mr. WU, by Harry M. Vernon and Harold Owen
    Times, 15/10/14, p. 13

Mrs. Jimmie Thompson, by Norman S. Rose and Edith Ellis
    Times, 18/4/20, Sec. 6, p. 2

Mrs. Partridge Presents, by Mary Kennedy and Ruth Haw-
    thorne
        Sun, 6/1/25, p. 16

Mud Turtle, by Elliott Manners
    World, 21/8/25, p. 11

Murray Hill, by Leslie Howard
    World, 30/9/27, p. 13

Music Box Revue, by Irving Berlin
    Herald, 24/10/22, p. 12

Music Master, The, by Charles Klein
    Times, 11/10/16, p. 12

Musk, by Leonie de Souiny
    Times, 15/3/20, p. 13

New Englander, The, by Abby Merchant
	Herald, 8/2/24, p. 9

New Gallentry, The, by F. S. Merlin and Brian Marlow
	World, 25/9/25, p. 14

New Morality, The, by Harold Chapin
	Times, 31/1/21, p. 10

New Poor, The, by Cosmo Hamilton
	Herald, 14/1/24, p. 9

New York Idea, by Langdon Mitchell
	Times, 29/9/15, p. 13

New World, The, by J. M. Barrie
	Times, 15/5/17, p. 11

Newcomer, The, by Michael Morton
	Times, 11/4/17, p. 11

Newcomers, The, by Joe Burrows and Will Morrissey
	Herald, 9/8/23, p. 8

Nice People, by Rachel Crothers
	Times, 3/3/21, p. 11

Nifties of 1923, by Sam Bernard and William Collier
	Herald, 27/9/23, p. 8

Night at an Inn, A, by Lord Dunsany
	Times, 24/4/16, p. 11

Night of Snow, by Roberto Brucco
	Times, 5/10/15, p. 11

Nightcap, The, by Max Marcin and Guy Bolton
	Times, 16/8/21, p. 18

Nightie Night, by M. M. Stanley and Adelaide Matthews
	Times, 10/9/19, p. 16

Nightstick, by John Wray
	World, 11/11/27, p. 13

Nine O'Clock Revue, by Harold Simpson and Morris Harvey
	(book) and Muriel Lillie and Others (music)
	Herald, 5/10/23, p. 12

Oh, Ernest, by Francis De Vitt (book and lyrics) and Robert
H. Bowers (music)
World, 10/5/27, p. 15

Oh! Mamma, by Wilton Lackays and H. W. Gribble
World, 20/8/25, p. 11

Oh, Please, by Anne Caldwell and Otto Harbach (book and
lyrics)
World, 22/12/26, p. 11

Old English, by John Galsworthy
Sun, 24/12/24, p. 5

Old Friends, by J. M. Barrie
Times, 15/5/17, p. 11

Old Lady 31, by Rachel Crothers
Times, 31/10/16, p. 11

Old Lady Shows Her Medals, by J. M. Barrie
Times, 15/5/17, p. 11

Old Man Out, by Paul Fox and George Tilton
Sun, 26/5/25, p. 22

Old Soak, The, by Don Marquis
Times, 23/8/22, p. 14

On Approval, by Frederick Lonsdale
World, 19/10/26, p. 15

On the Firing Line, by Henry O'Higgins and Harriet Ford
Times, 21/10/19, p. 13

On Trial, by Elmer Reizenstein
Times, 20/8/14, p. 11

One for All, by Ernest and Louise Cortle
World, 14/5/27, p. 13

One Glorious Hour, by Gerhardt Falkenburg
World, 15/4/27, p. 11

One Kiss, by Maurice Yvain and Clare Kummer
Herald, 28/11/23, p. 11

One Night in Rome, by J. Hartley Manners
      Times, 3/12/19, p. 20

One of the Family, by Kenneth Webb
      World, 23/12/25, p. 15

Only Girl, The, by Henry Blossom and Victor Herbert
      Times, 15/11/14, Sec. 7, p. 9

Only 38, by A. E. Thomas
      Times, 14/9/21, p. 22

Orange Blossoms, by Victor Herbert (music) and Bud de
   Sylva (lyrics)
      Times, 20/9/22, p. 18

Ostriches, by Edward Willbraham
      Sun, 31/3/25, p. 18

Othello, by William Shakespeare
      Sun, 12/1/25, p. 18

Other Rose, The, by George Middleton
      Herald, 21/12/23, p. 11

Ouija Board, The, by Crane Wilbur
      Times, 30/3/20, p. 9

Our Betters, by W. Somerset Maugham
      Times, 13/3/17, p. 9; World, 21/2/28, p. 13

Our Elsie, by Elsie Janis (book) and Elsie Janis, William
   Kernell, Richard Fechheimer and B. C. Hilliam (music)
      Times, 2/12/19, p. 11

Our Mrs. McChesney, by Edna Ferber and George V. Hobart
      Times, 20/10/15, p. 11

Our Nelly, by A. E. Thomas and Brian Hooker (book and
   lyrics) and George Gershwin and William Daly (music)
      Herald, 5/12/22, p. 12

Out of Step, by A. A. Kline
      Sun, 30/1/25, p. 18

Out of the Sea, by Don Marquis
      World, 6/12/27, p. 11

Pay Day, by Oliver D. Bailey and Lottie Meaney
    Times, 28/2/16, p. 7

Peasant Girl, The, by Herbert Reynolds and H. A. Alleridge
    (lyrics), Edgar Smith (book) and Oskar Nedbal and Rudolf
    Friml (music)
    Times, 3/3/15, p. 11

Peer Gynt, by Henrik Ibsen
    Herald, 6/2/23, p. 12

Peggy Ann, by Herbert Field (libretto)
    World, 27/2/27, p. 3M

Peg O' My Heart, by J. Hartley Manners
    Times, 15/2/21, p. 7

Pelican, The, by Fryn Tennyson
    World, 22/9/25, p. 13

Pelleas and Melisande, by Maurice Maeterlinck
    Herald, 5/12/23, p. 13

People Don't Do Such Things, by Lyon Mearson and Edgar M.
    Schoenberg
    World, 24/11/27, p. 19

Perfect Fool, The, by Ed Wynn
    Times, 27/11/21, Sec. 6, p. 1

Perfect Lady, A, by Channing Pollock, Rennold Wolf and
    Rose Stalk
    Times, 29/10/4, p. 11

Peripherie, by Frantisek Langer
    World, 3/1/28, p. 13

Personality, by Philip Bartholomae and Jasper E. Brady
    Times, 29/8/21, p. 14

Persons Unknown, by Robert Housum
    Herald, 26/10/22, p. 12

Peter Ibbetson, by John Raphael
    Times, 19/4/17, p. 13

Peter Pan, by James M. Barrie
    Times, 22/12/15, p. 11; Sun, 7/11/24, p. 28

Play's the Thing, The, by Ferenc Molnar
    World, 4/11/26, p. 13

Please Help Emily, by H. M. Harwood
    Times, 15/8/16, p. 7

Plot Thickens, The, by Thomas Beer
    Times, 6/9/22, p. 16

Plots and Playwrights, by Edward Massey
    Times, 22/3/17, p. 9

Plough and the Stars, The, by Sean O'Casey
    World, 29/11/27, p. 13

Pollyanna, by Elenor H. Porter
    Times, 1/10/16, Sec. 2, p. 9

Polly Preferred, by Guy Bolton
    Herald, 12/1/23, p. 8

Polygamy, by Harvey J. O'Higgins and Harriet Ford
    Times, 2/12/14, p. 13

Poor Fool, The, by Hermann Bahr
    Times, 22/3/17, p. 9

Poppy, by Dorothy Donnelly (book and lyrics) and Stephen
    Jones and Arthur Samuels (music)
    Herald, 4/9/23, p. 4

Porgy, by Dorothy and Du Bosse Hayward
    World, 11/10/27, p. 13; World, 18/3/28, p. 3M

Potash and Perlmutter, Detectives, by Montague Glass and
    Jules B. Goodman
    World, 1/9/26, p. 11

Pot-Luck, by Edward C. Carpenter
    Times, 30/9/21, p. 10

Power of Darkness, The, by Leo Tolstoy
    Times, 22/1/20, p. 22

Prince and the Pauper, The, by Van W. Brooks
    Times, 7/11/20, Sec. 7, p. 1

Princess Pat, The, by Henry Blossom (book and lyrics) and
    Victor Herbert (music)
        Times, 30/9/15, p. 11

Princess Turandot, by Carlo Gozzi
        World, 13/11/26, p. 13

Princess Virtue, by B. C. Hilliam and Gitz Rice (book) and
    Franz Liszt (music)
        Times, 5/5/21, p. 20

Processional, by John H. Lawson
        Sun, 13/1/24, p. 24; Sun, 27/2/25, p. 22

Prodigal Son, The, by Dario Niccodemi and Michael Morton
        Times, 8/9/14, p. 11

Professor's Love Story, The, by J. M. Barrie
        Times, 27/2/17, p. 9

Punch and Judy, The, by Abbe Caldwell and Hugh Ford (book)
    and Jerome Kern (music)
        Herald, 29/11/22, p. 8

Puppets, by Frances Lightner
        Sun, 10/3/25, p. 20

Puppets of Passion, by Rossi de San Secondo
        World, 25/2/27, p. 11

Purple Mask, The, by Matheson Land
        Times, 6/1/20, p. 9

Puzzles of 1925, by Elsie Janis, Blanche Merrill, Kalmer
    and Ruby, and Others
        Sun, 3/2/25, p. 20

Pygmalion, by G. B. Shaw
        Times, 25/3/14, p. 11; Times, 13/10/14, p. 11;
        World, 16/11/26, p. 13; World, 12/5/27, p. 13

Quarantine, by Tennyson Jesse
        Sun, 17/12/24, p. 30

Queen Victoria, by David Carb and Walter P. Eaton
        Herald, 16/11/23, p. 11

Queen's Enemies, The, by Lord Dunsany
        Times, 15/11/16, p. 9

Queen's Husband, The, by Robert E. Sherwood
        World, 26/1/28, p. 11

R. U. R., by Karel Capek
        Herald, 10/10/22, p. 8

Race with the Shadow, The, by Wilhelm von Scholz
        Herald, 21/1/24, p. 9

Rain, by John Colton and Clemance Randolph
        Herald, 8/11/22, p. 12

Rain or Shine, by James Gleason and Maurice Mack (book),
    Milton Aker and Owen Murphy (music), and Jack Yellen
    (lyrics)
        World, 10/2/28, p. 13

Rapid Transit, by Lajos N. Egri
        World, 8/4/27, p. 13

Red Blinds, by Edward Wilbraham
        World, 1/10/26, p. 15

Red Canary, The, by Harold Orlob (music), Will B. John-
    stone (lyrics) and William L. Baron and Alexander John-
    stone (book)
        Times, 15/4/14, p. 13

Red Dawn, The, by Thomas Dixon
        Times, 7/8/19, p. 8

Red Falcon, The, by Mrs. Tremble Bradley and George
    Broadhurst
        Sun, 8/10/24, p. 26

Red Light Annie, by Norman Houston and Sam Forrest
        Herald, 22/8/23, p. 8

Red Puppy, The, by Andre Picard
        Herald, 21/12/22, p. 8

Rented Earl, The, by Salisbury Field
        Times, 9/2/15, p. 9

Road to Mandalay, The, by W. H. Post (book), William
   McKenna (lyrics), and Oreste Vessela (music)
      Times, 2/3/16, p. 9

Road to Rome, The, by Robert E. Sherwood
      World, 1/2/27, p. 15

Robbery, The, by Clare Kummer
      Times, 1/3/21, p. 18

Robert E. Lee, by John Drinkwater
      Herald, 21/11/23, p. 11

Roger Bloomer, by John Howard Lawson
      Herald, 2/2/23, p. 8

Rolling Stones, by Edgar Selwyn
      Times, 18/8/15, p. 11

Rollo's Wild Oat, by Clare Kummer
      Times, 24/11/20, p. 14

Roly-Boly Eyes, by Edgar A. Woolf (book and lyrics) and
   Eddie Brown and Louis Gruen (music)
      Times, 26/9/19, p. 11

Romance, by Edward Sheldon
      Times, 6/3/21, Sec. 6, p. 1

Romantic Age, The, by A. A. Milne
      Herald, 15/11/22, p. 12

Romantic Young Lady, The, by Helen and Harley G. Baker
      World, 5/5/26, p. 17

Romantic Young Lady, The, by Martinez Sierra
      World, 5/5/27, p. 15

Romeo and Juliet, by William Shakespeare
      Herald, 28/12/22, p. 6; Herald, 25/1/23, p. 8;
      Herald, 2/2/23, p. 12

Rope, by David Wallace and T. S. Stribling
      World, 23/2/28, p. 13

Rosalie, by Guy Bolton and William A. McGuire (book),
   George Gershwin and Sigmund Romberg (music), and

P. G. Wodehouse and Ira Gershwin (lyrics)
World, 11/1/28, p. 19

Rosalind, by J. M. Barrie
Times, 7/9/15, p. 13

Rose Bernd, by Gerhart Hauptmann
Times, 27/9/22, p. 18

Rose Briar, by Booth Tarkington
Herald, 26/12/22, p. 10

Rose Girl, The, by William C. Duncan (book and lyrics) and
Anselem Goetze (music)
Times, 12/2/21, p. 11

Rose Marie, by Otto Harbarch and Oscar Hammerstein II
(book and lyrics) and Rudolf Friml and Herbert Stolhart
(music)
Sun, 3/10/24, p. 26

Rose of Stambowl, by Leo Fail and Sigmund Romberg (score)
and Harold Atteridge (book and lyrics)
Times, 8/3/22, p. 11

Roseanne, by Nan B. Stephens
Herald, 31/12/23, p. 7

Rosmersholm, by Henrik Ibsen
Sun, 6/5/25, p. 22

Round the Town, by Marc Connelly and George Kaufman,
and Others
Sun, 22/5/24, p. 20

Royal Family, The, by George S. Kaufman and Edna Ferber
World, 29/12/27, p. 13; World, 30/4/28, p. 11

Royal Fandango, A, by Zöe Akins
Herald, 13/11/23, p. 9

Rubicon, The, by Henry Baron
Times, 22/2/22, p. 13

Ruddigore, by W. S. Gilbert and A. S. Sullivan
World, 21/5/27, p. 15

Ruggles of Red Gap, by Harrison Rhodes and Leon Wilson (book), Sigmund Romberg (music) and Harold Atteridge (lyrics)
Times, 25/12/15, p. 7

Ruined Lady, The, by Frances Nordstrom
Times, 21/1/20, p. 10

Ruint, by Hatcher Hughes
Sun, 8/4/25, p. 18

Rule of Three, The, by Guy Bolton
Times, 17/2/14, p. 11

Sacred and Profane Love, by Arnold Bennett
Times, 24/2/20, p. 11

Sadie Love, by Avery Hopwood
Times, 30/11/15, p. 13

Saint, The, by Stark Young
Sun, 13/10/24, p. 18

Saint Joan, by G. B. Shaw
Herald, 29/12/23, p. 5

Salamander, The, by Owen Johnson
Times, 24/10/14, p. 18

Sally, by Guy Bolton (book), Clifford Gray (lyrics), and Jerome Kern and Victor Herbert (music)
Times, 22/12/20, p. 16

Salome, by Oscar Wilde
Herald, 9/5/23, p. 12

Salvation, by Sidney Howard and Charles MacArthur
World, 1/2/28, p. 13

Sam Abramovitch, by Francois Porche
World, 20/1/27, p. 13

Samson and Delilah, by Sven Lange
Times, 18/11/20, p. 18

Sandro Botticelli, by Mercedes de Acosta
Herald, 27/3/23, p. 12

Second Man, The, by S. N. Behrman
    World, 12/4/27, p. 13

Second Mrs. Tanqueray, by Arthur W. Pinero
    Sun, 28/10/24, p. 20

Secret Strings, by Kate Jordan
    Times, 31/12/14, p. 9

Secrets, by Rudolf Besier and Mary Edington
    Herald, 27/12/22, p. 12

See My Lawyer, by Max Marcin
    Times, 3/9/15, p. 9

See-Saw, by Earl D. Biggers (book and lyrics) and Louis A.
    Hirsch (music)
    Times, 24/9/19, p. 21

Seed of the Brute, by Knowles Entrikin
    World, 2/11/26, p. 15

Seremonda, by William Lindsey
    Times, 2/1/17, p. 19

Serpent's Tooth, A, by Arthur Richman
    Times, 25/8/22, p. 8

Servant in the House, The, by Charles R. Kennedy
    Times, 3/5/21, p. 20; Sun, 9/4/25, p. 22

Seven Chances, by Roi C. Megrue
    Times, 9/8/16, p. 9

Seventh Heaven, by Austin Strong
    Herald, 30/10/22, p. 6

Sganarelle, by Moliere
    Times, 22/3/17, p. 9

Shadow, The, by Dario Niccodemi and Michael Morton
    Times, 26/1/15, p. 11

Shadow, The, by Eden Phillpotts
    Times, 25/4/22, p. 14

Shall We Join the Ladies?, by J. M. Barrie
    Sun, 14/1/25, p. 24

Shame Woman, The, by Lulu Vollmer
    Herald, 17/10/23, p. 11

Shangai Gesture, The, by John Colton
    World, 2/27/26, p. 13

She Had to Know, by Paul Geraldy
    Sun, 4/2/25, p. 12

She Stoops to Conquer, by Oliver Goldsmith
    World, 15/5/28, p. 13

She Would and She Did, by Mark Reed
    Times, 12/10/19, p. 18

Shelf, The, by Dorrance Davis
    World, 28/9/26, p. 15

Sherman Was Right, by Frank Mendel
    Times, 27/10/15, p. 11

She's in Again, by Thomas J. Gray
    Times, 18/5/15, p. 13

She's My Baby, by Guy Bolton, Bert Kalmar, Harry Ruby
    (book), Richard Rodgers (music), and Lorenz Hart (lyrics)
    World, 4/1/28, p. 15

Shirley Kaye, by Hulbert Footnes
    Times, 31/12/16, Sec. 2, p. 4

Show Booth, by Alexander Blok
    Herald, 4/4/23, p. 12

Show Girl, The, by James Forbes
    Times, 1/1/15, p. 17

Show-Off, The, by George Kelly
    Herald, 6/2/24, p. 9

Shuffle Along, by Irvin C. Miller (book) and Maceo Pinkard
    (lyrics and music)
    Herald, 28/11/22, p. 12

Sign on the Door, The, by Channing Pollock
    Times, 20/12/19, p. 14

Skin Deep, by Lynn Starling
World, 18/10/27, p. 15

Skin Game, The, by John Galsworthy
Times, 21/10/20, p. 11

Skull, The, by Bernard J. McOwen and Harry E. Humphry
World, 24/4/28, p. 13

Sky High, by Harold Atteridge and Harry Graham (book) and
Robert Stolz, Alfred Goodman, Carlton Kelsey, Maurice
Ruben, and Clifford Gorey (music)
Sun, 3/3/25, p. 20

Smilin Through, by Allan L. Martin
Times, 31/12/19, p. 5

Smooth as Silk, by Willard Mack
Times, 23/2/21, p. 18

So Am I, by C. M. Selling
World, 28/1/28, p. 11

So Much for So Much, by Willard Mack
Times, 5/16/14, p. 13

So This Is London, by Arthur Goodrich
Times, 31/8/22, p. 18

Some Baby, by Zellah Covington, Jules Simonson, and Percival Knight
Times, 17/8/15, p. 9

Some Party, by Silvio Hein, Raymond Hubbell, Percy Wen-
rich, and Gustav Kerker
Times, 17/4/22, p. 22

Somebody's Luggage, by Mark E. Swan
Times, 29/8/16, p. 7

Son-Daughter, The, by George Scarborough
Times, 20/11/19, p. 11

Song and Dance Man, The, by George M. Cohan
Herald, 1/1/22, p. 17

Song of Songs, The, by Edward Sheldon
Times, 23/12/14, p. 13

Spring 3100, by Argyil Campbell and Willard Mack
  World, 16/2/28, p. 11

Springboard, The, by Alice D. Miller
  World, 13/10/27, p. 13

Springtime of Youth, by Matthey C. Woodward and Cyrus Ward (lyrics), and Walter Kollo and Sigmund Romberg (musical numbers)
  Herald, 27/10/22, p. 12

Squall, The, by Jean Bart
  World, 12/11/26, p. 13

Square Peg, A, by Lewis Beach
  Herald, 29/1/23, p. 8

Starlight, by Gladys Unger
  Sun, 4/3/24, p. 14

Steamship Tenacity, by Charles Vildrac
  Times, 3/1/22, p. 20

Step this Way, by Edgar Smith (book), E. Ray Goetz (lyrics) and Bert Grant (music)
  Times, 30/5/16, p. 7

Still Waters, by Augustus Thomas
  World, 2/3/26, p. 15

Stork, The, by Laszio Fodor
  Sun, 27/1/25, p. 12

Storm, The, by Langdon McCormick
  Times, 3/10/19, p. 19

Stranger than Fiction, by E. H. Sothern
  Times, 6/3/17, p. 9

Straw, The, by Eugene O'Neill
  Times, 11/11/21, p. 16

Strings, by C. K. Munro
  World, 27/4/26, p. 13

Strong, The, by Henry Baron
  Herald, 27/2/24, p. 9

Stronger Than Love, by Dario Niccodemi
World, 30/12/25, p. 11

Successful Calamity, by Clare Kummer
Times, 6/2/17, p. 10

Sugar House, The, by Alice Brown
Times, 8/10/16, Sec. 2, p. 6

Sunny, by Otto Harbach and Oscar Hammerstein (book and
lyrics) and Jerome Kern (music)
World, 23/9/25, p. 12

Sunny Days, by Clifford Grey and W. C. Duncan (book and
lyrics) and Jean Schwartz (music)
World, 9/2/28, p. 11

Sunshine, by Henry C. White
World, 18/8/26, p. 15

Sure Fire, by Ralph Murphy
World, 21/10/26, p. 15

Survival of the Fittest, by George Harrison
Times, 15/3/21, p. 14

Suzette, by Roy Dixon (book and lyrics) and Arthur H. Gutman
(music)
Times, 25/11/21, p. 18

Suzy, by Andre Bard
Times, 28/1/16, p. 10

Swan, The, by Ferenc Molnar
Herald, 24/10/23, p. 9; Sun, 29/8/24, p. 16

Sweet Nell of Old Drury, by Paul Kester
Herald, 19/5/2, p. 7

Swifty, by John Peter Toohey and Walter C. Percival
Herald, 17/10/12, p. 8

Swords, by Sidney Howard
Times, 2/9/21, p. 9

Sybil, by Harry Gesham (book) and Victor Jacobi (music)
Times, 11/1/16, p. 11

That Awful Mrs. Eaton, by John Farrar and Stephen V. Benet
    Sun, 30/9/24, p. 26

That Sort, by Basil Macdonald Hastings
    Times, 7/11/14, p. 11

These Charming People, by Michael Arlen
    World, 7/10/25, p. 11

These Modern Women, by Laurence Langner
    World, 14/2/28, p. 11

They Knew What They Wanted, by Sidney Howard
    Sun, 25/11/24, p. 22

Thief, The, by Henri Bernstein
    World, 23/4/27, p. 13

Thin Ice, by Perceval Knight
    Times, 2/10/22, p. 20

Third Party, A, by Jocelyn Brandon and Frederick Arthur
    Times, 4/8/14, p. 11

This Was a Man, by Noel Coward
    World, 24/11/26, p. 25

This Woman Business, by Benn W. Levy
    World, 8/12/26, p. 15

Thoroughbreds, by Lewis B. Ely and Sam Forrest
    Sun, 9/9/24, p. 18

Those Who Walk in Darkness, by Owen Davis
    Times, 15/8/19, p. 12

Thou Desperate Pilot, by Zöe Akins
    World, 8/3/27, p. 13

Three from the Earth, by Djuna Barnes
    Times, 9/11/19, Sec. 8, p. 2

Three Live Ghosts, by Frederic S. Isham
    Times, 30/9/20, p. 12

Three Musketeers, by Rudolph Friml (music), and P. G.
    Wodehouse and Clifford Grey (lyrics)
        World, 14/3/28, p. 13

Under Fire, by Roi C. Megrue
    Times, 13/8/15, p. 9

Under Sentence, by Roi C. Megrue and Irwin S. Cobb
    Times, 4/10/16, p. 9

Unknown Woman, The, by Marjorie Blaine and Willard Mack
    Times, 11/11/19, p. 11

Unwritten Chapter, The, by Samuel Shipman and Victor Victor
    Times, 12/10/20, p. 18

Up the Line, by Henry F. Carlton
    World, 23/11/26, p. 15

Vagabond, The, by William Collison
    Herald, 28/12/23, p. 9

Van Dyck, The, by Cosmo G. Lennox
    Times, 12/10/21, p. 18

Varying Shore, The, by Zöe Akins
    Times, 6/12/21, p. 24

Verge, The, by Susan Glaspell
    Times, 15/11/21, p. 23

Very Minute, The, by John Meehan
    Times, 10/4/17, p. 11

Very Wise Virgin, A, by Sam January
    World, 3/6/27, p. 13

Victim, The, by Ossip Dymow
    Times, 30/3/15, p. 11

Village Eyvind of the Hills, The, by Johann Sigurjonsson
    Times, 2/2/21, p. 14

Virgin, The, by Arthur Corning
    World, 23/2/26, p. 13

Virgin of Bethulia, by Gladys Unger
    Sun, 26/2/25, p. 20

Virginia Runs Away, by Sidney Rosenfield
    Herald, 9/11/23, p. 9

Vogues, by Fred Thompson and Clifford Grey (book and lyrics) and Herbert Stothart (music)
    Sun, 28/3/24, p. 28

Vogues of 1924, by Fred Thompson and Clifford Grey (book and lyrics) and Herbert Stothart (music)
    Sun, 29/5/24, p. 6

Voice from the Minaret, The, by Robert Hichens
    Times, 31/1/22, p. 11

Volpone, by Stefan Zweig
    World, 10/4/28, p. 13

Voltaire, by Leila Taylor and Gertrude Purcell
    Times, 21/3/22, p. 17

Vortex, The, by Noel Coward
    World, 17/9/25, p. 15

Wait Till We're Married, by Hutcheson Boyd and Rudolph Bonner
    Times, 27/9/21, p. 14

Wake Up Jonathan, by Hatcher Hughes and Elmer Rice
    Times, 18/1/21, p. 14

Wall Street, by James N. Rosenberg
    World, 21/4/27, p. 15

Waltz of the Dogs, The, by Leonid Andreyev
    World, 26/4/28, p. 13

Wanderer, The, by Maurice V. Samuels
    Times, 2/2/17, p. 9

Wandering Jew, The, by E. Temple Thurston
    Times, 27/10/21, p. 22

Wasp, The, by Thomas F. Fallon
    Herald, 28/3/23, p. 8

Watch Your Step, by Irving Berlin (music and lyrics) and H. B. Smith (book)
    Times, 9/12/14, p. 13

Way of the World, The, by William Congreve
    Sun, 29/11/24, p. 7

Way Things Happen, The, by Clemence Dane
    Herald, 29/1/24, p. 9

We Girls, by Frederic and Fanny Hatton
    Times, 10/11/21, p. 20

We Moderns, by Israel Zangwill
    Herald, 12/3/24, p. 9

Wedding Bells, by Salisbury Field
    Times, 13/11/19, p. 11

Welded, by Eugene O'Neill
    Herald, 18/3/24, p. 11

Werewolf, The, by Rudolph Lotlar
    Sun, 26/8/24, p. 14

What Every Woman Knows, by J. M. Barrie
    World, 14/4/26, p. 17

What Happened at 22, by Paul Wilstack
    Times, 22/8/14, p. 7

What Is Love, by George Scarborough
    Times, 21/9/14, p. 7

What It Means to a Woman, by E. H. Gould and F. White-
    house
    Times, 23/11/14, p. 11

What Money Can't Buy, by George Broadhurst
    Times, 12/10/15, p. 11

What Never Dies, by Alexander Engel
    World, 29/12/26, p. 11

What Price Glory?, by Maxwell Anderson and Laurence Stal-
    lings
    Sun, 6/9/24, p. 3

What's in a Name, by Anonymous (musical revue)
    Times, 20/3/20, p. 14

Wife with a Smile, The, by Denys Aimel and Andre Obey
Times, 29/11/21, p. 20

Wild Birds, The, by Dan Totheroh
Sun, 10/4/25, p. 24

Wild Duck, The, by Henrik Ibsen
Sun, 25/2/25, p. 20

Wild Man of Borneo, The, by Marc Connelly and Herman
Mankrewicz
World, 14/9/27, p. 13

Wild Oats Lane, by George Broadhurst
Times, 7/9/22, p. 12

Wild Westcotts, The, by Ann Morrison
Herald, 25/12/23, p. 13

Wildflower, by Otto Harbach and Oscar Hammerstein (book
and lyrics) and Herbert Stothart and Vincent Youmans
(music)
Herald, 8/2/23, p. 12

Will Shakespeare, by Clemence Dane
Herald, 2/1/23, p. 12

Willow Tree, The, by J. H. Benrimo and Harrison Rhodes
Times, 7/3/17, p. 9

Windows, by John Galsworthy
Herald, 9/10/23, p. 8

Winter's Tale, A, by William Shakespeare
Times, 5/2/21, p. 14

Wisdom Tooth, The, by Marc Connelly
World, 16/2/26, p. 13

Wise Crackers, The, by Gilbert Seldes
World, 17/12/25, p. 15

Witch, The, by H. Wiers-Jenssen
World, 19/11/26, p. 17

Within Four Walls, by Glen MacDonald
Herald, 18/4/23, p. 10

Ziegfeld Follies, by Victor Herbert, George M. Cohan,
   Frederick Lonsdale, and Others
         Herald, 22/10/23, p. 9

Ziegfeld Follies, by William A. McGuire and Will Rogers
   (book), Gene Buck and J. J. McCarthy (lyrics) and Victor
   Herbert, Raymond Hubbell, David Stamper, Harry Tierney,
   and Dr. A. Szirmai (music)
         Sun, 31/10/24, p. 24

Ziegfeld Girls of 1920, by Anonymous (A Revue)
         Times, 9/3/20, p. 18

INDEX

Footnotes, which appear at the end of each chapter, are indexed for the page in the text on which the footnote occurs.

Abbott, George: Coquette, 56
Abel, Walter, 125
Actors Equity, 16
Actor's Fund, 122
Actors' Strike, 123
Actors' well-being, 122-23
Adams, Franklin P., 9, 10, 13
Adams, H. Austin, 141
Adams, Maude, 53, 56, 61
Adams, Samuel Hopkins, 3, 5
Age of Innocence, 113
Ainsworth, Harrison, 2
Akins, Zoë, 13: Déclassée, 42, 43; A Royal Fandango, 43
Alcott, Louisa M., 2
Algonquin Hotel, 9
Algonquin Round Table, 9
Algonquin Wits, The, 10
Allen, Fred, 19
Ambush, 130
American in Paris, The, 145
And Ye Took Me In, 9
Anglin, Margaret, 76, 78
Arnold, Benedict, 32
Artistic development of actors, 121-22
As You Were, 32
Ashton, Ivy, 3
Atkinson, Brooks, 20, 22, 23, 24, 28-29, 30, 31-32, 64
Atlantic Monthly, 32
Austen, Jane, 2

Bachelor's Baby, The, 6
Ballentine, Edward J., 129
Bankhead, Tallulah, 10
Banks, Leslie, 29
Barker, Granville, 138

Barrett, Lillian: The Dice of the Gods, 40
Barrie, James M., 27, 80, 109: The Twelve Pound Look, 42; What Every Woman Knows, 55
Barrymore, Ethel, 16, 44, 46, 50, 51, 59, 61, 63, 64, 65, 92, 112, 121: Woollcott's evaluation of her, 41-43; in A Scrap of Paper, 41; as Berthe Tregnier in The Shadow, 41; in Our Mrs. Mc-Chesney, 42; as Lady Helen Haden in Déclassée, 42; in The Twelve Pound Look, 42; in A Royal Fandango, 43; as Portia in The Merchant of Venice, 43; touring in Dé-classée, 43
Barrymore, John, 4, 41, 59, 61, 63, 64, 65, 85, 92, 154; Woollcott's evaluation of him, 43-49; as Chick Hewes in Kick In, 43-44; as William Falder in Justice, 44, 49; in The Jest, 45; in Peter Ibbet-son, 45; as Richard III in Richard III, 45-46; as Gwym-plaine in Claire de Lune, 46; as Hamlet in Hamlet, 47-49, 62, 77; use of imagination, 68-69
Barrymore, Lionel, 41, 45, 49, 59, 61, 63, 64, 65, 92, 135: Woollcott's evaluation of him, 49-51; as Colonel Ibbetson in Peter Ibbetson, 49; as Milt Shanks in The Copperhead, 49-50; in The Jest, 50; as

277

ment of actors, 120-21; on
artistic development, 121-
22; on actors' well-being,
122; on Negro actors, 122;
on repertory theatre, 123-27;
on ensemble acting, 128-29;
on the Theatre Guild, 129-
33; on designers, 134, 137,
151; evaluation of Robert
Edmond Jones, 133-39; on
the new stagecraft, 139-41;
on directors, 141-42; on artist's business, 143; on theatre as a collaborative art,
146; use of sarcasm, 151-
52

Woollcott, Frances (mother), 1
Woollcott Reader, The, 27
Woollcott, Walter (father), 1,
2
World, The, 15, 16, 17

Yellow Jacket, The, 32
Young, Roland, 125, 129
Young, Stark, 22, 29, 134
Yurka, Blanche, 16

Zangwill, Israel, 116; We Moderns, 54-55
Zolotow, Maurice, 61